A HISTORY OF
Juab County

A HISTORY OF

Juab

County

Pearl D. Wilson
with June McNulty
and David Hampshire

1999
Utah State Historical Society
Juab County Commission

ISBN 0-913738-20-4
Library of Congress Catalog Card Number 98-61328
Map by Automated Geographic Reference Center—State of Utah
Printed in the United States of America

Utah State Historical Society
300 Rio Grande
Salt Lake City, Utah 84101-1182

Contents

General Introduction

When Utah was granted statehood on 4 January 1896, twenty-seven counties comprised the nation's new forty-fifth state. Subsequently two counties, Duchesne in 1914 and Daggett in 1917, were created. These twenty-nine counties have been the stage on which much of the history of Utah has been played.

Recognizing the importance of Utah's counties, the Utah State Legislature established in 1991 a Centennial History Project to write and publish county histories as part of Utah's statehood centennial commemoration. The Division of State History was given the assignment to administer the project. The county commissioners, or their designees, were responsible for selecting the author or authors for their individual histories, and funds were provided by the state legislature to cover most research and writing costs as well as to provide each public school and library with a copy of each history. Writers worked under general guidelines provided by the Division of State History and in cooperation with county history committees. The counties also established a Utah Centennial County History Council to help develop policies for distribution of state-appropriated funds and plans for publication.

Each volume in the series reflects the scholarship and interpretation of the individual author. The general guidelines provided by the Utah State Legislature included coverage of five broad themes encompassing the economic, religious, educational, social, and political history of the county. Authors were encouraged to cover a vast period of time stretching from geologic and prehistoric times to the present. Since Utah's statehood centennial celebration falls just four years before the arrival of the twenty-first century, authors were encouraged to give particular attention to the history of their respective counties during the twentieth century.

Still, each history is at best a brief synopsis of what has transpired within the political boundaries of each county. No history can do justice to every theme or event or individual that is part of an area's past. Readers are asked to consider these volumes as an introduction to the history of the county, for it is expected that other researchers and writers will extend beyond the limits of time, space, and detail imposed on this volume to add to the wealth of knowledge about the county and its people. In understanding the history of our counties, we come to understand better the history of our state, our nation, our world, and ourselves.

In addition to the authors, local history committee members, and county commissioners, who deserve praise for their outstanding efforts and important contributions, special recognition is given to Joseph Francis, chairman of the Morgan County Historical Society, for his role in conceiving the idea of the centennial county history project and for his energetic efforts in working with the Utah State Legislature and State of Utah officials to make the project a reality. Mr. Francis is proof that one person does make a difference.

ALLAN KENT POWELL
CRAIG FULLER
GENERAL EDITORS

Introduction

In the history of the State of Utah, Juab County has often been seen as a rather quiet rural area, yet it also has exerted an enormous influence and had a great impact on much of the development of Utah. The county, in north-central Utah, includes the major north-south route through the state, present-day Interstate 15 and its earlier forerunners. Its land area, encompassing some 3,392 square miles, includes fertile valleys, lakes and streams, mineral-bearing mountains and the majestic Mount Nebo, and vast desert stretches that long have tested the survival skills of all peoples who have traveled in them. Juab, recognized as a Ute Indian word meaning a flat or level plain, witnessed all of the major forces evident in the general history of Utah—prehistoric peoples and Native Americans; Spanish exploration; trappers, traders, and adventurous travelers; Mormon settlers; railroad builders; gold and silver miners; ranchers and farmers; community builders; military interests; recreational activities; business and industrial development; and technological advancements.

Juab County, as does each of Utah's other twenty-eight counties, exhibits unique characteristics. The history which follows highlights specific elements of Juab's past—touching upon various developments and their impacts that have been relevant to towns and settlements. Specific themes rise as important factors in Juab County's history. Prehistoric cultures, and the physical remains of that habitation, can still be seen on the landscape. Juab's agricultural emphasis is also evident, and the culture that created it, which was in turn influenced by this farming and ranching, continues of importance and significance. Mining also played a critical role in county development—both economically and socially, creating a diversity somewhat unusual in rural Utah. The Tintic Mining District looms as one of Utah's richest producers of mineral wealth. How people played out their lives in these different arenas forms the story of this study.

In viewing Juab County, there exists a dichotomy of landscapes, economies, and societies. The eastern end is very much a part of the Wastach Front—along Utah's main north-south interstate highway, the latest in the traditional historic major north-south corridors of travel through Utah. This section also provided the agricultural land and initial economic basis for the county. The western portion of Juab is a somewhat different land; it contained much of the mineral wealth as well as the vast desert regions. Contrasts still remain evident, as exemplified by the neatly organized rolling checkerboard Mormon farming villages of Levan, Mona, and Nephi, compared to the zig-zagging randomness of Eureka streets and lots, from necessity laid out according to the geography of mining. Such contrasts permeate the story of the county, which still has remained in great part unified in its citizens' outlooks and aspirations. Juab County, one of Utah's first counties, has survived because of the adaptability and drive of its residents. This has been a mutual effort from all sectors of society.

A variety of sources allows readers to see diverse views of Juab County. Eyewitness accounts provide readers with contemporary observations of early peoples and land. The diary of the 1776 Domínguez-Escalante expedition, including the incredible map prepared by cartographer Don Bernardo Miera y Pacheco, offers intriguing perceptions and commentary on the geography of eighteenth-century Juab land near Nephi, Mona, and Mills through which the intrepid Catholic friars and their small band of explorers traveled. The diary and map represent magnificent portraits of life and land in the area that was to become Juab County.

Likewise, an early perspective from fur trader and trapper Jedediah Strong Smith offers a glimpse of the foreboding west desert. Smith's reports of his traverses of the region of west Juab still convey to readers the urgency he and his companions experienced while crossing an unknown arid land. Always in search of food and water on the journeys, Smith offers poignant glimpses of those crossings in his journals.

A critical view from a young journalist who later became a world-famous author allows for another interesting first-person account. Samuel Clemens, better known to the world as Mark Twain, journeyed along the overland trail in 1861, passing through a portion of Juab County. The author sarcastically put forward his observations, thoughts, and opinions of Mormons, Goshutes, and the west desert. Twain's stagecoach ride, with a stay at Callao, provided material for the future author of *The Adventures of Huckleberry Finn* to hone his writing skills. His book of his western experiences, *Roughing It,* also provides an early glimpse of the people and terrain of west Juab County.

Contemporary sources, both written reports and especially newspaper accounts, provide much material in this glimpse at early Juab County. The *Times News* of Nephi and the *Eureka Reporter,* with news of the Tintic Mining District, furnished much valuable information about the life and times of Juab County. These weeklies were considered by many the life blood of their respective communities. Several key secondary sources supplied much-needed research and material for this book, which can be seen to stand on the efforts of others who ventured into the writing of local Juab County history. Local studies on Levan, Mona, Nephi, the Tintic Mining District, and an early county history, *History of Juab County* by Alice P. McCune, written under the auspices of the Daughters of Utah Pioneers for the Mormon pioneer centennial of 1947, represent the gleaning of much information, some of which is no longer available. The present volume offers glances at Juab County history, attempting to place the county into a broader perspective—looking at both east and west Juab County.

This study utilizes many historic and contemporary photographs that form a visual record of the past, allowing viewers a glimpse of past eras. Photography is a powerful medium. The "reading" of a photograph can sometimes better help one understand aspects of history than even the written word. Issues of landscape and its stark reality, geographical location and challenges, architecture, social interaction, social customs, physical adaptability, the world of work, and the role of technology can all be evident in photography.

In the final analysis, a county history is a product of many efforts. I would like to express sincere appreciation to all who supported and encouraged the writing of this history as well as to those who provided photographs and shared their family histories and other information of historical interest. Among them were the Tintic Historical Society and Fred J. Chapman, who made available their photographs of the early days, and Wayne Christiansen, who took contemporary photographs of Juab County. Thanks also to the many friends who searched their personal photo albums for pictures to be used in the book.

Thanks go to Steele McIntyre, Maurine Bates, Ann Alloway, Betty E. Thomas, and others for family histories and material about the early days in Juab County. Last but certainly not least, thanks to members of the Utah State Historical Society who have worked on the Utah Centennial county history project for all their encouragement and help. It was a tremendous undertaking—one that I am sure will be appreciated even more in the future.

JUAB COUNTY

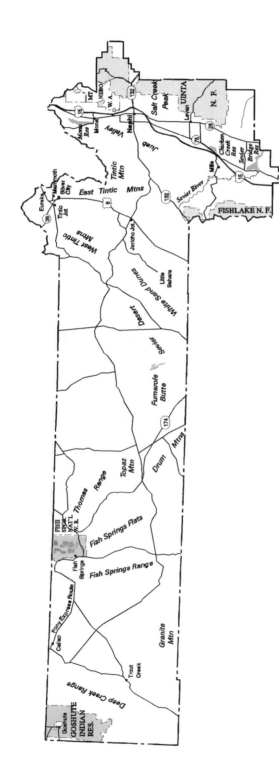

CHAPTER 1

THE LAND

Because of its shape, Juab County is sometimes referred to as the "key" county. The county is located in west-central Utah and extends westward from the mountains of the Uinta National Forest, near the center of the state, to the desert lands of the Nevada border. It measures approximately 125 miles from east to west and twenty-five miles north to south. Juab's climate would be classified as semiarid, as is almost all of Utah. Temperatures range from a high of more than 100 degrees Fahrenheit in summer to below zero in winter months. During the summer, flash floods are common; in winter, rapidly developing snowstorms can appear out of nowhere, especially in the western part of the county.

Geology

In the study of history it is valuable to understand the physical characteristics of the land upon which people lived, because land can exert a definite impact upon the events that shape lives. The present-day visible geology of Juab County includes surface exposures of Precambrian quartzites and agrillites that are some 560 million years

1

old. The exact origin of these rocks is uncertain, but some resemble old outflows of possible volcanic origin. These Precambrian quartzites can be observed in the northeast part of the Tintic Mining District, the West Tintic Mountains, and the Deep Creek Range.

The Ordovician period, when material was deposited in these areas, began around 505 million years ago when land areas were uplifted, rising from the shallow seas that had covered much of the area that is now the western United States. This uplifted area generally was located north of Juab County, and the rising sea floor formed shallow-water limestones and quartzites from areas near the old shore lines. Ordovician period rocks may be observed in both the Thomas Range and East Tintic Mountains. The Devonian period commenced about 408 million years ago and lasted about 50 million years. Rocks of this age, which thicken to the west and thin to the east in the county, were formed from sea sediments and windblown sands. This indicates that the ancient seas covered this area and periodically retreated to the west during this time.

Pennsylvanian period rocks began forming 320 million years ago as a basin developed and thick layers of limestones and shales were deposited. The formation of these rocks in this basin continued through Permian time, and the deposition ended around 245 million years ago as the basin filled. The layers of rock previously formed in what is called the Oquirrh Basin can now be seen on the upper parts of Mount Nebo, the Canyon Range, and the Confusion Range.

At the beginning of the Triassic period (the dinosaur age), 245 million years ago, western Utah, including Juab County, was covered by a shallow sea that deepened to the west. Sedimentary rocks up to 2,000 feet thick were formed but were subsequently essentially eroded from the Juab County area. Small remnants of these formations can be observed on the lower parts of Mount Nebo's southern flank. Toward the end of Triassic time this area began to be uplifted and the inland sea covering the area retreated to the east. The western part of future Juab County became highlands covered by sand dunes.

The future county during the Jurassic period, beginning about 200 million years ago, still consisted of highlands and mountains to the west and sand dunes along the eastern margins of the county. During the middle and later parts of this period a basin developed

Mount Nebo from the Goshen-Eureka Branch of the Rio Grande Western Railway. (C. R. Savage, Utah State Historical Society)

with a generally north-trending low area. Thick sequences of shale, gypsum, and salt were deposited in this basin, and they can be readily observed from Salt Creek to Deep Canyon, continuing on to a point near the southern boundary of the eastern part of the county. Throughout the Cretaceous period, beginning some 144 million years ago, rocks were pushed (thrust) from the west and older rocks overrode younger formations. This movement has been called the Sevier Orogeny, or mountian-building period. As mountains were pushed up and built to the west, they drained eastward, and large alluvial sand and gravel deposits can be observed at the present day in the conglomerate rock in parts of Chicken Creek and above Four Mile Creek.

During Paleocene and through Eocene time, approximately 65 to 37 million years ago, mountains and highlands to the west continued to be eroded away. Areas to the east contained inland seas into which sand and gravel deposits were carried by streams and rivers. These deposits would later form the North Horn and Green River Formations on the Gunnison Plateau. In western Juab County granite rock intruded into the Deep Creek Mountains around 39 million years ago from deep underground volcanic pressure.

Granite Canyon, West Desert, 1998. (Wayne Christiansen)

In the Oligocene-Miocene epoch, 37 to 5 million years ago, volcanic activity increased in this area with intrusive granite and other molten rock invading sedimentary strata in the Tintic and West Tintic Mountains, Keg Mountains, Desert Mountain complex, and the Thomas Range (Topaz Mountains). Eroded remnants of this intrusive rock can be seen at each of these areas. Extrusive volcanic flows on the surfaces cover an extensive area. These rock flows cover much of the Tintic Mountains south of Eureka and can be seen in Ferner, Sage, and Dog Valleys. They also cover major portions of Lone Ridge. During this period of volcanic activity many of the ore bodies containing lead, zinc, silver, gold and copper were deposited in the intrusive volcanic rocks, resulting in many of the ore bodies presently existing in the county.

Approximately 12 to 15 million years ago, during the late Miocene epoch, the present landforms that we now see began to take shape. The region began to rise in elevation, and, as the rock strata rose, north-south-trending faults (fractures in the rock) developed. As the displacement, or movement, of these faults increased, the mountain ranges rose in relation to the valley floors, and the mountain ranges and valleys began to take on the familiar forms we see today.

During Quaternary time, 100,000 to 10,000 years ago, glaciers formed on Mount Nebo and the Deep Canyon mountains. These glaciers carved out cirques (large basins) that can be readily seen near the top of Mount Nebo on its western side. Ancient Lake Bonneville covered much of the area some 30,000 to 10,000 years ago and formed many ancient shorelines that can still be seen along the faces of many of the mountain ranges in western Juab County. This lake covered approximately 20,000 square miles of the Great Basin and was over 1,000 feet deep at its highest stage.

Like the earth everywhere, the landforms of the county are still being reshaped. Valleys continue to be filled with alluvial material. Mountains are slowly being eroded down and fault movement continues to produce earthquakes and the building of new mountain areas. Volcanic activity and plate tectonics could still create great areas of elevated land.

The existence of mineralization in the county is a significant feature of the area's geology. Juab County has many organized mining districts. The most notable, the Tintic District, is located in the Eureka, Mammoth, and Silver City area. The district is ranked second in the state in terms of the total value of all minerals mined. The major metals and ore produced from this area are lead, silver, gold, copper, and zinc. Other organized mining districts are the Desert (Desert Mountain), Detroit (Drum Mountain), Fish Springs, Granite Creek, Johnson Peak (Trout Creek), Juab, Leamington, Mount Nebo (Timmins), Spring Creek, North Tintic, and West Tintic (West Tintic Mountains). All of these districts have had varying amounts of lead, zinc, silver, gold, copper, and manganese.

Spor Mountain, located immediately west of the Thomas Range in southwestern Juab County, contains large deposits of beryllium that are currently being mined and processed at the Brush Wellman plant. Spor Mountain also has fluorspar deposits that are mined and shipped to steel plants. Ash Grove Cement West, Inc., is using limestones, shales, gypsum, and some iron procured from the county.[1]

Fish Springs Range, Looking North, 1998. (Wayne Christiansen)

Mountains

Eastern Juab County is bordered by the southern part of the Wasatch Range, long spur of the western Rocky Mountains. The Wasatch Range begins at the Idaho border and extends south to Mount Nebo, the last peak on the north side of Salt Creek Canyon. Mount Nebo begins near Rocky Ridge, south of Santaquin, and ends northeast of Nephi, near Salt Creek Canyon. Mount Nebo, directly east of Mona, has three distinct peaks. Because the trails to the top of the mountain began on the south side from Salt Creek Canyon, South Peak became the best known. It was also the first to be climbed and documented. On 24 August 1869 W.W. Phelps went to the top to make scientific observations. Four years later, in 1873, Lt. George M. Wheeler of the U.S. Topographical Survey erected an observatory on its summit after he and several men from Mona hewed a trail up the mountainside in order to carry lumber and scientific instruments on the backs of mules.[2]

Because of Juab County's irregular east border, two of Mount Nebo's peaks are in Utah County. South Peak, at 11,877 feet, is in Juab County. North Peak, which is 11,928 feet, is in Utah County, making it the highest peak in that county.[3] A sign consisting of a

Ponds at Fish Springs Wild Life Refuge, 1998. (Wayne Christiansen)

metal pole and a flag-shaped piece of metal was placed on the summit of South Peak in 1923 by the Wasatch Mountain Club. Patrick Christian, writing in the *Provo Herald,* 22 September 1978, wrote of the view from the summit: "From that high point one can see all the way to Nevada. . . . We could see the sand dunes and other mountains in that same area. Utah Lake seems larger from the top of Nebo, Mt. Timpanogas seems smaller and everything looks impressive. Standing in the wind, higher than everything except the hawks, I felt an uncommon sense of how small I am compared to the world. At the same time, I felt a sense of well being."[4]

Salt Creek Canyon, on the east side of Mount Nebo, has been improved to accommodate recreational activities. Improvements have been made by Juab County and the U.S. Forest Service. Ponderosa and Bear Canyon Campgrounds provide tables, stoves, water, restrooms, and recreational areas. In the fall of 1934 the Nebo Loop Road was completed. This road extends from Salt Creek to Payson and reaches an elevation of 10,000 feet. The beautiful scenery features rugged rock formations, high mountain streams, green foliage, and breathtaking changes of color in the fall. Widening and resurfacing of the loop road was begun in November 1983 and was completed at the end of 1984 at a cost of about $555,000.

South of Salt Creek is Red Cliffs, which is part of the San Pitch Mountains of the Gunnison Plateau. Salt Creek Peak, east of Nephi, is 9,991 feet high. Horse Haven Peak, southeast of Levan, is 8,487 feet high.

The western area of Juab County generally does not get as much attention as the east side. Mountains there are equally as beautiful and interesting. The Tintic Mining District encompasses the central portion of the East Tintic Mountains, which begin in Tooele County and run northeast, following the border between Utah and Juab Counties almost to Ferner Ridge in east-central Juab County.

The West Tintic Mountains are farther west, on the west side of Tintic Valley. They also begin in Tooele County and extend into Juab. Topaz Mountain, in the Thomas Range, in west-central Juab County, is 7,046 feet high. Beginning on the Tooele County border, the Fish Springs Range runs north and south almost to the southern border of Juab County at about the western third of the county. Its highest peak, George H. Hansen Peak, reaches an elevation of 8,523 feet.

Haystack Peak, at 11,989 feet, and Ibapah Peak, at 12,101 feet, are located in the Deep Creek Range near the Goshute Indian Reservation. Ibapah is the highest peak in Juab County. In October of 1979 Darrell Berkheimer, *Provo Herald News* editor; Patrick Christian, staff member and photographer; and Bevan Killpack, a Bureau of Land Management landscape architect from the Fillmore office, climbed to the summits of both Ibapah and Haystack peaks. At about 8,800 feet they reported that they encountered massive granite cliffs, cold mountain streams, and a surprising amount of vegetation. The change from desert to green mountains is so abrupt that the term "oasis" came to mind. The Deep Creek Mountains were once an island floating in the middle of ancient Lake Bonneville. In 1992 Winford Bloodworth climbed to the top of Ibapah Peak. He stated that Haystack and Ibapah formed a saddle mountain about one mile apart, and that it was his toughest climb of a Utah mountain.[5]

Nebo Loop. (Utah State Historical Society)

Valleys

Juab Valley is located at the foot of Mount Nebo and the San Pitch Mountains to the east, with the Tintic Mountains to the west. It runs somewhat southwesterly, in the same general direction as modern-day I-15, and extends the full width—from north to south—of the widest part of the county. There are a number of creeks running through the valley that have helped to make it Juab County's largest agricultural area. North Creek and Willow Creek both rise on the west side of the Wasatch Mountains above Mona and empty into Mona Reservoir. Salt Creek rises in the Wasatch Mountains east of Mount Nebo and flows southwesterly and then westerly through Nephi. It then flows in a northerly direction until it also empties into Mona Reservoir. Currant Creek flows down Goshen Canyon to Goshen. Currant Creek Canal joins Kimball Creek and flows north to Elberta. Four Mile Creek rises in the San Pitch Mountains approximately six miles south of Nephi, flowing north

Sand Dunes West of Eureka. (Utah State Historical Society)

and west into Juab Valley. Pigeon Creek rises east of Levan and flows westerly to Chicken Creek Reservoir east of Mills.

Little Salt Creek begins in the mountains about six miles south of Levan and also empties into Chicken Creek Reservoir. Dog Valley, about six miles west of Nephi, lies between Ferner Ridge on the west and Long Ridge and West Hills on the east. This valley has been a successful dry farming area for many years. Sage Valley is located about seven miles west of Levan. Mills Valley joins Sage Valley at its south end.

The Sevier River is the only water source of any significant size in Juab County. It enters the county by way of the Sevier Bridge Dam and Yuba Lake, which is located in the extreme southeastern corner of Juab County. It then meanders north through Mills Valley and northwest into Sevier Canyon, where it turns south and west through Leamington Canyon into Millard County. During most years, the water has been completely expended for irrigation purposes by the time it reaches the now normally dry bed of Sevier Lake.

Yuba Reservoir is located twenty-six miles south of Nephi and was completed in 1916 by local ranchers and farmers. Older farmers who worked on the dam stated that for many years it was called U.B. Dam, a name taken from an old workers song that portrayed the workers "as damned if they worked and damned if they didn't work. You be damned either way." The Utah Division of Parks and Recreation has developed recreational facilities at two locations on the reservoir: Yuba State Park, located on the west shore, and Painted Rock State Park on the southwest shore. The area has become a very popular area for boating and camping, especially on Memorial Day and Labor Day weekends. It was estimated that there were up to 20,000 visitors over the Easter weekend in 1994.[6]

Fish Springs Flat is an extremely isolated desert area located between the Fish Springs and Thomas Ranges. At the north end, bordering Tooele County, is the Fish Springs National Wildlife Refuge. It is 104 miles southwest of Tooele and seventy-eight miles northwest of Delta. The area was used by Native Americans for centuries before white men came to Utah. Mountain man Jedediah Strong Smith visited the area on one of his treks from California. Both the Overland Stage and the Pony Express maintained stations at Fish Springs. The first transcontinental telegraph crossed the area in 1861, and early in the twentieth century the first transcontinental automobile road, the Lincoln Highway, traversed the area.

The present refuge contains a 10,000-acre spring-fed marsh, which has been developed to increase waterfowl utilization. The springs arise from a fault zone along the east edge of the Fish Springs Range and provide water for nine large impoundments. The 18,000-acre refuge was established in 1959 and development was finished in 1964.

The east-central portion of Juab County is part of the Sevier Desert, and the White Sands Dune area is located near the center of this area. The sand originated from sandbars which were deposited along the southern shoreline of Lake Bonneville during the late Pleistocene epoch. Little Sahara Recreational Area has been developed there by the Bureau of Land Management and has become a very popular place for recreational all-terrain vehicle (ATV) use from early spring until late fall. The Rockwell region of the area is protected and is being preserved in its natural state. There is unique plant and animal life as well as more common lizards, kangaroo rats, coyotes, bobcats, and hawks. Some areas are reserved for sand play, campgrounds, and picnics. Probably the most popular areas are those reserved for off-road vehicles (ORVs). It was reported that there were approximately 17,000 people at the sand dunes on Easter weekend of 1994.

The variety of recreational opportunities found in the county make it a popular destination for many different types of recreational enthusiasts. The natural beauty and importance of the natural ecosystems provided by the county attract others, and still others have looked to the land for centuries as a place to live.

ENDNOTES

1. Glen Miller, "The Geology and Mineral Deposits of Juab County," 1998, written especially for this study and in author's possession.

2. Alice Paxman McCune, *History of Juab County, 1847–1947* (Springville, Utah: Art City Publishing Co., 1947), 264.

3. Lynn Arave, "Utah's Expert on Peaks Identifies Highest Points in all Counties," *Deseret News,* 14–15 December 1992.

4. *Provo Herald,* 22 September 1978.

5. Ibid.; Arave, "Utah's Expert on Peaks."

6. *Times News* (Nephi), 9 June 1993.

CHAPTER 2

THE ORIGINAL PEOPLES
OF JUAB COUNTY

The knowledge and understanding of prehistoric cultures in Utah is in a state of exciting development. New archaeological discoveries, improved methodologies of study, and a growing body of reliable knowledge suggest innovative theories and ideas about prehistoric Native Americans who lived in Utah and the West. Some of these new methods of study include genetics, climatology, volcanic and tectonic activities, the study of pollen, and comparative analysis. Although new understanding has brought some lack of certainty, researchers believe they can understand the basic developments of prehistoric Indians both in Utah and Juab County. Significant to our understanding of prehistoric Indians is a better conception of the environment and climate in which they lived. It is clear that the occupation of prehistoric Indians in areas of the West was directly associated with the availability of water for themselves as well as the flora and fauna resources they gathered and hunted. Availability of water has always been critical to the occupation of areas by humans in Juab County, in Utah, and in the West. Like us, ancient inhabitants developed a rudimentary understanding of their environment and were able to work within that environment to provide themselves with food, clothing, and shelter.

The earliest inhabitants of North America, the Great Basin, and Utah are called the Paleo-Indians. Archaeologists, based on their study of fluted projectile points, have dated Indian occupation of the Great Basin and western Utah to about 12,000 years ago.[1] These prehistoric people are identified with the use of stone implements in the hunting of big game and in their preparation of food. Archaeologists call this period the lithic (rock) stage or culture. Using materials at hand, Paleo-Indians fashioned fluted stone points to hunt megafauna—the large, now-extinct, prehistoric camels, mammoths, long-horned bison, and sloths, among others—and formed crude stone choppers and scrapers to prepare their food. Lithic projectile points, a primary means of understanding Paleo-Indians, are classified by archaeologists to aid in their chronological placing and cultural studies of these earliest American people. Two types of stone projectile points which provide some of the earliest evidence of human occupation in the West are Folsom and Clovis fluted points.

Widely scattered Clovis and Folsom point sites in Utah suggest that ancient Indians hunted in the Great Basin and the northern Colorado Plateau country of eastern Utah as early as 10,000 B.C. and perhaps even earlier. Isolated discoveries of these projectile points have been found in Emery County, the Sevier Desert south of Juab County, and at the Ouray National Bird Refuge in the Uinta Basin.[2] A Clovis point site was located near the northernmost bend of the Sevier River in southeastern Juab County.[3] These and other possible Paleo-Indian sites are associated with ancient as well as contemporary lakes, marshes, and streams. It is believed that these sites were probably kill sites where big game roamed and where Paleo-Indians prepared food. In ancient times, the flat area around the Deep Creek Mountain Range and eastern Juab County provided an abundance of flora for prehistoric big game to feed upon. It is very likely that Paleo-Indians using stone projectile points on spears hunted big game in parts of Juab County. Parts of Juab County, then, have probably occupied from those times to the present.

Sometime around 9,000 B.C. a different classification of people, which archaeologists call the Desert Archaic Culture, either evolved

Deep Creek Mountains, 1998. (Wayne Christiansen)

from the Paleo-Indians or moved into the Great Basin and Utah and displaced them. Archaeologists define the Desert Archaic Culture of the Great Basin region as lasting from about 9,000 B.C. to A.D. 500 and as "broadly based . . . , with subsistence varying from season to season as it focused first on one species or community of species and then on another . . . a fundamental lifeway not geared to any one ecosystem."[4]

The Desert Archaic people in Utah lived most of the time in flat areas near marshes like Fish Springs in western Juab County or near lakes and streams where a constant supply of flora and fauna was available. Marshes provided an abundant supply of food for the early people. An acre of marsh reportedly can yield as much as 5,500 pounds of edible flour ground from cattail roots and tubers. Cattail flour nutritionally equals or exceeds an equal amount of rice or wheat flour.[5]

The Desert Archaic people developed a more effective hunting weapon, the atlatl, or spear-thrower, as well as a wide variety of fluted projectile points to hunt the smaller game that inhabited the area after the extinction of the great megafauna. They used flat milling stones to grind seeds, clothed themselves with fur robes, used hide to fashion footwear, wove baskets to carry and store food, and made extensive use of caves and rock overhangs located near streams, lakes, and marshes for shelter.

Several significant archaeological sites of the early Desert Archaic culture have been discovered and studied to some degree by archaeologists in western Utah and Juab County. Scribble Rock Shelter, Fish Springs Caves in western Juab County, and Smith Creek Cave and Amy Shelter along the Utah-Nevada border in White Pine County, Nevada, indicate long-term occupation of the area by Desert Archaic people. Danger Cave in western Tooele County and Hogup Cave in western Box Elder County remain significant sites for understanding the Desert Archaic people. By comparing these sites in western Utah and eastern Nevada, archaeologists have determined that various Desert Archaic groups used similar sources of food. Over forty species of animals, including rabbit, antelope, deer, bison, and mountain sheep, were hunted and used by the Desert Archaic people living in western Utah. Other foods included pickleweed, sedge, and marsh birds. Archaeological digs at Danger and Hogup Caves reveal that these people were afflicted by lice, ticks, penworms, roundworms, and a thorny-headed worm that sometimes proved fatal.[6]

Beginning about 5,500 years ago the Desert Archaic people of the region are believed to have increased in population, placing a greater burden on the area's limited marshes and flatlands for their food supply. There is some evidence that these people began to use the upland areas of the Deep Creek Mountains and similar areas in the Great Basin as places for hunting and foraging flora and fauna.

Sometime around A.D. 400–500, Desert Archaic people seemed to no longer inhabit Juab County and other areas in the Great Basin. It is difficult to know what caused this lapse of occupation, but around A.D. 500 a new prehistoric Indian culture occupied most of Utah. Archaeologists identify this new group as the Fremont culture. It generally corresponded in time with the Puebloan or Anasazi culture found south of the Colorado River in Utah and in the Four Corners area of Utah, Arizona, Colorado, and New Mexico.

People of the Fremont culture adopted some of the Desert Archaic traditions, occupying the same natural shelters and caves. In addition, they constructed dwellings and small food-storage bins out

Ibapah Peak, West Desert, 1998. (Wayne Christiansen)

of sun-dried adobe (clay) bricks, logs, brush, and field stone. They expanded the harvest of various plants, roots, and seeds, improved the making of stone projectile points, adopted the use of bows and arrows, became proficient in making ceramic jugs and pots, wove baskets using the one-rod-and-bundle method, formed small humanoid images from clay, and painted and incised artwork on canyon walls. Most importantly, they were much more sedentary, living in small hamlets organized around the extended family, and adopting horticulture, including the planting and harvesting of corn, squash, and beans, to supplement their food supply. Like their predecessors, the Fremont people continued to rely heavily on hunting and gathering for much of their subsistence. However, they were not limited to flatlands and marshes, extending their food gathering and hunting to other environmental zones including the mountains. From existing shelters and caves as well as surface dwelling sites, Fremont Indians hunted the Deep Creek Mountains in western Juab County and the Wasatch Mountains east of Nephi for deer, pinyon nuts, and many other foods.

Archaeologists have divided the Fremont culture into five smaller complexes associated with specific geographical regions of the state:

Great Salt Lake, Uinta, San Rafael, Parowan, and Sevier. The Sevier complex or variant of the Fremont culture encompassed Juab County and extended roughly east of Garrison, Nevada, to Ephraim and the Wasatch Plateau and Mountains, and from Garrison and Kanosh on the south to Grantsville and Tooele on the north. Each Fremont variant seems to have developed their own identifiable ceramics. The Sevier Fremont ceramics have been identified as "a distinctive volcanic glass tempered pottery" fashioned within the area and with its own distinctive coloring.[7]

The Sevier Fremont people hunted and gathered most of their food. Unlike the San Rafael Fremont and Anasazi to the south, the Sevier Fremont either did not grow corn, beans, or squash or were severely limited in their horticultural subsistence. A number of temporary Sevier Fremont sites have been located in and around the Deep Creek Mountains. Generally, these temporary sites are located at the mouths of canyons and in canyon bottoms near available water. Most of these sites were probably used seasonally on hunting and gathering trips.

Nephi Mounds

The Nephi Mounds are located approximately two miles north of Nephi and were excavated by University of Utah researchers in 1965 and 1966. The mounds were there when Nephi was first settled in 1851 but soon were plowed over and planted with crops, Of course, no one was aware of what was under the wheat and alfalfa. However, over the years, many small artifacts were unearthed, leading many people to believe that the area had been inhabited many years ago. According to the researchers,

> The site consists of 30 or more mounds of marked variability in height and diameter. The mounds represent accumulations of occupational debris on low prominence that were, at the time of occupation, situated along the Salt Creek distributary system. The drainage pattern has been extensively displaced since the site was occupied, and the mounds now stand in fields, isolated from any stream.[8]

Juab Valley at the time of this occupation was almost a perfect place for nomadic people to settle. With the mountains to the east and plenty of water for agricultural and other needs, the fertile val-

General location of the Nephi Mounds site. (University of Utah)

ley provided the inhabitants with a variety of food and material for clothing shelter.

Five of the mounds were excavated, one in 1965 and four in 1966. The 1965 excavation was dug with hand tools, while the 1966 dig was excavated by selective backhoe trenching and scraping. Mound One, excavated in 1965, was found to have had three successive occupations—evidence of each was separated by a layer of debris. It appeared to have been a dwelling built of adobe and containing a clay-rimmed firepit, central roof-support postholes or pole remnants, and a bell-shaped storage pit. Pottery, worked bone, food scraps, chipped stone, and ground stone were found in the mound.[9] The researchers later wrote of their findings:

> In the five mounds excavated, 19 major structures were encountered: 8 coursed adobe coil granaries; 4 coursed adobe-coil dwellings; 3 pit house mud-and-pole dwellings; 1 surface mud-and-pole dwelling; 1 jacal surface (?) dwelling; 1 pit house mud-and-pole dwelling or ceremonial structure; 1 dwelling unknown.[10]

The structures were of various shapes—circular, rectangular, square, trapezoidal, and irregular in plan. Most of them were built of

Circular pit house, Nephi Mounds. Note the central fire hearth and that charred roof support beams are still visible. (University of Utah)

about 12-by-8-inch coils of adobe placed on top of each other and smoothed inside and out to become an adobe wall. The floors were of packed clay. Firepits were centrally located and circular in shape. They ranged from clay-lined and rimmed to merely scooped-out depressions. Roofs of surface dwellings were apparently made from mud-covered thatch over wood beams, and the entry was probably from the top. The roofs of some structures were supported by four posts placed around the fire pit and the corners. Secondary support posts seem to have been common. Other structures lacked central supports. According to scholars,

> A distinct prototype of adobe-coil surface dwellings is not to be found in the surrounding areas of the Great Basin, Plains or Southwest. Probably, it is better considered a Fremont innovation (along with the coursed adobe-coil granaries) than a copy of an Anasazi Pueblo.
>
> The surface mud-and-pole lodge is a structural form found, to date, only at the Nephi site . . . and in the Uinta Basin. . . . Absence of central supports suggests a conical arrangement of poles with a mud cover, although a wattle-and-daub dome is not

Nephi Mounds adobe-walled dwelling with small attached storage structure to the left. A clay-rimmed fire hearth, in the center, remains a prominent feature. (University of Utah)

> precluded. Entry was probably through the wall rather than the roof. . . .
>
> Nephi site structures are perfectly typical of Fremont architecture in that they seldom duplicate, but are similar to, structures at other Fremont sites; and structures within the site seldom duplicate one another, but are similar to other structures at the site.[11]

Among the artifacts found in the mounds were pottery, pottery shards, unfired clay smoking pipes, pottery discs, potter scraping tools, clay figurines, projectile points (knives, drills, scrapers), jewelry, hammerstones, and gaming pieces. Some of the artifacts have been Carbon-14 dated at about from A.D. 850 to 920. Archaeologists concluded that the Nephi site is distinctively of the Sevier Fremont type.

The Fish Springs Caves

Sevier Fremont peoples also occupied the Deep Creek Mountains and surrounding areas, including the Fish Springs Range and the area that is now the Fish Springs National Wildlife Refuge. Two caves, Barn Owl Cave and Crab Cave, have been excavated and their contents studied by archaeologists. From artifacts found there it has been concluded that the caves were probably occupied seasonally from 5,000 to 2,000 years ago. They would have provided protection from the weather when it was cold, while also being near to the flora, roots, seeds, and berries which were a major part of their inhabitants' diets. There also probably were small game and birds in the area. The abundance of pinyon nut hulls suggests that the inhabitants must have spent time in the Deep Creek Mountains, because that is the closest place where the pine nuts were available. Scholars concluded that, "If the occupation of the Deep Creek Mountains and Fish Springs area are considered together, it is probable that one-quarter to one-third of the year was spent in the procurement of wild foods."[12]

One burial at a nearby dune was found and examined. Researchers wrote:

> The body was in a flexed position on its right side. The skeletal material was badly disturbed by roots, water, insects, and rodents, precluding determination of possible pathologies. Neither could the sex be determined, although size and shape of several elements suggest it was a male. Dental wear is characteristic of a young adult 18 to 24 years of age.[13]

The Fremont culture, including the Sevier Fremont variant, did not last much beyond A.D. 1300 and was perhaps in decline in areas as early as A.D. 1100. What happened to the Fremont, where they went, and where they came from remain mysteries for archaeologists. Some have postulated that the Fremont people originally came from the Plains culture and retreated back to it as a result of increased pressure from Numic-speaking Ute, Paiute, and Shoshoni people who were expanding into the Great Basin from southern California and extreme northern Mexico. Other archaeologists suggest that the Fremont were absorbed into the Numic peoples.[14] Still others argue that the Anasazi and Fremont abandoned Utah and the Four Corners region because of prolonged drought. One history text maintains that,

> At the end of the thirteenth century a cultural regression occurred among the Fremont peoples which paralleled the retreat of the

Goshute Mother and Child. (Utah State Historical Society)

Anasazi from Utah and may have had similar causes. They were replaced, displaced, or absorbed by peoples of different cultural and linguistic background, who probably began to move into the region after A.D. 1000.[15]

Southern Paiutes have a tradition that bridges the gap between the ancient peoples and those who occupied the land in later time. According to one account,

> It describes a people who anciently made an arduous trek eastward from a land of high mountains and endless waters to the red mountains. There, under the benign influence of their gods, Tobats and Shinob, they developed a happy way of life in which irrigated gardens, abundant game, and wild seeds amply met their needs. Then came many years without moisture, and the streams dried up and the game fled. As famine threatened, they appealed to Tobats and Shinob, and after three days Shinob appeared, heard their problem, and instructed them to take counsel from the animals. Since that time the Southern Paiutes have been nomads, "leaving their homes in the caves, they have followed the game from high land to low and gathered in gratitude the foods which the gods distribute every year over the face of *tu-weep*, the earth."[16]

Historic Indian Cultures of Juab County

Employing linguistics to study Native Americans, ethnographers and others indicate that Western Shoshoni peoples, who spoke a variant of the Numic language, occupied a vast territory of the Great Basin, from present-day Box Elder and Weber Counties in northern Utah extending in a large broad swath through central Nevada to east-central California south of Mono Lake. The territory extended east, where Ute Indians ranged well into the Rocky Mountains of present-day Colorado. The Northern Shoshoni, other Western Shoshoni, the Goshutes, the Southern Paiutes, and Utes all speak variants of the Numic language. The Goshutes occupied west-central Utah including future Juab County at the time of the coming of whites to the area. The Goshute Indians living in future Juab County would have contact with early Spanish and American explorers, traders, and fur trappers.

The Goshutes were hunters and gatherers, hunting small game and collecting seeds and other vegetation in season. Unlike the Sevier Fremont, the Goshutes did not build permanent structures in which to live but instead occupied caves and overhangs or built brush huts. Because resources were scarce, Goshutes roamed the country in small bands of a few families, with no specific leader, searching for food

Goshute Rider at Ibapah, 1924. (Utah State Historical Society)

and other necessities. They depended on a medicine man to cure their ills and give them other instructions. They used the bow and arrow for hunting but rarely for warfare. More aggressive Ute raiding parties on horseback frequently stole Goshute women and children and sold them into slavery to the Spanish and the Mexicans in New Mexico.

Most Goshutes historically lived in the Deep Creek region and in Rush, Skull, and Tooele Valleys. This was harsh country and their lives were hard, but they became extremely skilled in adapting to and living off of the resources of the land. They wandered from one place to another as the seasons changed and the supplies of food became scarce or new ones became available. Their food consisted of roots, plants, berries, nuts (particularly pine nuts), seeds, and greens. This was supplemented by lizards, snakes, fish, insects, rodents, rabbits, birds, and occasionally by mountain sheep, deer, bear, and elk, which they hunted in the mountains.[17]

In late 1849 Mormon pioneers began to settle in Tooele County. In January 1850 Tooele townsite was established, and the next year the settlers built a wall around their town to protect themselves from the Indians. Increasing numbers of whites moved onto traditional Native American lands throughout the region, gradually displacing the Indians and consuming their traditional resources. By 1860 the population of whites in the Tooele region had increased to more than 1,000 and they had taken over a good share of the land which had been used exclusively by the Goshutes. Their cattle, sheep, and horses grazed over the ranges, and the Pony Express and Overland Mail constructed stations on Goshute land.

The Indians increasingly began to raid the settlements and the stations, motivated by revenge and also because it was becoming increasingly more difficult for them to survive on what the land produced. By the spring of 1859 Jacob Forney, the Superintendent of Indian Affairs for Utah, became interested in establishing permanent farms among the Goshutes. He instructed Indian agent Robert Jarvis to proceed to Deep Creek and Ruby Valley and open farms at those places. The "miserably starving fragments of the Gosha-Utes" were to be induced to try farming at Deep Creek.[18]

On 25 March 1859 Jarvis met with about one hundred Goshutes from several bands and convinced them to try farming and stop raiding and stealing from whites. The Indians left for Deep Creek on 3 April. Later a hostile group arrived at Jarvis's camp, but with the help of Howard Egan and George Chorpenning, Jarvis convinced them to join those who had agreed to try farming.[19] A third group also joined who were anxious to obtain farm implements as well as instruction.

No agent had ever visited them, but they had used sticks to turn up the ground and they had already planted forty acres of wheat that year.

In September 1859, Superintendent Forney of Salt Lake City wrote that the Goshute band was broken and subdivided into small groups, but that some sixty had a "quiet and well-disposed chief to control them" and were at that time "permanently located on the Deep Creek Indian farm."[20] Most of the Indians, however, found it hard to adapt to a totally new way of life. By 1860 many were destitute and some were beginning to threaten whites in the region, including their telegraph and Overland Mail enterprises. By the winter of 1862–63 Goshutes had attacked mail stations, killing three whites.

Territorial Superintendent of Indian Affairs Benjamin Davis was sympathetic to the plight of the Goshutes and urged the government to extend the "reservation" in 1861, but it did not materialize at this time. However, in 1863 the government concluded a series of treaties with the Utah and Nevada Indians. As part of the treaty the Goshute Indians agreed to cease all hostilities against the whites; allow several routes of travel through their country to be unobstructed by them; and allow the establishment of military posts and station houses wherever deemed necessary. Telegraph, stage lines, and railways also could be constructed without molestation through any portion of Goshute country, and mines, mills, and ranches could be established and timber taken. The Goshutes agreed to abandon their nomadic life and become settled as herdsmen and farmers whenever the President of the United States deemed it expedient to remove them to reservations. The United States, in consequence of driving away and destroying game along the routes traveled by white men, and by the formation of agricultural and mining settlements, agreed to pay the Goshutes $1,000 a year for the next twenty years. The treaty was ratified in 1864 and proclaimed by President Lincoln on 17 January 1865.[21]

Even before the treaty was signed, steps had been taken to remove all territorial Indians to the Uinta Basin. Many of the Indians went, but not the Goshutes; they refused to leave the Deep Creek region. Between 1863 and 1870 other treaties were made and not ratified. By that time the Goshutes of necessity had become less hostile toward the whites due to the ever-increasing dominance of the latter, and they were beginning to farm seriously in Deep Creek and Skull Valley. In 1869 thirty acres of wheat, potatoes, and turnips were under cultivation by Native Americans at Deep Creek. Various attempts were made to move the Goshutes to Fort Hall, the Uinta Valley, and even to Indian Territory (present-day Oklahoma), but they stubbornly resisted. They did not want to live with strange people nor leave the land of their ancestors.[22]

In 1873 John Wesley Powell and George W. Ingals were appointed by the U.S. government to examine the condition of some western Indians. Once again it was recommended that they be sent to the reservation at the Uinta Basin. The Indians were very concerned, and their leaders met with General H.A. Morrow at Camp Douglas. Morrow went to the national Commission of Indian Affairs and told its members that the "valley now occupied by them is unfit for the purpose of farming by white men and if abandoned by the Indians it would relapse into a desert."[23] William Lee, a Mormon farmer and interpreter, agreed with Morrow, but apparently believed that the Indians were capable of successfully farming in the area. Ingals continued to recommend that the Goshutes be sent to the Uinta Valley, and Lee continued to write letters requesting aid to help the Indians become more self sufficient.

The situation basically continued from the 1870s to the end of the century, although by that time the Goshutes had largely been forgotten. Two reservations finally were established by executive orders in the twentieth century. On 17 January 1912 President William Howard Taft set aside eighty acres in Skull Valley for the exclusive use of the Goshute Indians residing there. On 7 September 1919 the small reserve was enlarged by an additional 17,920 acres by order of President Woodrow Wilson. The Deep Creek Goshute Reservation in western Tooele County and eastern Nevada was established on 23 March 1914, when some 34,560 acres in Utah was declared an Indian reservation by President Wilson.[24]

The Goshutes today are located primarily in northwestern Utah and northeastern Nevada. Their reservations are located in western Juab and Tooele Counties. The Goshute experience, with the establishment of these reservations, illustrates the continuation of traditional Indian-white relationships. The pattern of contact, encroachment, treaties, peace, white demands for additional concessions, Indian protest followed by white retaliation, and finally Indian acceptance of more restrictive reservations marks Goshute history as it does that of most other Indian groups.

ENDNOTES

1. Alan R. Schroedl, "Paleo-Indian Occupation in the Eastern Great Basin and Northern Colorado Plateau," *Utah Archaeology* 4 (1991): 6–7.

2. Jesse D. Jennings, "Prehistory of Utah and the Eastern Great Basin," University of Utah Anthropological Papers Number 98 (1978): 17–21. See also LaMar W. Lindsay and Kay Sargeant, "Prehistory of the Deep Creek Mountain Area, Western Utah," *Antiquities Section Selected Papers* 6 (1979): 22 for a brief discussion on a possible Paleo-Indian surface site located between Trout and Granite Creeks.

3. James M. Copeland and Richard E. Fike, "Fluted Projectile Points in Utah," *Utah Archaeology* 1 (1988): 26.

4. Jesse D. Jennings, *The Prehistory of North America* (New York: McGraw-Hill, 1974), 110–11.

5. David B. Madsen, "The Human Prehistory of the Great Salt Lake Region," in J. Wallace Gwynn, ed., *Great Salt Lake: A Scientific, Historical and Economic Overview,* Utah Department of Natural Resources Bulletin No. 115 (1980), 20, 24.

6. Jesse D. Jennings, "Prehistory of Utah," 84–85; David B. Madsen and James F. O'Connell, eds., *Man and Environment in the Great Basin,* Society of American Archaeologists Papers No. 2 (1982), 214.

7. Madsen and O'Connell, *Man and Environment,* 213.

8. Floyd W. Sharrock and John P. Marwitt, "Excavations at Nephi, Utah, 1965–1966," University of Utah Anthropological Papers No. 88 (1967), 49.

9. Ibid., 5–10.

10. Ibid., 49.

11. Ibid., 45, 49.

12. See David B. Madsen and Richard Fike, "Archaeological Investigations in Utah at Fish Springs, Clay Basin, Northern San Rafael Swell, Southern Henry Mountains," Bureau of Land Management, Utah Cultural Resource Series No. 12 (1982), 54.

13. Madsen and Fike, "Archaeological Investigations in Utah at Fish Springs," 48.

14. John P. Marwitt, "Fremont Cultures," in *Handbook of North American Indians: Great Basin,* Vol. 11, Warren L. D'Azevedo, ed. (Washington, D.C.: Smithsonian Institution, 1986), 171–72; William D. Lipe, "The Southwest," in *Ancient North Americans,* Jesse D. Jennings, ed. (New York: W.H. Freeman and Company, 1983), 480–82.

15. Richard D. Poll, Thomas G. Alexander, Eugene E. Campbell, and David E. Miller, eds., *Utah's History* (Provo, Utah: Brigham Young University Press, 1978), 26.

16. Ibid.

17. James B. Allen and Ted J. Warner, "The Gosiute Indians in Pioneer Utah," *Utah Historical Quarterly* 39 (1971): 163.

18. Ibid., 164–66.

19. Ibid., 166.

20. Ibid.

21. Ibid., 168.

22. Ibid., 174.

23. Quoted in ibid., 175.

24. Ibid., 177.

CHAPTER 3

EXPLORATION AND EARLY SETTLEMENT

Early Exploration

Various references lead historians to believe that Spaniards traveled into the Utah area before 1776; however, the most thoroughly documented account comes from the expedition of that year led by Franciscan friars Francisco Atanasio Domínguez and Silvestre Velez de Escalante. Earlier expeditions under the command of Juan Maria Antonio de Rivera twice entered the Utah region. The first expedition occurred in June and July 1765; it was followed by a second in October and November of the same year. Both went into the Four Corners region of the southeastern corner of the future state—the first in the vicinity of Aneth, and the second, farther north into the Moab area. The journeys were to verify the existence of the Colorado River and scout Native Americans in the region, with a secondary objective being the discovery of precious metals. Rivera's instructions for the second trek were, in part, "to reconnoiter the land along the trail, at the crossing, and on the other side of the [Colorado] river; to determine the names of the nations they encountered; and to ascer-

Sketch of the Domingez-Escalante Expedition. Artist Unknown. (Utah State Historical Society)

tain the languages of the native groups and their attitude toward the Spanish; and to make a journal account of the trip and map the trail to the crossing."[1] With Rivera's reports of friendly Utes that they encountered, this expedition helped set the groundwork for the Domínguez-Escalante journey.

Father Francisco Atanasio Domínguez had been instructed to search for a route from Santa Fe to Monterey, California. He ordered Father Silvestre Velez de Escalante to accompany him. Eight additional men were selected to participate, including Don Bernardo Miera y Pacheco, who served as the group's cartographer. After some delay, the group left Santa Fe on 29 July 1776.[2] The Domínguez-Escalante journal and Miera's map remain significant documents in the understanding of the history and geography of early Utah, including a portion of future Juab County. The expedition arrived in Utah on 11 September 1776 near Jensen and then traveled west to the banks of the Green River. They then proceeded southwest to the junction of the Uinta and the Duchesne Rivers and along Diamond Creek to the Spanish Fork River, which they followed to the shore of Utah Lake; an area they named *La Valle de Nuestra Senora de la Merced* (the Valley of Our Lady of Mercy).[3]

After spending a couple of days with the Laguna, or Timpanogos, Ute Indians, the padres headed south along the western flank of the Wasatch Mountains. By 27 September, they were in future Juab County and provide the first eyewitness account of Juab Valley:

> This [Valle de las Salinas, today Juab Valley] is one of those just mentioned above, and it must extend fourteen leagues from north to south and five from east to west. It is all level land, greatly abounding in water and pasturage, even though no river flows through it other than a small one. There a great number of fowl breed, . . . We went another four leagues south over the valley floor and stopped by a copious running spring of good water, which we named Ojo de San Pablo [Burriston Ponds, about 1.3 miles south-southwest of Mona].[4]

Throughout the expedition, Spanish names were given to many locations, including some in Juab. The padres in entering Juab from Utah County crossed a gentle pass through which Interstate 15 now passes. That pass, on the county line, was called *Puerto de San Pedro,* the Gate of St. Peter.

On 28 September the expedition reached Salt Creek. Escalante wrote:

> . . . having traveled four leagues we arrived at a small river [Four Mile Creek] which comes down from the same eastern part of the sierra in which the salt flats are, according to what they told us. We stopped here a short time in the shade of the cottonwoods on the bank to get some relief from the great heat, and we had scarcely sat down when, from among some thick clumps of willows, eight Indians very fearfully approached us, most of them naked except for a piece of buckskin around their loins. We spoke to them and they spoke to us, but without either of us understanding the other, because the two Lagunas [Utes] and the interpreter had gone ahead. By the signs we gave them to understand that we were peaceful and friendly people. We continued toward the south, and having traveled three leagues we swung southeast half a league and

another half to the south and camped [near Levan], while still in the valley, near a spring which we named San Bernardino.—Today eight leagues [twenty-one miles] almost all to the south.[5]

The following day, the expedition continued in a south-south-westerly direction, meeting six Indians with whom they talked and preached. Traveling farther to the southwest, leaving *El Valle de las Salinas* (Juab Valley, on the route of the future Old Botham Road) they met an old Indian living alone in a small brush hut. They described the old Indian as having a beard "so thick and long that he looked like one of the hermits of Europe." The men explained to the padres that within a short distance they would cross a river, describing for them the country in which they would travel. Later in the day, the expedition came to that river after having crossed "some little valleys and dry hills" (present-day Washboard Valley). They arrived at the river, as Escalante described, "not discovering it until we were on its very bank."[6]

Domínguez and Escalante were at a point on the Sevier River approximately where present-day U.S. Highway 91 crosses the river. They described their campsite as "a meadow with good pasturage, which we named Santa Ysabel." The Sevier River was named the *Rio de Santa Isabel.*[7] Here they took latitudinal bearings and estimated that they were at 39 degrees 4 minutes latitude. Again, Indians met with the party, informing the Spaniards of the terrain and water sources ahead.

On the day of 30 September the expedition encountered twenty Indians wrapped in blankets made from rabbitskins. They were peaceful and friendly, and, like those encountered earlier, the men wore heavy beards, heavier than those of the Lagunas met earlier at Utah Lake. Of this, the friars stated,

> Now these ones, more fully bearded than the Lagunas, have their nostril-cartilage pierced, and in the hole, by way of adornment, they wear a tiny polished bone of deer, fowl, or some other animal. In their features they more resemble the Spaniards than they do all the other Indians known in America up to now, from whom they differ in what has been said. They employ the same language as the Timpanogotizis. From the river and site of Santa Isabel onward begin these full-bearded Indians.[8]

These "Yutas Barbones," or Bearded Utes (probably Southern Paiutes), so intrigued the cartographer Don Berdardo Miera that he sketched them on one version of his map. By the end of the day, the expedition had departed future Juab County heading in a south-southwesterly direction.

Within a few days, Domínguez and Escalante encountered foul, stormy weather in central Beaver County. Here, rather than trying to push on to California with the possibility of being trapped in deep snows in the mountains to the west, they decided to return to Santa Fe. In early January 1777 the expedition, after much hardship, arrived in Santa Fe and submitted a report to their superiors.[9]

Domínguez and Escalante had promised the Utes they would return in a year, but political difficulties prevented the establishment of Spanish settlements in the Utah area. However, other Spaniards subsequently traded frequently with Utah Indians. The Spanish discovered that they could obtain good beaver pelts from the Indians. Also, the Indians captured women and children from rival tribes and sold them to the Spaniards. They, in turn, sold them as slaves to other Spaniards and Mexicans. A legacy of this trade was the creation of the Old Spanish Trail from New Mexico through Utah to California to the south and east of Juab County.

The Mountain Men

Beginning in the 1820s fur trappers and traders used and popularized paths through the West that later often became the routes traveled by people who came to settle. These men were known to history as the mountain men. At that time, beaver pelts were bringing ten dollars or more in St. Louis and the demand for them was great, as beaver felt hats were highly fashionable. On 20 March 1822 William H. Ashley placed the following notice, "To Enterprising Young Men," in the *Missouri Republican* of St. Louis:

> The subscriber wishes to engage ONE HUNDRED MEN to ascend the Missouri to its source, there to be employed for one, two or three years.—For particulars enquire of Major Andrew Henry, near the Lead Mines, in the County of Washington, (who will ascend with, and command the party) or to the subscriber at St. Louis. [10]

Artist's sketch of Jedediah Strong Smith (1798–1831). Sketch allegedly made by a friend, from memory, after Smith's death. (Utah State Historical Society)

Among those who answered were men who later became famous in history including Jedediah S. Smith, James Bridger, David E. Jackson, Thomas Fitzpatrick, James Clayman, William L. Sublette, Daniel T. Potts, Hugh Glass, John H. Weber, Milton G. Sublette, Moses (Black) Harris, James Beckwourth, and others. Most of the men eventually made their way into Utah, and some discovered that some of the country southwest of the Great Salt Lake was a promising area to trap beaver.

In 1825 Ashley made his way as far as Sevier Lake, which was given the name of Ashley Lake at the time. (It is interesting to note that Don Bernardo Miera of the Domínguez-Escalante expedition had named Sevier Lake after himself, *Laguna de Miera*—Miera Lake.) On 18 July 1826 Ashley sold his company to Jedediah S. Smith, David E. Jackson, and William L. Sublette, who established the firm of Smith, Jackson & Sublette. By October 1827 the men were able to pay off their indebtedness to Ashley and to lay the foundations of comfortable fortunes for themselves.[11] William H. Ashley had "fired the minds of everyone with visions of wealth. . . . He had brought down in 1824 one hundred packs, in 1826 one hundred and twenty-three packs, in 1827 one hundred and thirty packs." From 1823 to 1826, an estimated $250,000 worth of beaver pelts had been delivered to St. Louis.[12]

Jedediah Strong Smith concentrated on exploring the area between Utah and California. In August 1826 he and a party of fifteen men left on a "South West Expedition." From a rendevzous in Cache Valley, the group traveled to the Great Salt Lake and into Utah Valley. This proved to be the first foray of "American" trappers into the area. Smith handed out gifts to the Utes residing at Utah Lake but could not understand anything of their explanation of what lie ahead. According to historian Dale Morgan, "Jedediah carried seven hundredweight of dried buffalo meat. He was soon glad of his forethought, for after leaving Utah Valley he saw no more buffalo, nothing but an occasional antelope, a mountain sheep or what was most plentiful, 'black-tailed hares.'"[13]

Three days after departing the Utes, Smith reached the Sevier River, which proved to be at that time from three to four feet deep and about twelve yards wide. The long valley through which the river wound was arid and devoid of timber. The soil was dry, but where side streams had flooded the bottoms, grass grew to the horses' bellies.[14] Smith traveled southwest through the Sevier Valley and on to the Virgin River, then to San Gabriel and San Diego, California, where the men were considered spies and trespassers and eventually were ordered to leave.

Smith, Robert Evans, and Silas Goble eventually crossed the Sierra Nevada in 1827, making their way across Nevada and the Goshute region of western Utah. Jedediah Smith's own journal offers a keen insight into the region north of present-day Gandy in Millard County:

> North 25 Miles. My course was nearly parallel with a chain of hills on the west [Deep Creek Mountains], on the tops of which was some snow and from which ran a creek to the North East. On this creek [Thomas Creek] I encamped. The Country in the vicinity so much resembled that on the south side of the Salt Lake that for a while I was induced to believe that I was near that place. During the day I saw a good many Antelope but could not kill any. I however, killed 2 hares which when cooked at night we found much better than horse meat. June 23d N E 35 Miles. Moving on in the mourning I kept down the creek on which we had encamped until it was lost in a small Lake. We then filled our horns and continued on our course, passing some brackish as well as some very salt springs [Salt Wells], and leaving on the north of the latter part of the days travel a considerable Salt Plain [the Salt Desert, the northern reaches of which he had seen the year before]. Just before night I found water that was drinkable but continued on in hopes of finding better and was obliged to encamp without any.[15]

Smith and his companions barely survived this ordeal, returning to Bear Lake for the 1827 rendezvous.

In 1830 Jedediah Smith sold his partnership in the fur trade and left the mountains. His tragic death at the hands of a Comanche hunting party occurred on 27 May 1831 while he was serving as guide for a Santa Fe-bound wagon train and scouting for water in the Cimmeron Desert in New Mexico. He was thirty-one years old.[16] By about 1842 the fashion in men's hats had changed from felt to silk. The sale of beaver pelts was no longer profitable. The number of beaver in the West had been severely reduced by that time anyway, and many mountain men began to guide parties of settlers to and through the West. In ensuing years the settlers who came west followed the trails blazed and charted by these adventurous men.

Pony Express Cabin, Callao. Supposed resting place for Mark Twain when he journeyed through the area by stage in 1861. (Tintic Historical Society)

Government Exploration

Although the territory that became Utah was technically controlled by Mexico, increasing numbers of Americans were looking westward for expansion of their nation and their own personal fortunes, creating a movement called at the time Manifest Destiny—that is, that it was the destiny or mission of the United States to control the continent from ocean to ocean. As a result, a number of private adventurers and government explorers began to travel the region, becoming acquainted with its features.

The United States gained control of much of the West in 1848 as a result of the Treaty of Guadalupe Hidalgo ending the Mexican War. Mexico ceded most of its claims to land north of the present border, including all of Utah. This development spurred both government and Mormon exploration of the interior West.

Although the Great Basin was somewhat forbidding due to the treacherous desert expanse to the west of present-day Juab County, a few explorers are known to have passed through parts of the future county, especially along the natural north-south corridor of travel at the foot of the Wasatch Mountains. Captain John C. Frémont is thought to have traveled along this route in the course of his first

Pony Express Marker, Callao, 1939, taken by Dick Seal. (Tintic Historical Society)

western expedition in 1843–44. His published reports were influential in the decision of Mormon leaders to relocate to the region.

After the arrival to the region of the Mormons in 1847 other government explorers mapped and traveled through the region. Notable among them were the Captain James H. Simpson survey of 1858–59, which traveled across large sections of the county traveling both east and west in its search for routes to and from California. Earlier, in 1853, Captain John W. Gunnison traveled through a corner of the county before being killed with members of his survey party in Millard County. The county continued to be studied by men developing both north-south and east-west routes, as the county was favorably situated for such undertakings—something of which residents later boasted as they attempted to promote visitation to the area.

Mormon Exploration

With permanent Mormon settlement beginning in 1851, Juab has become an area of agriculture, mining, and recreation. The Church of Jesus Christ of Latter-day Saints, commonly known as the

Mormon or LDS church, was organized in 1830 by Joseph Smith, Jr., in Palmyra, New York, and, although its membership steadily grew, members were not readily accepted by the people of other denominations. Their zealous preaching and claims that all other churches were false met with opposition expressed in political and even physical conflict. The Latter-day Saints moved from Palmyra to Kirtland, Ohio, and from there to Jackson County, Missouri. In the winter of 1838–39 they were forced to leave Missouri and go to Illinois, where they settled on the banks of the Mississippi River. The land was transformed from swampland to a city of perhaps 12,000 people by 1845.

On 27 June 1844, however, Joseph Smith was killed while in custody at Carthage, Illinois, and Brigham Young became the leader of the Mormons. He and his associates decided in 1845 to go to the West. The establishment of the Mormons and their "Kingdom of God" in the Great Basin and what has been called "its ultimate accommodation to secular political, economic, and social pressures and influences would prove to be the central theme in the history of Utah," according to some historians.[17]

Brigham Young entered the Salt Lake Valley on 24 July 1847. The first arrivals immediately began to plow the ground, plant crops, and prepare to establish the community they had dreamed of. Young also began to explore the surrounding areas for likely places where other settlements could be situated both within and outside the borders of the present state. A party of eighteen led by Captain Jefferson Hunt of the Mormon Battalion, which had served in the Mexican War, left Salt Lake City on 13 November 1847, traveling south to California. The men traveled through future Juab County on a route closely approximating that of later U.S. Highway 91, returning in February 1848 with livestock and other supplies. A party of Mormon Battalion members in California followed Hunt's trail in the spring of 1848, arriving in Salt Lake in June. They were the first to use a wagon on the trail. Hunt and others subsequently used the trail that was being rapidly developed.[18]

Another route west developed at about this time was known by Utahns as the Egan Trail and went through parts of western Juab County. Howard Egan had been a major in the Nauvoo Legion and became a well-known guide and mountaineer after coming to Utah.

Nephi Plaster Mill Site, 1998. (Wayne Christiansen)

He worked for Livingston and Kinkead, driving cattle to California. He also guided gold-seeking Forty-niners to California in 1849. Egan probably searched out and mapped the Egan Trail while he was driving cattle and later used it after he carried the mail for George

A photograph of Nephi Depot, looking south, 1974, taken by Jim Ozment. (Utah State Historical Society)

Chorpening, who had established a mail and freight service between Salt Lake City and San Francisco—the "Jackass Mail."

In his diary for 1855, Egan penned the following notes about the trail:

> Commencement of trail . . . was ninety miles to the right (or south) of the sink of Humboldt. Across a valley twelve miles—little water in canyon over a mountain five miles; little water to the right in the creek across a valley one mile from the road at foot of mountain, good grass and water. Thirty miles to summit of mountain. Ten miles to left, one mile over small mountain creek. Fifteen miles to Ruby Valley. Twenty miles down to valley; forty miles in same valley, creek fifteen miles [perhaps Shell Creek] on the side of a small mountain is a large spring. Twenty miles over mountain five or six springs [Spring Valley]. Twelve miles to summit of a little mountain; twenty five miles to Deep Creek; thirty miles to desert; twenty miles over summit of mountain; forty five miles to Salt Spring. To creek sixteen miles.[19]

The trail was later used by the Pony Express.

On 23 November 1849 Parley P. Pratt and fifty other men were instructed to look for likely locations for more colonies south of Salt Lake City. They traveled through what is now Juab, Sanpete, Sevier and Iron Counties. They also went as far south as the Virgin and Santa Clara Valleys. Their report became a basis for a line of colonies from Utah Valley to the Sevier and Virgin Rivers.[20] Mormon leaders planned to build a string of settlements from Salt Lake City to San Bernardino, California, which became known as the Mormon Corridor to the Pacific. They felt it would be easier for immigrants from other countries to get to Utah by sea instead of making the trip across the North American continent. The corridor also would provide a route for trade. Since a good water supply was of prime importance to their survival, they searched for and placed towns near creeks or lakes. This effort led to the settlement of Nephi and other towns in the Juab Valley.

Early Settlements of East Juab County

Juab was among the first six counties created by the legislature of the Provisional State of Deseret in December 1849. Originally the boundaries were loosely defined, but, when later formalized, they extended from the highest summit ridgeline of Mount Nebo to the eastern boundary of California. The western portion was reduced in 1861 and 1866, when the Territory of Nevada was organized and then made a state. Nephi and Mona (Clover Creek) were the only settlements in Juab County when Governor Brigham Young of Utah Territory approved an act of 7 February 1852 appointing probate judges for several counties in the territory.

George W. Bradley was appointed probate judge of Juab County, and under his direction the county organization was completed on 1 August 1852. The following were either elected or appointed: John Carter, Charles H. Bryan, and William Cazier, selectmen (commissioners); Israel Hoyt, sheriff; Amos Gustin, clerk of the county and probate courts; Z.H. Baxter, assessor and collector. Amos Gustin also acted as recorder and Z.H. Baxter served as county surveyor.[21]

Nephi. Salt Creek, as it was called early, was along the Mormon Corridor and was first explored by Parley P. Pratt. The settlement was

The Old Searles Home at Starr. (Tintic Historical Society)

located at the mouth of what was later called Salt Creek Canyon, so named because the water coming from the canyon had a salty taste. The name, at the suggestion of Brigham Young, was soon changed to Nephi, a name from the Book of Mormon, but it was not until 22 May 1882 that the U.S. Postal Department approved the name change.

It was the custom of Mormon church authorities to send or "call" individuals to settle the communities of what they first called the State of Deseret, a huge territory soon officially reduced by Congress to the (still large) Territory of Utah in 1850. One man was given the authority to head the settlement and others were called to take their families and help. Some were given specific assignments according to what was needed and available at that time.

In the summer of 1851 Joseph L. Heywood was called to supervise the settlement of Salt Creek. According to the journal of his wife, Martha Spence Heywood, they arrived on the evening of 21 September and Joseph Heywood held a council meeting on 23 September to assign certain tasks to some of the men. She wrote that a vote was taken

> appointing Brother Foote the captain of the guard and also to have an oversight in reference to the brethren having fire arms and in good order with the privilege of calling them out for examination and drill when he thought suitable. Next Mr. H. [Heywood] pro-

Trout Creek, 1998. (Wayne Christiansen)

posed Father Gifford to preside over the meetings. . . . Mr. H. also made some observations as to the right of individuals taking up and following their own particular branch of business and counseled Br. Baxter to build a grist mill and Brother Camp to build a saw mill. [22]

Jesse W. Fox, the territorial surveyor, with the help of Joseph L. Heywood, surveyed a townsite one-half-mile square. According to Martha's journal, the site was to be divided into blocks which would be twenty-six rods square, each block would contain four lots and the streets would be six rods wide, with the exception of the state road which passed north and south, which was to be eight rods wide. Two blocks were to be reserved for public purposes. The house of Timothy B. Foote was the first to be finished, but others soon followed and the little settlement began to grow. There was plenty of wood nearby for fires to keep the settlers warm, but that which could be used for lumber was higher in the hills and roads had to be built before they could get to it.

The first thing done was to clear and plant the land so the settlers would be able to have crops for the needs of both their livestock and themselves. A dam was built across Salt Creek in order that the water

Site of Joy. (Utah State Historical Society)

could be used to irrigate their crops. The industrious people soon planted gardens, fruit trees, grain, hay, shade trees, and even kept a few beehives in the area.

In the spring of 1854 Brigham Young instructed the settlers to build a fort to protect themselves from the Indians, as troubles had erupted between Mormons and followers of the Ute leader Walkara (Walker) the previous year. The fort was begun in May of that year. Its walls enclosed three square blocks and were twelve feet high, six feet wide at the bottom, over two feet wide at the top, and were made of mud and straw. Each man was given a portion of the wall to build. When the structure was completed it was about 420 rods long and cost approximately $8,400. Two heavy gates were erected, one on the north side and the other the south side.[23] After the Walker War ended later that year the settlers began to build outside of the fort, where their homes could be larger and they could also have corrals, barns, and yards large enough to plant gardens.

Mona. Soon after the first settlers came to Nephi some of them began to make improvements near Clover Creek Spring, about seven miles north of Nephi. In February 1852 Andrew Love and his family, as well as James A. Bigelow and his family settled there. John A. Wolf and his family joined them in March 1852. According to Love's journal, in the following spring they built a canyon road and cut timber. When the Walker War began in July 1853, they moved back to Nephi, where they felt they would be safer.

In January 1860 Edward Kay was called to start a settlement at Clover Creek. The following spring, John Vest was called to join him, and others soon followed. The town was first called Clover Creek and then Willow Creek. Dr. Matthew McCune later suggested the name of Mona for the town, after his former home on the Isle of Man in the British Isles, and the other settlers agreed.

While they were building homes and clearing the ground, they also found time to erect a building which would serve as a schoolhouse, a chapel, and a place to hold other meetings and social gatherings. They built a look-out platform by the chimney to watch for Indians. Brigham Young later suggested that they move the settlement farther east to a better site and the settlers complied, moving the town to its present location.

Mormon Apostle Erastus Snow was sent to aid in the laying out and planning of the town. The site was initially surveyed in the spring of 1867 by Juab County Surveyor Charles Price and expanded over the years.[24]

Cheney's Ranch (Starr). Starr was located about three and one-half miles north of Mona on the route of Highway 91. In 1858 the federal soldiers of Johnston's Army established a ranch near the springs, built a livestock corral, and kept stock there until the following fall. Ike Potter located a ranch near the springs and sold it to Elam Cheney in 1859. Cheney lived there alone for about four years. Eventually, Uriah Stewart of Springville settled near him, and in 1870 Cheney sold his ranch to Jackson Stewart. A few years later most of the property was purchased by the Albert W. Starr family, and William A. Starr operated the ranch until about 1910. By 1900 about a dozen families were living there. In 1880 settlers had constructed a school, which was also used for church and social gatherings. According to Juab School District minutes for 13 July 1915, local students were sent to Mona the following fall. Ranches continue to occupy the area.

Levan (Chicken Creek). The original settlement of Chicken Creek was about three miles southwest of present-day Levan. During 1860 William Cole and Samuel Cazier established a ranch at Chicken Creek; others soon followed.[25] By 1867 it was evident that the soil at this location was not as good as it could have been and that the settlers were too far away from water sources for irrigation purposes. Since Chicken Creek was a branch of the LDS church, church authorities were consulted about moving the settlement. In September, James Wilson wrote to Apostle Erastus Snow asking him to use his influence to have the settlement moved. When Snow came to Chicken Creek, he and the settlers decided on a site about one-half mile west of the mountain and halfway between Chicken Creek and Pigeon Creek Canyons, the present-day location of Levan.[26]

According to one historian,

> The Seth Ollerton II family arrived in Utah in 1864 and settled at Chicken Creek, Juab County. They stayed there only a short time then moved to Parawan but returned shortly thereafter to Chicken Creek. He took up 160 acres of land where Levan now stands . He also filed on a spring. When that area was chosen for a new community he was asked to turn the tract of land over to the settlers. He did and later helped to survey the town.[27]

Arthur Meade filed on the quarter section of land that included the former settlement of Chicken Creek and built a shearing corral. By 1876, however, all that was left there were a few foundations and fireplace rocks.

Juab County Surveyor Charles Price surveyed the new townsite in December 1867. The settlement consisted of fifty-six blocks. Each block was twenty-six rods square with streets six rods wide. The town was seven blocks by eight blocks. The fields west of town were also surveyed and were made into plots of ten and twenty acres. A married man was given twenty acres and a single man was given ten acres. Families gradually moved from Chicken Creek to Levan. The population increased and soon there was a mercantile business, a

Mining Structure, Joy. (Utah State Historical Society)

molasses factory, a broom-making shop, a livery stable, and a black-smith shop.

Places for meetings and celebrations formed central locations for townfolks. In 1869 the first meetinghouse was built in Levan. This adobe building also was used for school classes until 1892. On 24 July 1869 Pioneer Day was celebrated by the people of Levan, and towns-folk have kept the tradition alive.

The water supply was a constant concern for the pioneer settlers of Levan. In 1873 a site was chosen between Chicken Creek and Pigeon Creek for the construction of a reservoir. The dam was about thirty feet wide at the base and ten feet wide at the top. When water was turned into it for testing, however, the builders discovered it had been built over a fault and would not hold water. This was very dis-appointing for them.

In 1874 a branch of the Mormon church's United Order was organized in Levan to help bring about cooperation in temporal affairs. Material possessions were turned over to the order, and all

Mary Laird ran a boarding house, saloon, and store at Joy. (Utah State Historical Society)

produce from the cooperative enterprises was put into a common storehouse and distributed to each according to their needs. Such a cooperative living arrangement was too difficult for most to practice, and, as elsewhere in other Mormon communities, the local order was soon dissolved.

Farming was the main local industry, and cash was very scarce in the early years. To gain currency, some of the men supplemented their income by working on the railroad; others sold vegetables, eggs, butter, meat, cheese, and flour to the railroad workers or to other communities. Some locals sheared sheep in the spring.

Little Salt Creek. In 1870 and 1871 a small polygamous settlement began at the mouth of Little Salt Creek, six miles south of Levan. It consisted of the families of Martin, Norman, and Crispin Taylor. A one-room schoolhouse was built which also served as a church. The settlers became part of the Levan LDS Branch. In about 1881 the Taylor families sold their ranch and moved away.[28]

York. In 1875 the Utah Southern Railroad built south from Provo and established a terminus about four miles south of Santaquin and fifteen miles north of Nephi on the main north-south transportation corridor. The station was named York and quickly became a prosperous little town. For two years it was the closest railroad station to the rich Tintic mines and shipped thousands of tons of ore to the smelters in the Salt Lake Valley. Hundreds of carloads of produce also were shipped out by the farmers, while building material and hardware was brought in. According to one account,

> The town consisted of railroad buildings—a depot, water tower, coal station, turning wye and warehouses, plus several homes for railroad employees. Several farmers also built their homes in town; a busy hotel, store and restaurants were erected. The town remained quit active as the railroad started building south again in 1877. One reason was that it took an unexplained two years to lay 28 miles of track through Nephi to Juab. In 1879 much of the railroad operation was switched to Juab and York lost its glamour and its business as a terminal city.[29]

Juab. In 1876 John C. Whitbeck secured from the government a quarter section of land six miles south and west of Levan. He named it Juab and moved his mail station from Chicken Creek in order to have better water and feed for his animals. By 1879 the railroad reached Juab and it became the terminus. A town quickly grew and soon had a brick schoolhouse, two hotels, a store, and a saloon. In the early days of the railroad terminal, mine owners in Marysvale had their ore hauled to Juab for shipment to the smelters in Salt Lake City. However, according to one history,

> Just as the town was settling down to become a terminal railroad city, the millionaire banker Jay Cooke cajoled the railroad officials to build on down to Milford, thence up to Frisco where Cooke owned the famous Horn Silver mine. The railroad built to Milford without an intervening pause, and during that short year Juab remained the terminus.[30]

Most of the area's residents followed the railroad on to Milford. Others moved to Nephi or Levan, leaving Juab to eventually become a virtual ghost town, with just scattered ranches in the area in subsequent years.

Mills. In 1877 a Mr. Winigar settled in what is now Mills on land west of the Sevier River, about twenty-four miles southwest of Nephi. At that time it probably looked as if it would be an ideal place for homesteading. There was plenty of water, the land was flat, and there was grass to feed livestock. Soon other settlers followed, but they found it a very difficult task to make a living. The alkaline soil, abundance of snakes, and mosquitoes made living in the area somewhat unpleasant. The location soon was called Suckertown because of the mosquitoes. During this time the Utah Central/Utah Southern Railroad which was being built between Juab and Milford went through the valley. Henry Mills, one of the first group of settlers, worked for the railroad and the little town was named after him. From 1883 to 1896 it was officially listed as the Wellington Branch of the LDS church, and in 1900 the branch became a part of the Juab LDS Ward.

Nortonville. A small ranching community about four miles north of Nephi, Nortonville was first settled by three men from Arizona— John Holland, Joseph Marble, and Nathaniel Marble. They did not stay very long, however. The land was later homesteaded by brothers Wesley, Isaac, and John Norton, for whom the community was named. In about 1881 the land was purchased by Edward Jones and William Tolley. Jones's two sons, Edward and William, worked the

West Desert School, Partoun, 1998. (Wayne Christiansen)

land and raised their families there. The also constructed ditches from the canyon streams and eventually piped the water close to their homes. Citizens petitioned the school board at Nephi requesting a school. The petition was granted, and in 1888 Nebo School District 9 was established for the area. School was held in a small one-room building; when it became too small, residents built a larger one. By 1911, however, the population had declined such that the few remaining students were sent to Nephi.

Early Settlements of West Juab County

Pleasant Valley. Pleasant Valley lies west of Snake Valley. Part of it is in Utah and part is in White Pine County, Nevada, The town was first known as Uvada. It was founded in 1851 by H.J. Faust, Howard Egan, and Al Huntington, who were establishing a mail route to California. During the Pony Express days the area housed a sleeping station. When the Pony Express was discontinued, the station was abandoned for a few years.

In 1870 two men, named Dooley and White, were driving cattle to California. The story goes that they stumbled across Pleasant Valley early one morning in March as the sun was rising. One of the

Fish Springs National Wildlife Refuge, 1998. (Wayne Christiansen)

men mentioned that the beautiful, peaceful valley was a pleasant place—thus, it subsequently became known as Pleasant Valley. Both Dooley and White settled there and for several years ran longhorn cattle in the area.

Several springs supplied water for irrigation and the occasional runoff from Water Canyon was also used. People moved into the valley to take up homesteads, some of which proved profitable while others did not. Some people always remained, however, and ranchers continued to inhabit the area to the present day.[31]

Trout Creek. Located in the west-central part of Juab County's portion of Snake Valley, Trout Creek was settled by ranchers who were looking for a place to graze their sheep during the winter months. There was also some mining in the vicinity. At one time the population was listed at fifty and the town supported a store, schoolhouse, and a post office. Most of the original buildings have been destroyed by fire, however, as the town area is largely abandoned.

Joy. In 1872 the Drum Mountain Mining District was organized in the mountains straddling the Juab-Millard County line. In 1879 Harry Joy and Charles Howard, two mining engineers from Michigan, reorganized it into the Detroit District, named after their hometown, and established mining operations and a smelter at the new town of Joy. The town became a supply center for miners and ranchers in the area. Dwellings were erected as well as a hotel, cafe, and store. The Howard Mine attempted to operate a smelter in Joy, but it was too expensive to haul fuel to it, so it did not last long. The Ward Leasing Company worked a mine about one mile southeast of Joy until 1946.[32]

Fish Springs. George Chorpening used Fish Springs for a watering station on his overland freight route. It later became a station for the Pony Express, stage lines, and the telegraph. By 1899 the Galina and Utah mines were operating in the area, and by 1904 the mining camp had 250 miners. Ranching and other ventures also found their way to Fish Springs. In 1902 John Thomas established a ranch near the station.

The Pony Express

Howard Egan, mentioned earlier, was born on 15 June 1815 in Ireland. Soon after his mother died, when he was five years old, his father took his family to Montreal, Canada, where he died five years later. Egan grew, married, and he and his wife subsequently became members of the LDS church in 1842 and went to Nauvoo, Illinois. He was among the first company of Latter-day Saints to arrive in the Salt Lake Valley. Egan was associated with a mail and freight service that held the first U.S. mail contract for service between Salt Lake City and San Francisco, California. The firm of Russell, Majors, and Waddell purchased the mail and transportation contracts in 1860 and established the Central Overland, California, and Pike's Peak Express Company. This company continued until its contract was lost to Ben Holliday in 1862. The trail, which was mapped out by Egan, consisted of fifty-six stations and covered a distance of 658 miles—the distance between Salt Lake City and the California border.[33]

Russell, Majors, and Waddell also established the Pony Express, which operated for less than two years in 1860–61. The portion of the Pony Express route between Salt Lake City and Robert's Creek (now in Nevada) was under the direct supervision of Howard Egan. His knowledge of the roadometer (used in measuring distance) undoubtedly aided in his responsibility to lay out the Pony Express stations within his division. Egan's two sons, Howard Ransom and Richard Erastus, both rode for the Pony Express.[34] The route through Juab County began a few miles north and east of Dugway Valley and continued west to Fish Springs, on to Callao (then known as Willow Springs), and then north to Ibapah in Tooele County.

The first mail from California reached Salt Lake City on 7 April 1860. Mail from St Joseph, Missouri, arrived in Salt Lake City on 9 April. The fastest ride, which carried President Abraham Lincoln's inaugural address, took a little over seven days. The Pony Express proved to be faster than any previous mail service, but with the necessity of 190 stations, approximately 420 horses, and sixty riders it was not profitable. The financial burden together with the completion of the transcontinental telegraph in 1861 brought an end to the Pony Express.[35] In 1870 the main route of transcontinental travel was changed to be adjacent to the new transcontinental railroad, which was north of the Great Salt Lake.

A Famous Traveler in the County

In addition to Spanish padres, mountain men, Mormon scouts, and Pony Express riders, at least one other person of note traveled through the territory of Utah in the early settlement period, touching the northern portion of Juab County. Samuel Clemens, better known as Mark Twain, ventured west in 1861 to assist his brother, who had been made Secretary of Nevada Territory. Enduring the trip along the Overland Stage route, the then budding author recounted some of his experiences in 1871 in a book entitled *Roughing It.* The book's informal nature, describing Twain's journey via stagecoach from Missouri to Nevada, allows an insight into the author as well as to his interpretation of the sights and sounds along the trail.

Twain's look at the land of northern Juab County, from Camp Floyd through to Callao and the land of the Goshutes, offers a brief eyewitness account of the area. Twain had fun in (or made fun of) Salt Lake City and wrote of his observations of the Mormons and Brigham Young. Upon leaving the territorial capital he wrote, "I left Salt Lake a good deal confused as to what state of things existed there—and sometimes even questioning in my own mind whether a

Cabin at Utah Mines, Fish Springs Mining District, 1998. (Wayne Christiansen)

state of things existed there at all or not."[36] This style marked Twain's writing of the entire trip.

From Salt Lake City, the stagecoach moved on to Camp Floyd, then headed southwest. Twain recounted,

> And now we entered upon one of that species of deserts whose concentrated hideousness shames the diffused and diluted horrors of Sahara—an "*alkali*" desert. For sixty-eight miles there was but one break in it. I do not remember that this was really a break; indeed it seems to me that it was nothing but a watering depot in the midst of the stretch of sixty-eight miles. If my memory serves me, there was no well or spring at this place, but the water was hauled there by mule and ox teams from the further side of the desert. There was a stage station there. It was forty-five miles from the beginning of the desert, and twenty-three from the end of it.[37]

For Twain, the novelty of a desert crossing soon gave way to reality. He continued,

> We plowed and dragged and groped along the whole live-long night, and at the end of this uncomfortable twelve hours we finished the forty-five-mile part of the desert and got to the stage sta-

tion where the imported water was. The sun was just rising. It was easy enough to cross a desert in the night while we were asleep; . . . but now we were to cross a desert in *daylight.* . . . The sun beats down with dead, blistering, relentless malignity; the perspiration is welling from every pore in man and beast, but scarcely a sign of it finds its way to the surface—it is absorbed before it gets there; . . . When we reached the station on the farther verge of the desert [Callao], we were glad, for the first time, that the dictionary was along, because we never could have found language to tell how glad we were, in any sort of dictionary but an unabridged one with pictures in it.[38]

The "Mark Twain Cabin," as one early structure is called, remains in Callao. The small log structure continues to capture the imagination of Twain's 1861 visit.[39]

The last section of Mark Twain's journey through the Juab area concentrated on his observations of the Goshute Indians. While perhaps "tongue in cheek," Twain's comments offer some insights into the common white men's view of this tribe.

On the morning of the sixteenth day out from St. Joseph we arrived at the entrance of Rocky Canyon, two hundred and fifty miles from Salt Lake. It was along in this wild country somewhere, and far from any habitation of white men, except the stage stations, that we came across the wretchedest type of mankind I have ever seen, up to this writing. I refer to the Goshoot Indians . . . who produce nothing at all, and have no villages, and . . . who inhabit one of the most rocky, wintry, repulsive wastes that our country or any other can exhibit.[40]

The resourcefulness of the Goshutes was lost on Twain and most other whites, who did not appreciate the Indians' skills in living on such harsh land. It was an attitude typical of how outsiders viewed these Indians of western Juab County and the surrounding region. White settlers of the area should have been more appreciative of the skills of the Native Americans, as they themselves increasingly faced difficulties in their attempts to wrest a livelihood from the land of Juab County.

ENDNOTES

1. G. Clell Jacobs, "The Phantom Pathfinder: Juan Maria Antonio de Rivera and His Expedition," *Utah Historical Quarterly* 60 (Summer 1992): 203.

2. Richard D. Poll, et al., *Utah's History,* 39–40.

3. Ibid., 40.

4. Ted J. Warner, ed., and Fray Angelico Chavez, trans., *The Dominguez-Escalante Journal* (Provo, Utah: Brigham Young University Press, 1976), 62.

5. Herbert E. Bolton, *Pageant in the Wilderness: The Story of the Escalante Expedition to the Interior Basin, 1776* (Salt Lake City: Utah State Historical Society, 1972), 188.

6. Ibid., 189.

7. Ibid.; Warner, *Dominguez-Escalante Journal,* 63.

8. Warner, *Dominguez-Escalante Journal,* 64.

9. Ibid., 118.

10. Dale L. Morgan, *Jedediah Smith and the Opening of the West* (Lincoln: University of Nebraska Press, 1969), 19–20.

11. Hiram Martin Chittenden, *The American Fur Trade of the Far West* (New York: Press of the Pioneers, 1935), 273, 276.

12. Ibid., 276–77.

13. Morgan, *Jedediah Smith,* 195–96.

14. Ibid., 196.

15. Ibid., 211.

16. Poll, et al., *Utah's History,* 63.

17. Ibid., 110.

18. Alice P. McCune, *History of Juab County,* 20–21.

19. Howard R. Egan, *Pioneering the West 1846–1878. Major Howard Egan's Diary* (Richmond, Utah: Howard R. Egan Estate, 1917), 197.

20. Poll, et al., *Utah's History,* 129.

21. Noble Warrum, ed., *Utah Since Statehood* (Salt Lake City: J.S. Clark, 1919), 1:197.

22. Juanita Brooks, ed., *The Journal of Martha Spence Heywood 1850–56* (Salt Lake City: Utah State Historical Society, 1978), 65–66.

23. McCune, *History of Juab County,* 68.

24. Clark M. Newell, ed., *Mona and Its Pioneers* (n.p.: Daughters of Utah Pioneers, 1991), 8.

25. McCune, *History of Juab County,* 152.

26. Ibid., 5–6.

27. Maurine Stephensen, *A History of Levan* (n.p.: Daughters of Utah Pioneers), 9.

28. Ibid., 27.

29. Stephen L. Carr, *The Historical Guide to Utah Ghost Towns* (Salt Lake City: Western Epics, 1972), 99.

30. Ibid.

31. Marlene Bates, "North Snake Valley, Part 1," 71, typescript, courtesy of Marlene Bates, Gandy, Utah.

32. Carr, *Utah Ghost Towns,* 107.

33. Egan, *Pioneering the West,* 197–98.

34. Richard E. Fike and John W. Hadley, *The Pony Express Stations of Utah in Historical Perspective,* Bureau of Land Management Cultural Resources Series No. 2. (1979), 4.

35. Ibid., 5.

36. Mark Twain, *Roughing It* (New York: Holt, Rinehart and Winston, 1953), 92.

37. Ibid., 95.

38. Ibid., 95–98.

39. *Salt Lake Tribune,* 29 November 1945.

40. Twain, *Roughing It,* 98–99.

CHAPTER 4

JUAB COUNTY'S MORMON SETTLEMENTS IN THE TERRITORIAL PERIOD

Agriculture

Mormon pioneers had come to Utah in search of a place where they could live and worship God as they chose. They did not expect life to be easy, knowing they would have to work hard to survive. The first job in Juab County as elsewhere was to clear the land and plant crops which would provide food for themselves and their livestock. Dams were built across creeks and ditches were dug so they could use the water to irrigate the land. Among the crops the Juab pioneers planted from seeds brought with them were wheat, oats, barley, corn, potatoes, peas, beans, melons, squash, corn, and sugar cane. In 1852 Charles Bryan planted some peach seeds, but most of them winter killed. A few survived and produced fruit in 1858.[1] Residents of both Mona and Levan moved their settlements east of the original sites to be closer to water and, in Levan's case, to improved soil.

Dry Farming. East of Mona, the bench area was steep and gravelly and the water was almost impossible to control until rock culverts were built.[2] According to a letter published in the *Deseret News*

Looking down First North from Seventh East, Nephi, ca. 1900. (Fred Chapman)

of 11 July 1870, written by James Wilson of Levan, the previous four years had been very dry and grasshoppers had eaten their crops. Area farmers did not expect to raise 200 bushels of wheat. Then, Wilson reported,

> About this time Brother Hans C. Koford and Brother David Broadhead found a cave in which had been stored a container of wheat. Most of the wheat had deteriorated into chaff but there were a few kernels which appeared to be good. There was not enough to divide so brother Koford took the kernels home and planted them. The first year he was successful in raising a bucket of good wheat which he saved for seed. The next year he raised more and each succeeding year he produced more. Enough so he could begin to sell it. It was a soft, beardless type of wheat which could be grown as an irrigated or dry land crop. It became known as Koford wheat and was used widely as a dry land crop.[3]

At this time David Broadhead and his family were farming at the mouth of Four Mile Creek, about midway between Nephi and Levan at the foot of the mountains. The stream was small and the

Broadheads used it to water their trees and hay. Some years there was adequate water, other years there was not. They accidentally success-fully dry farmed some of the area. One year they planted wheat on the south and west a long way from the water source. They made fur-rows in order to irrigate it once or twice when the high water came in the spring, and they did not expect a crop unless the high water came. The high water did not come and the wheat was not irrigated; however, the crop did mature and produce a fair harvest.[4]

In 1880 Elberta Dam, which created Mona Reservoir, was built northwest of Mona. It was drained through Currant Creek to Goshen Reservoir. A canal was constructed between Currant Creek and Kimball Creek, with the water flowing north to Elberta, where it was used for irrigation. This project was finished in 1891 and, according to Utah State Agricultural College records, Elberta farmers cleared $5,000 from ten acres of apples under irrigation in 1892.

Ranching. When the first settlers came to Juab Valley they found plenty of forage for the stock they had brought with them and also water to irrigate crops. The region was ideal for raising stock. The sheep owners in Levan soon banded together, and after their sheep were sheared and branded in the spring they hired someone to take this "Town Herd" to the mountain east and southeast of Levan for the summer. When winter came, the animals were brought back to town and divided, each owner taking care of his own sheep during the winter.[5]

Most of the sheep eventually were sold to the Malmcrest Company, owned by Cleo Malmgren and his brother-in-law, a man named Secrest, from California. The range permit was later sold to Sanpete County sheepmen. Alma Dalby, Cleo Malmgren, and Farrell Wankier continued to raise sheep, and Dalby became well known for his Rambouillet sheep and Malmgren and Wankier for their Suffolk sheep. A blooded Clydesdale stallion was imported and purebred Durham cattle were bought to improve the local horse and cattle stock.[6]

In 1859 Rodney Degrass Swasey brought his family to help settle Mona. He also brought with him a large herd of cattle, which he herded in western Millard and Juab Counties. Swasey built a large barn west of his home in Mona where he kept and raised purebred

Steam engine with owner Elias Worwood (in suit), at Nephi farm. (Fred Chapman)

horses, most of which he sold to the army.[7] Ephraim Ellertson dry farmed land near Mona and herded about 3,000 sheep on Mount Nebo.[8]

John E. Ingram was among the early sheep owners in Nephi. At the age of sixteen, he began working for W.I. Brown. He worked about three years herding sheep for Brown, then herded for Joseph and William Wright, who paid part of Ingram's wages with sheep. John and his two brothers, Alvin and Albert, became partners. By the time John Ingram was twenty-one years old the brothers owned 500 sheep, which they divided among them. After a few years, John Ingram bought out both of his brothers.

Agriculture in Western Juab County

The McIntyre family came to Utah from Grimes County, Texas. Three sons, Robert, Samuel, and William, accompanied their mother, Margaret, and stepfather, John M. Moody, to Salt Lake City. Moody received a LDS mission call to St. George. William and Samuel left there and went to Tintic Valley, where they found the land covered with wild hay and decided it would provide a good place for raising cattle. The young men and their mother went back to Texas to sell their father's property, which their brother Robert had been caring for. They started buying cattle in October and by April they had between 6,000 and 7,000 head of longhorns.

It took them eight months to get their cattle to Tintic, arriving in December 1871. They wintered there and sold their cattle, for which they had paid about $3.75 each, for $25.00 a head. They returned to the Omaha, Nebraska, area and purchased more cattle, which they then brought to Utah. They bought land from homesteaders in the Leamington area of Millard County and claimed other land for themselves. Their land in the Leamington and Tintic ranches totaled 6,200 acres. They obtained rights to Sevier River water and claimed all of the land with any water source in the Tintic Range. The ranches they owned were known as: the Rockwell Ranch, near Cherry Creek; the Company Ranch and the Summer Ranch, west of Mammoth; the Dry Farm, in Tooele County; and the Tintic Ranch.

At one time Porter Rockwell owned land adjoining the McIntyre property, calling his section Government Creek. Samuel McIntyre and Porter Rockwell were friends. During Rockwell's later years, in September 1877, he was taken to trial for some of his alleged misdeeds. After he had spent a week in prison, Samuel McIntyre and two of his associates in the Mammoth Mining Company, J.A. Cunningham and Orin Dix, posted $15,000 in bonds for Rockwell's release. After Rockwell's death in 1878, Samuel McIntyre acquired his claim, although it is not known whether the land was given to McIntyre by Rockwell's family to pay off debts or if Samuel McIntyre bought it from the family.[9]

Livestock ranching had a significant impact on the West Desert area of the county. The Ekker Ranch is located about fifty miles southwest of Eureka, on the edge of the desert, with property on both sides of the Juab-Tooele County line and on the southern drainage of the Sheeprock Mountains. This cattle ranch has been owned and operated by members of the Ekker family since the late 1880s. Albert Ekker went to the Sheeprock area in 1887, settling near his brother Henry's ranch. He built a cedar cabin and planted a field of alfalfa and then returned to Salt Lake City. The next spring his brother sent

McIntyre's Tintic Ranch, Tintic Valley. (Tintic Historical Society)

word to him that "the lucerne was coming up good," so he brought his wife and two children with him and settled on the ranch. He filed on the land and on water in Cottonwood Canyon in 1899, receiving a patent on it in 1914.

Gypsum, Salt, and Flour Mills

Mineral deposits proved critical to the economic development of Juab County. The Tintic Mining District, discussed later, developed as the most significant; however, other mining operations provided the county with additional commerce.

The settlers of Nephi were aware very soon after they arrived of the large deposit of gypsum located at the mouth of Salt Creek Canyon. In her journal, Martha Spence Heywood mentioned that she and a friend had gone to see the "Plaster Paris Mountain" on 25 October 1851. However, it was not until 1885 that John Hague began making plaster by grinding the material between two stones, cooking the fine dust in a boiler, and stirring it with a hoe.[10]

Alonzo Hyde and George Whitmore built the first gypsum mill in 1887 and sold shares of stock. They also owned a mercantile store and paid the workers with merchandise they could use as well as

McIntyre's Summer Ranch, on the road to Cherry Creek. (Tintic Historical Society)

some cash. In 1889 the Nephi Mill and Manufacturing Company was incorporated. It was leased by Fowler Brothers of Kansas City, Missouri, which improved the mill and built a large frame building. The mill operated until it burned to the ground in 1906.[11]

Just days after the settlers came to Nephi they discovered that the water coming from the mountains to the east was salty. A salt industry soon grew in the area. In 1854 T.B. Foote constructed a toll road to his salt works. In 1855 Jacob G. Bigler reported to the *Deseret News*, "Brother T.B. Foote is making a large amount of salt by evaporation in vats at our salt springs, which is of an extra quality. the salt mountain six miles east of us is of a superior quality, but is mixed with clay, so that it is hard to separate."[12]

Samuel G. Coulson hauled salty brine from the canyon to his home, boiled and evaporated it, and sold or bartered the salt to people in Sanpete and Juab Counties. The Nebo Salt Company, which was located at the foot of Red Creek Canyon, was organized in 1893 and began to successfully market its product. The *Blade* reported in 1895, "Mr. A. Cazier, Supt. of the Nebo Salt Mfg. Co. returned from

Denver on Thursday. While absent, Mr. Cazier was successful in placing Nephi's incomparable salt product on the Colorado Market, having sold six carloads and arranged with the principal grocery house
of Denver to handle the Nebo Salt."[13]

An article in the *Deseret News* of 24 July 1897 stated in part that
the Nebo Salt Company's salt was "the only salt made in the state
which can be used for preserving butter and packing meats. About
12 tons a day are produced and it is sold as far east as Colorado and
as far west as California."[14]

Martha Spence Heywood's journal indicated that one of the first
assignments of Mormon church leaders to settlers was for Zimri H.
Baxter to build and operate a gristmill. According to Alice McCune,
Baxter was joined by Abraham Boswell and George W. Bradley. John
Hoile established a burr mill in 1859 in Nephi that later was sold to
John Hague and some associates, who later sold it to the Juab Mill
and Elevator Company. Joseph Birch established a mill at the mouth
of Salt Creek Canyon called the Fort Birch Mill. He sold his mill to
John Vickers and A. Milton Musser; however, it was destroyed by fire
in 1870.[15]

Joel Grover and others established a flour milling company
known as the Standard Milling Company at the mouth of Salt Creek
Canyon in 1877. This mill was later purchased by J.A. Hyde of Nephi
and Andreus Jensen of Fountain Green and was known as the Hyde
and Jensen Company. T.C. and Robert Winn later bought the mill,
and it then became known as the Nephi Mill and Elevator Company.
In 1917 the Winn brothers built a large roller mill in Nephi near the
railroad tracks.[16]

Government Development

On 10 January 1866, by an act of the territorial legislature, Nephi
was declared the county seat of Juab County. Under the laws of the
Territory of Utah, the county court consisted of a probate judge and
three selectmen, and although the probate judge handled estates and
some of the court work, the county court was the principal governing
and administrative body of the county—similar to the Board of
County Commissioners today.[17] The probate judge was elected by the
legislature for a four-year term, and the selectmen by the electors of

Will Morgan's sheep herd in Tintic Valley, near Jericho. (Fred Chapman)

the county, one each year to a three-year term. In 1874 the probate judge became elected by the voters of the county, and in 1887 the United States Congress passed a bill providing that the probate judge be appointed by the president of the United States. The term of the selectmen was changed in 1888 to two years by the legislature. When Utah became a state in 1896, the county courts were abolished and a board of county commissioners established. The judicial powers of the probate judge and the U.S. District Courts passed to the justice courts and state district courts.[18]

The county seat at Nephi needed a courthouse. Reportedly, the first such building was located on the corner of First North and First East; later, in 1883, a more substantial structure was planned for the corner of Main and Center Streets. The building was constructed at about that time, with a later addition to the rear in 1937. The *Deseret News* of 24 July 1897 featured a sketch of the courthouse prominently pictured in a full-page article on the "History of Nephi City."[19] The courthouse was part of a county complex for the site. In back of the courthouse, Juab County officials erected the county jail in 1892.

Records indicate that on 13 July 1892 a contract was awarded to the Pauley Jail Building and Manufacturing Company of St. Louis, Missouri, to construct the jail. Juab County records stated,

> Said Pauley Jail Building and Manufacturing Company agreeing to put up an entirely new jail at Nephi and remove the iron cages in the present County jail at Nephi to Eureka and place said cages in proper working order in the building to be erected [there] by Juab County for the above sum. All work to be done in accordance with plans and specifications approved by the County Court.[20]

The jail was a two-story, rectangular brick building on a sandstone foundation with a hip roof. A concrete, basement-level heating plant was added in about 1915. Architecturally, the structure exhibits nice detailing on the exterior. Brick arches over the windows and doors and bands of corbeled brick below the eaves adorn the edifice.

Communications, Transportation, and Commerce

Nephi was designated as the county seat of Juab County, but it was not incorporated as a city until 1888. Businesses and other enterprises were established soon after the first settlers arrived. Zimri H. Baxter, for example, owned the first nail factory in Nephi. Samuel Adams and Edward Lunt gathered old wagon tires and other scrap metal and made nails from them.[21]

In 1861 transcontinental telegraph wires were laid across Utah and in 1866 the Deseret Telegraph System was in operation. It reached Nephi in December 1866, and, according to an article in the *Deseret News* of 19 April 1869, Mona was listed as one of the offices on the Deseret Telegraph line, open for the receipt and dispatch of messages. William A.C. Bryan, who was Nephi's first operator, trained Elizabeth Parkes, Elizabeth Claridge, and Mary Ellen Love. Bryan stated that "the girls were good students, soon building fair to excell [sic] their teacher, and by the summer of 1867 Miss Parkes could take my place in handling the telegraphy business." Elizabeth Parkes became Bryan's wife. Mary Ellen Love served as the first operator in Mona, while Parkes and Elizabeth Claridge worked in Nephi. The company opened an office in Levan on 11 August 1870.[22]

Transportation has always played a key role in the economic development of Juab County. Alice McCune, in her *History of Juab*

The "Old Creamery," located at 960 North Main, Nephi, where farmers sold cream which was retailed out to people in butter, cream, and cheese. (Fred Chapman)

County, stated that, "Grants were given the residents to build road-ways into the canyons to secure lumber and wood and salt in the early days of Nephi. Twenty-five cents toll was charged for a load of wood, while a higher toll was expected for a load of lumber."[23] With the coming of the railroad, transportation in Juab entered a new era.

When the railroad arrived in York in 1875 all the towns in East Juab began to prosper. York developed as a railroad town, and featured a depot, water tower, coal station, turning wye, warehouses, private homes, restaurants, and hotels. For several years, York functioned as the main railhead for the rich Tintic Mining District. A business publication of the late 1870s described York as follows:

> The place owes its present prosperity to the fact that stage lines start from the terminus of the road to the various populous mining districts that lie beyond. . . . At present, we find here G.T. Mills, who keeps a good eating house, deals in groceries, clothing, wines and liquors, is post master and agent for the Pioche stage line. R.

Stoddard, saloon, Earll Bros., forwarding merchants; A.M. Stephens, agent for the Utah Forwarding Company; John P. Bush, station and express agent.[24]

The town grew and also provided some employment for farmers in surrounding communities who used their teams and wagons to haul freight and passengers to and from the railroad. York remained active primarily because crews required nearly two years to lay twenty-eight miles of track through Nephi to Juab. In 1879 much of the railroad business had been shifted to Juab, and York ceased functioning as a busy railroad center.

In 1859 a deposit of coal was discovered near Wales in Sanpete County, but it was not until 1874 that a way was found to ship it economically. Knowing that the Utah Southern Railroad would soon be coming to Nephi, grading for the narrow-gauge San Pete Valley Railway was begun, but the money to lay the tracks was not available. At about this time, Simon Bamberger, who had with W.S. McCornick and W.W. Chisholm made a major strike at the Centennial-Eureka Mine in Eureka, became interested in the coal mine in Wales. He left for England, where he raised a million dollars which he used to build the railroad. The coal had been stockpiled, but, by 1882, when the railroad was completed, most of the coal had been mined out. Therefore, the coal traffic soon ended and most of the shipments consisted of livestock, grain, hay, and wool. Passenger service from the Sanpitch Valley to Nephi lasted until 1931.[25]

Nephi. In May 1879 the railroad tracks reached Nephi. This meant even greater prosperity for Nephi and surrounding towns. Nephi increasingly became the business center of the county, and its population grew to about 2,000 by 1890. Many new businesses were started and new homes built. Nephi's economic future looked very bright. The Union Pacific Railroad bought the Utah Northern, Utah Central, and Utah Southern lines, however; and in the early 1900s it moved the main line farther west through Lynndyl and Delta, leaving Nephi with only a branch line. The city still was active due its other communication and transportation connections, but its growth did slow from what it was during the railroad boom period of the late nineteenth century.

A shipment of elk, from Wyoming, unloaded in Nephi, March 1913. (Fred Chapman)

The railroad provided a great boost to the commercial development of Nephi and the rest of Juab County. In 1879, when the railroad came to Nephi, with highways entering from four directions and railroad tracks from three, the city became a center from which livestock, wool, grain, and other commodities were shipped. Goods also were shipped into Nephi and freighted to surrounding towns. By this time wool had become one of the leading products of the area and Nephi became the shipping point for much of Utah and southern Nevada. The wool was hauled to Nephi and then baled and shipped to eastern markets.

The Boston Wool Company had an office and storage warehouse at Second South and Main Street in Nephi. In an article written for the *Deseret News* in 1887, Samuel Pitchforth stated that,

No one can really believe the importance and immensity of this industry until he visits Nephi and sees for himself. Nephi is the market for all the wool of this section and towards this port all the wool gravitates. In May and June the wool business is at its height, and Nephi is alive with bustle with activity. The wool clip last season was over 3,000,000 pounds. Two million and a half was clipped in the spring. Nephi last season exported 3,000,000 pounds of wool and received for it $700,000. The wool merchants are enabled to offer the highest market price for the product and the poor man thereby receives the benefit. Juab County is a natural winter range for sheep, and within the immediate vicinity of Nephi there are 200,000 sheep wintered. Success of great commercial interest is steadily increasing.[26]

He also wrote that there were large herds of cattle pastured in the region. Between wool growing, stock raising, and railroad shipping prosperity was coming to the region.

New businesses began and many of those already established grew and prospered. The town became such a hub that it was referred to by some as "Little Chicago." By 1900 the *Utah State Gazetteer & Business Directory* listed some sixty-five businesses operating in the city.[27]

George Carter Whitmore was one of the merchants who prospered during Nephi's boom years. He settled in Nephi in 1872 and began his entrepreneurial activity, establishing the First National Bank of Nephi in 1886. He later incorporated the State Bank of Payson, Fillmore Commercial and Savings Bank, and the Fountain Green State Bank. In 1907 the Nephi National Bank was chartered, with J.S. Ostler as president and J.W. Bond as cashier.[28] His prestige rose in both economic and political circles.

Between 1898 and 1900 Whitmore constructed a magnificent home in what was then Nephi's commercial district. The house was designed and built by Oscar Booth, a local architect. The three-story home, in a variant Queen Anne architectural style, was said to display "all the ornamentation, shingles, finials, moldings, latices, carved panels, friezes, balusters, that characterize the style." Built on a sandstone foundation from stone quarried in nearby Andrews Canyon, the lavish residence featured a domed turret and continues to be a Nephi landmark.[29]

Nephi's first newspaper, the *Ensign,* was published by James T. Jakeman, who was also the editor of the *Manti Sentinel.* The first edition was dated Friday, 10 June 1887. On 14 March 1888 ownership changed hands and the paper was published and edited by John S. Rollo and John T. Field.[30] According to the *American Newspaper Directory* for 1888, the weekly publication was printed "Fridays, Democratic, 4-pages, 21 x 30, $2, Field and Rollo, editors and publishers." Another source noted,

> "The Ensign is the only purely Democratic sheet in the territory. They are offering their paper for $2 a year, cash in advance, and will give one half of each subscription to the Democratic campaign fund. (Now is the time for all good men to come to the aid of their party)." says the Manti Sentinel, November 7, 1888.[31]

In September 1889 Rollo retired and James H. Wallis became Field's partner. In January 1891 Wallis sold to W.J. Shimmin, and by 29 August 1892 the *Ensign* was under the management of S.B. Freed and E. Carroll. The name was changed to the *Nephi Courier.*[32]

The *Juab County Standard* appeared next, beginning in January 1895. This newspaper lasted only about six months, however, being replaced by the *Nephi Blade,* edited by J.F. Gibbs.[33] Management soon changed:

> In the issue of November 30, 1895, appears this: "Transferred—With this issue of the Blade, the business of publication is transferred to Messrs. E.H. Pulver and Alfred Orme, and the writer retires from the editorial and business management. During the last eight years the above named gentlemen have done nearly all of the literary work, excepting the editorials, and they have furnished Blade readers with a bright, newsy paper, and will continue to do so. They are young and capable, and are practical printers. . . . J.F. Gibbs."[34]

Other newspapers became important and sometimes humorous voices in the life of Nephi. The *Republic,* first published in 1896 by the Republic Publishing Company, was edited by W.L. Roe. The *Nephi Times,* edited and managed by Henry Adams, received various barbs from other local papers. According to one source, the *Republic* of 29 August 1896 quipped, "If this man [Adams] of might and valor knew as much about grammar as an eight year old school boy . . . by publishing that, Friend Adams, you have dispelled the idea."[35] The

Horse Shoe Tires, owned by John Robertson; and Enterprise Grocery owner Jude Pexton, Nephi. (Fred Chapman)

Nephi Record first appeared about 1900 under the editorship of T.L. Foote, with R.J. Henroid, manager.

Mona. A post office was established on 1 June 1884, and an irrigation company was organized in Mona in 1896. The railroad was completed to York, four miles north of Mona, on 2 February 1875 and reached Mona in 1877. Many of the settlers from Mona and from Nephi became freighters, hauling freight by wagon to towns around the area. A lumber mill was built by Jack Smith in 1880. Charles Carrow constructed a sawmill in 1881, and William Newton built another one on the east bench that was later moved up Willow Creek.[36] The church building burned in 1883, destroying all of the records to that time. A new building was started almost immediately and completed in 1884.

Levan. During the winter of 1869 and 1870 a group of Levan residents formed a corporation and built a store called the Levan Co-Op Store. The Bosh butcher shop was built next to the co-op store and was operated by Delbert Bosh and his sons. The Bosh family built a slaughterhouse and also operated a freighting business between Levan and Eureka, taking fresh meat, eggs, and butter to the mining communities.

During the late 1800s and the early 1900s Levan's population grew, many people who settled there coming from Scandinavian countries, particularly Denmark. When the railroad came to Juab, a small spur was built directly west of Levan. A small station was built there with a metal arm on which was hung a bag containing the outgoing mail. As the train went by the bag would be snatched up; incoming mail was thrown off the train and was then picked up and taken to Levan.[37]

Juab County's early commercial and economic development rested heavily on agriculture and transportation. Mining and mineral resources became increasingly important, especially the fabulously rich deposits of precious metals in the Tintic Mining District. With Nephi's prime geographical location, on both east-west and north-south corridors, the city and county prospered, with much commercial activity. The label "Little Chicago," for Nephi reflected the bustle of activity in the cattle and milling industries as well as the significance of railroad-related business. Polk's 1912–13 *Utah State Gazetteer and Business Directory* labeled Nephi as "the most important distributing point in central Utah."[38] With increases in commerce and business, Juab County would develop other ways, including social organizations and government offices.

Schools

As was customary in Mormon settlements, a combination school, church, and community building was soon built in Nephi. The first was constructed at the corner of Main and Center Streets. Among the first school teachers were Martha Spence Heywood, Amy Bigler, George Spencer, Andrew Love, Amos Gustin, Thomas Ord, and Jane Bailey.[39]

As settlements spread throughout Utah, establishing schools became a priority for settlers in Juab County as elsewhere. In 1852 the county courts were assigned the responsibility to organize school districts within counties. Thus, when any portion of a county had

Engine on the Sanpete Valley Railroad, ran from Wales, Sanpete County, to Nephi. Later became part of the Denver & Rio Grande Railroad. (Fred Chapman)

sufficient children to justify a school, the court was petitioned to create a school district. This law, with very slight modification, remained in force until 1866 when the legislature created the office of county superintendents of schools to supervise and improve the quality the local schools.[40]

In 1888 a bill was introduced in the territorial legislature to consolidate all schools within a county, but the measure failed. Territorial superintendent Jacob Boreman recommended in 1891 that county school districts be created by popular vote of constituents in each county. In 1895 Superintendent T.B. Lewis recommended reorganization of school districts. His plan, apparently, was to create county school districts in more populous communities wherever a high school could be justified. In 1896 John R. Park, Utah's first State Superintendent of Public Instruction, recommended the establishment of county school districts in addition to city school districts of the first and second class.[41]

Governor Heber M. Wells appeared before the legislature in 1897 proposing the recommendations of Superintendent Park. He enumerated the problems of small school district systems and urged that education problems be studied. Some changes were made between then and 1914, when state superintendent A.C. Matheson urged the legislature to permit any county so desiring to reorganize its school district regardless of the school population.[42]

Nephi's first school was built on what is now the northeast corner of Main and Center Streets. It was a one-room, eighteen-by-twenty-foot building, with windows on the south and east and a door to the west. The roof of the building was made of log stringers, covered with willows, and a layer of hay covered with mud. The building also was used for church services and for recreation. In 1854 this building was torn down and a new one built.[43] An elementary school—the Central School—was later built at First East and First North Streets. By 1884 Nephi had three schools: the Central School, the North School at First East between Fifth and Sixth North, and the South School on Main between Fourth and Fifth Streets. Students of various ages all attended classes together.

Prior to 1880 the Nephi School Board, in order to obtain opportunities for higher education for students, encouraged young men and women to attend the University of Deseret in Salt Lake City. The board agreed to pay their tuition; in return, the students were required to teach for at least one year upon the completion of the university's normal course. From 1881 to 1885, several students agreed to this proposal.[44]

In 1884 a graded elementary school was established, with Fred W. Chappell as principal and Elizabeth A. Schofield as teacher. An article in the *Salt Lake Herald* of 23 January 1884 praised the work of Chappell and Schofield at the Central School, stating:

> The other schools are located in different parts of the city and it is a lamentable fact, and a rare one, that the accommodations are unequal to the number of applicants. It is said 100 or more students would attend if accommodations could be found for them. This is not due to a lack of interest, but to a sudden awakening of interest, which has been so rapid that facilities could not be had to keep up with the remarkable growth of the demand.[45]

Remnants of the Gem Flour Mill, Nephi, 1998. (Wayne Christiansen)

Problems of inadequate facilities continued. At the beginning of the 1894–95 school year, the local school board found they were short a teacher for the eighth grade. Many older students had returned to school for advanced instruction. Elizabeth Schofield Adams was now principal of the Central School and also taught the eighth grade. W.I. Brown was hired and placed in charge of the advanced students. At the end of the year Adams retired and Brown became principal.[46]

Some of the students Brown had been teaching expressed an interest in having a high school in Nephi and he told them that he would be willing to teach them high school courses but they would have to gain the support of the townspeople in this endeavor. The matter was placed before the school board, who presented it to the people. The majority voted in favor of the proposal, and in 1899 Nephi High School became the third high school in the State of Utah. The graduating class of 1899 consisted of Elva Bailey, Claude Bryan, Frances Ellison, Will Latimer, Allen McPherson, Jane McPherson, Hattie Scott, Willard Sells, and Kate Wilson. On 11 May 1900, graduation exercises for Nephi High School were held at the Juab LDS Stake Tabernacle. With the motto, "The End Crowns the Work," the class of 1900 held a "Class Farewell Ball" at the local opera house, and an essay entitled "The Coming Woman" was presented by Ada Salisbury.[47]

Mona's first school, which was built of logs, was completed in 1866; William Palmer was the first teacher. A few years later, the school burned and classes were held in homes until a new one could be erected. The new school was built of blue clay adobe bricks. It was torn down and replaced by a two-story brick structure in 1907.

One of the first area teachers was John Z. Brown, who became the first principal; he was followed by O.M. Sanderson and Heber and George Olson. From 1891 to 1895 Fred W. Chappell from Nephi was principal. In 1904 Archibald Henry Anderson arrived from Fairview to assume that position. The first graduating class completed their course of instruction in 1901. Other early teachers in Mona included a Mr. Crumley, Alfred Keyte, Daniel F. Tibbs, Melvin McArthur, and Henry Young. Also, it was reported that William Newton taught night school without any salary.[48]

In 1868 James Wilson was teaching school in a room of the Seth Ollerton home in Levan. According to a local historian,

> the one room log cabin near the center of town which served as a church and meeting house until a church could be built was used as a classroom. There were 15 to 20 students in the group. There were no grades and no uniformity of text books nor were there any promotions as we know them today. The parents furnished the meager supplies for the school and also paid a fee of $2.50 for each child. The fee served as a salary for the teacher during the 5 months that school was held.[49]

About 1869 or 1870 Levan's new church building was used for a school. John Shepherd taught older students in the church while Josie Rawlins taught younger children in the Ollerton home. An evening school was conducted by Robert Hill; John W. Shepherd taught music and Isaac W. Pierce taught music and dancing.[50]

A Relief Society Hall was built in Levan in 1884, leaving the old church building to be used for a school. The one-room building had a curtain hung through the center so it could be used on one side by the younger students and on the other side by the older ones. About

Home of George W. Whitmore and family, Nephi. (Utah State Historical Society)

1888 a new four-room school was begun, financed by state funds. This was enlarged and modernized in 1912 with two rooms on each of two floors and central heating.

As will be mentioned in the following section, Protestant denominations established quality schools throughout the territory in the late nineteenth century in an attempt to combat Mormon polygamy through educating Mormon children. Schools were established by the Methodist church in both Nephi and Levan in the 1880s, Nephi's being built in 1889. In September 1887 the Methodist church's mission in the territory acquired land and began to build a school in Levan; it opened in December 1888. The first year's attendance reached forty students, all Mormons. After new public school requirements were enacted with Utah statehood, the number of students attending the Methodist school dwindled. It ceased to operate in 1905.[51]

Society and Religion

As mentioned previously, certain men were "called" or given specific assignments by LDS church leaders to lead a group of people in the settlement of an area. The leader along with other men approved by the authorities of the LDS church constituted the governing body of the settlement. Joseph L. Heywood, chosen to lead and supervise the settlement of Nephi, served as president of the Nephi LDS Branch until the spring of 1852, also directing the temporal affairs. At that time a government was organized, with the following officers elected in Nephi: mayor, Josiah Miller; aldermen, Timothy B. Foote, Charles H. Bryan, John Carter, and Isaac Grace; counselors, Amos Gustin, John Cazier, David Webb, James Crabb, Cleon Elmer, Levi Gifford, Ichabod Gifford, Thomas Tranter, and Miles Miller; recorder, assessor, and collector, Z.H. Baxter; treasurer, William Cazier; marshal, Israel Hoyt; and supervisor of streets, Charles Sperry.[52]

According to a local history, at first civil authorities had little to do, for the church had directed matters. But the gradual transition from church leadership to civil government brought some problems. One incident occurred in March 1853 when Jacob G. Bigler was presiding as LDS bishop of Juab County and Joseph Heywood was president of the Nephi branch. George W. Bradley was probate judge of Juab County and Josiah Miller was mayor of Nephi. There were only a few people, and soon some differences among the officers were manifest, particularly between Heywood, Bradley, and Bigler, perhaps due to jurisdiction questions. On 13 March a conference was held in which the people could vote as to whether they wanted to sustain the present officers. There was some opposition, but the majority voted to sustain the officials.[53]

About 1859 or 1860, Nephi residents built a structure on Center Street where they could hold dances, dramas, and other recreational activities. It was built with financial and labor donations and was known as the Social Hall. Each person who contributed received shares in the building according to the amount of his or her donation. The dividend on the shares was two free tickets to various amusements.

Dancing was a popular form of recreation. Residents often took their children, who played together in an adjacent room or a corner of the room while their parents danced. Charles Sperry played the fiddle for dances, and Charles Haynes and Alfred Gowers acted as caller for those dances which required one. Dances of the day have

A day of fun for the Nephi Plaster Mill—sports, games, and refreshments for all its employees and families. (Fred Chapman)

been identified as the quadrille, waltz quadrille, polka, schottish, lancers, Scotch reel, Sir Roger de Coverly, and the Danish tucker. Music also was an integral part of the social scene. One source indicated, "There is a discrepancy as to when the first brass band was organized in Nephi, dates varying from 1854 to 1861, but there is no disagreement as to the quality of the band. It was one of the outstanding bands in the territory of Utah."[54] In 1900 the *Utah State Gazetteer* listed Sperry's Orchestra, led by C.H. Sperry, in its pages devoted to Juab County.[55]

William M. Evans was "called and set apart" in 1853 by Brigham Young to organize and conduct a choir. The group practiced in the homes of members and played with no accompaniment until 1880 when they were able to obtain an organ. Both the local choir and brass band accompanied Young on some of his visits to the region. They also were invited to sing at some of the general conferences of the church.[56]

Sports and other recreational activities provided a release from everyday life. Children played all sorts of games and enjoyed numerous other activities. Men pitched horseshoes and raced horses, and horseback riding was enjoyed by both men and women. Alice McCune reported that some women rode side-saddle and that "Their elegant 'riding-habit' consisted of a long, black skirt, a tight fitting bodice and high-topped hat."[57]

The first baseball game played in Nephi occurred on 1 January 1875 and reportedly was also the first game played in Central Utah. Alice McCune quoted Charles Haynes as having written,

> Mr. Samuel H. Gibson, at that time a resident of Nephi, challenged Mr. George C. Whitmore in the following language: "We will play a game of baseball and I will give you the right to pick your nine men first, and when you are through I will pick nine men from the town at large and beat you." (Each man on the winning team was to receive a quarter of beef).[58]

Gilson should have chosen first, or perhaps played at a more propitious time. As reported, the score ended with Gilson's team scoring 17 runs and Whitmore's team 87! Baseball would continue to be an important pastime in Juab, especially in the Tintic Mining District.

The Fourth and Twenty-fourth of July were traditionally celebrated in Nephi until 1937, at which time they were replaced by the Ute Stampede, which is celebrated annually during the first part of July. The first Juab County Fair was held at Nephi on 27 September 1862, and it is still held every year in the fall.

Religious affiliation and participation helped guide most citizens of the county. Even in multicultural Tintic there existed a cooperation between various religions and denominations uncommon in most other mining areas. In Nephi and east Juab the dominance of the LDS Cchurch was significant, but later inroads by Protestant denominations and the immigration of others to the area provided some religious diversity. Jacob G. Bigler was ordained LDS bishop of Juab County in November 1852, becoming president of the Nephi Branch in 1854 and president of the Juab Stake when it was organized in 1868.

In October 1853 the Nephi branch had eighty-seven male priesthood holders, 164 others not ordained, five persons over eight years of age not baptized, and 140 children under eight years of age. After returning from a general conference in Salt Lake City in 1855, Bishop Bigler instructed the brethren and sisters of the church to sit together at meetings, instead of the men on one side and the women on the other, as they had been doing up to this time.[59]

A Mormon priesthood Quorum of Seventies was organized on 18 May 1857 including John A. Wolf, Samuel Pitchforth, Timothy H. Hoyt, George Kendall, Miles Miller, John Borrowman, and David Webb. Other early priesthood holders included Edward Ockey, Samuel Claridge, Edwin Harley, Daniel Miller, John Kienke, Charles Sperry, and Benjamin Riches.[60]

A women's Relief Society was organized on a stake basis, as were all Mormon auxiliary organizations at first, on 23 June 1868. Amelia Goldsbrough was the first president, with Elizabeth Kendall and Jane Picton as counselors and Amy S. Bigler as secretary. By 1876 it was determined that the organization needed a building of its own. The building was constructed and dedicated on 30 November 1881. By 1890 there were two LDS wards in Nephi, so the old building was sold and two new ones built.

The Young Ladies Retrenchment Society was organized on 19 March 1874. Charlotte H. Evans was president, Alice H. Evans and Matilda Picton counselors, Roxy Bigler secretary, and Louise L. Foote assistant. The organization had six members. On 30 June 1875 they were reorganized and the name was changed to Young Ladies Mutual Improvement Association (YLMIA). The following officers were then installed: Hannah Grover, superintendent; Ann M. McCune, assistant superintendent; Matilda Picton, local president; M.A. Parks, Elizabeth E. McCune, Emma Bryan, Mary Udell, Mary Hoyt, and Mary E. Harley, counselors; Roxy L. Blackburn, secretary; and Louise L. Foote, assistant secretary.[61] A Young Mens Mutual Improvement Association was organized sometime in the 1870s.

A Sunday School was established in 1859 but for unknown reasons was discontinued and not reorganized until 1868. At that time, Jonathan Midgley became superintendent. In 1868 a local School of the Prophets was also organized. This was somewhat akin to a chamber of commerce or later civic club, with some re4ligious instruction also added. A Primary auxiliary for children was organized in 1879; the officers were Hannah Grover, president; Matilda E. Teasdale, first counselor; Mary E. Cazier, second counselor; Adelaide Schofield, secretary; and Anna Schofield, treasurer.

On 21 and 22 October 1877 Nephi was divided into two LDS wards. Joel Grover became bishop of the South Ward, with Edward Harley and William A.C. Bryan as his counselors. The North Ward bishop was Charles Sperry; his counselors were William F. Tolley and Charles Cazier.

In 1860 work was begun on what was to become the Juab Stake Tabernacle. Timothy B. Foote was appointed by Brigham Young to supervise the building's construction. Zimri H. Baxter was the architect; Charles Foote, Reuben J. Downs, Alex Gardner, and Isaac Sowby were the carpenters. It was said that Sowby walked from Nephi to Salt Lake City to obtain tools for the work. The lath was sawed at the mill of Charles Price. J.H. Runnell of Salt Lake City did the plastering, using plaster from the gypsum deposit east of Nephi. He also made the cornice and the rosettes for the ceiling, assisted by a Mr. Pickering. Abraham Boswell, who came to the area from the gold fields of California, reportedly brought $500 with him and used some of it to purchase glass for the windows. The building was finished and dedicated in 1865. A large tower was built on the front.[62]

In 1877 a vestry was built on the east end of the building. A time-capsule box was placed in the cornerstone containing coins, grains, church records, and local publications. Some time after 1883 a gallery was placed in the assembly room under the direction of Charles Foote. A.W. McCune, who had moved to Salt Lake City, donated $1,500 to improve the front of the building. An addition was constructed at the front and the tower was remodeled. In 1930 the tower was removed and the front given a more modern look.[63]

Mona. Edward Kay was presiding elder of the Mona Branch of the Juab Stake from 1860 until 1 July 1877 when it became a ward. At this time, John Madison Haws became bishop, with William Newton as first counselor. The Mona Relief Society was organized in July 1868; Eliza Somerville was president, with Alice Bascom as first counselor and Martha Newton as second counselor. The Primary Association was organized on 1 June 1879 with the following officers: president Elinor J. Somerville, first counselor Emma J. Keyte, second counselor Emma Sommerville, secretary Elizabeth Harrison, and treasurer Ann Somerville.[64] The local YWMIA was organized on 28 January 1878 with officers Emma Sommerville, president; Emma Jane Kay, first counselor; Elzada Carter, second counselor; Luella Webb, secretary; Sarah Sommerville, assistant secretary; Rowena Partridge, treasurer.

Levan. On 26 June 1865 the settlers at Chicken Creek (Levan) petitioned Mormon church authorities for a branch organization. On 11 February 1866 Apostle Erastus Snow visited them accompanied by Nephi Bishop Charles H. Bryan, Jacob Bigler, Samuel Pyper, Timothy S. Hoyt, and others and organized a branch of the church in Levan. Abraham Palmer was appointed presiding elder, with J. Wilson and W. Morgan as his assistants.[65]

Soon after this, the people at Chicken Creek moved to the present location of Levan. A Mormon conference was held in Levan on 3 May 1869 and Samuel Pitchforth of Nephi became president of the Levan LDS Branch, with Christian Christiansen and Elmer Taylor as his counselors. John Worlock Shepherd was choir leader, Herbert Hartley was clerk, and William Dye was sexton. A Sunday School was also organized at this time; its officers were Superintendent James Wilson and counselors Clarence Isaac Pierce and Heber Hartley.

Samuel Pitchforth lived in Nephi and served as branch president in Levan, while his wife served as Levan Relief Society president for three years. The Relief Society held annual social parties, one of which was mentioned on 21 March 1871 by the *Deseret News,* saying the Levan meetinghouse was "beautifully decorated for the occasion with choice selections of pictures, banners, mottoes and evergreens."[66]

In 1872, Elmer Taylor became president of the Levan Branch, with John C. Whitbeck and Christian Christiansen as counselors. Taylor was appointed to the regional church high council on 9 October 1876 and Christiansen acted as presiding elder in Levan until 1 July 1877. On 21 April 1874 a branch of the United Order was organized in Levan by Juab Stake President Joel Grover. The following officers were chosen: president, Elmer Taylor; vice-president, Christian Christiansen; secretary, Peter Thygersen; assistant secretary, Heber Hartley; directors, John C. Whitbeck, Niels J. Aagard, and George Gardner; treasurer, Eli Curtis. Not every one joined the order, however, although between 1875 and 1878 the membership grew to

273 members. On 8 October 1876 Christian Christiansen became president of the order, and on 1 July 1877 Levan became a ward, with Niels J. Aagard as the first bishop. Aagard worked diligently to keep the united order going, but the experiment in cooperative living was soon disolved.[67]

A Young Men's Mutual Improvement Association was organized in Levan in 1876, and on 29 May 1879 a Primary was organized with Esther Gardner as president and Eliza Curtis and Diantha Ollerton as counselors. The local Young Ladies Mutual Improvement Association was organized on 3 November 1879, with Diantha Pierce as president and Olive Taylor and Hansene Peterson as counselors.[68]

Protestant Denominations. With the coming of the railroad and the development of commercial mining in Utah, an increasing number of immigrants of other faiths came to the area and many Protestant denominations began actively proselytizing in Utah. By the latter part of the nineteenth century Utah's population included a large number of Scandinavians, some of whom were disaffected Mormon converts, others new immigrants. Several Protestant ministers saw an opportunity to minister to these people and others. Many ministers could speak the Scandinavian languages.

Protestant denominations also attempted to combat Mormon polygamy by aggressively trying to convince Mormons of the error of their ways. One attempt was to reach out through children by opening quality schools throughout the territory. As a result, various faiths, particularly the Methodists and Presbyterians, opened schools and churches in a large number of communities. Many Mormons sent their children to the schools, which had qualified teachers and generally were well attended. Methodist schools were established in both Nephi and Levan. A Presbyterian church was built in 1886 in Nephi and was called the Huntington Chapel. Fidelia Gee and a Miss Hulbert were the first teachers at the associated school. The first church minister was Rev. W.N.P. Dailey, who came to Nephi in 1888. The building stood until the 1930s, when the property was sold and it was torn down.[69] Nephi's Methodist school was opened in 1889. Reverend D.J. Gillilan began teaching in an old saloon and the Nebo Hall, but a brick church was later built. Gillilan was assisted by a Reverend Smith and L.M. Gillilan.[70]

In September 1887 the Methodist church purchased land and built a school in Levan. The building consisted of one large classroom with a small coat room in the front and a room in back that served as living quarters for the teacher. There was a belfry, and a bell was rung when it was time for school to begin. The teacher was a Miss Burkholder. The school opened in December 1888, and the first year forty students attended; in 1890 the attendance reached forty-four.

Statehood brought improvements in education, including the establishment throughout the territory of free public schools, leading to the closing of most Protestant schools, including those in Juab County. The Methodist school building in Levan was finally torn down and its bell was placed over the firehouse.[71]

Though Protestants were becoming more numerous in the Mormon villages of Juab County, it was in the mining districts of the county that diversity really flourished and from which wealth flowed to all the inhabitants of the county in the late nineteenth and early twentieth centuries.

Endnotes

1. Alice P. McCune, *History of Juab County,* 63.

2. M. Clark Newell, ed., *Mona and Its Pioneers,* 11.

3. Maurine Stephensen, *A History of Levan,* 43.

4. Stephen R. Boswell, *History of Dry Farming on the Levan Ridge,* 4, Special Collections, Utah State University Library, Logan.

5. Stephensen, *Levan,* 73.

6. Ibid., 27.

7. Newell, *Mona,* 145–46.

8. Ibid., 95.

9. Sherry Scoville, "Samuel McIntyre: Founder and Builder in Utah History," (1980), manuscript, copy in possession of Pearl Wilson.

10. McCune, *Juab County,* 96.

11. Ibid., 96–97.

12. Keith N. Worthington, Sadie H. Greenhalgh, and Fred Chapman, *They Left a Record. A Comprehensive History of Nephi, Utah, 1851–1978* (Provo, Utah: United States of America Community Press, 1979), 40.

13. Ibid.

14. Ibid., 40–41.

15. Ibid., 42.

16. George A. Sperry, C.W. Johnson, Sadie H. Greenhalgh, Grace J. McCune, Martha C. Eager, and Iris Garrett, "Nephi's Centennial Jubilee," pamphlet in possession of author, 36–37.

17. McCune, *Juab County*, 31.

18. Ibid.

19. *Deseret News*, 24 July 1897; McCune, *Juab County*, 33–34. See also Juab County Courthouse File, Historic Preservation Files, Utah State Historical Society, Salt Lake City, Utah.

20. Juab County Records, Juab County Courthouse, Nephi, Utah, as quoted in the National Register of Historic Places form for the Juab County Jail, Historic Preservation Files, Utah State Historical Society.

21. McCune, *Juab County*, 90–91.

22. Ibid., 92; Stephensen, *Levan*, 23.

23. McCune, *Juab County*, 75.

24. *Wolf's Mercantile Guide, Gazetteer, and Business Directory* (Omaha, Nebraska: Omaha Republican Book and Job Printing House, 1878), 257. The *Utah Directory and Gazetteer for 1879–80* (Salt Lake City: H.L.A. Culmer & Co.), 40, lists York as one of Utah's post offices. See also Carr, *Utah Ghost Towns*, 99.

25. Stephen L. Carr and Robert W. Edwards, *Utah Ghost Rails* (Salt Lake City: Western Epics, 1989), 166. See also Helen Z. Papanikolas, ed., *The Peoples of Utah* (Salt Lake City: Utah State Historical Society, 1981), 209.

26. Worthington, et. al., *They Left a Record*, 29.

27. Ibid., 31; *Utah State Gazetteer and Business Directory, 1900* (Salt Lake City: R.L. Polk & Co.), 160–62.

28. Noble Warrum, ed., *Utah Since Statehood*, vol. 1 (Salt Lake City: J.S. Clark Publishing Co., 1919), 317.

29. George Carter Whitmore Mansion, National Register of Historic Places Inventory Nomination Form, Utah State Historical Society.

30. J. Cecil Alter, *Early Utah Journalism* (Salt Lake City: Utah State Historical Society, 1938), 135.

31. Ibid., 135–36.

32. Ibid., 138–39.

33. Ibid., 138.

34. Ibid., 140.

35. Ibid., 141.

36. McCune, *Juab County*, 144.

37. Stephensen, *Levan,* 63.

38. *Utah State Gazetteer 1912–1913,* 154.

39. McCune, *Juab County,* 76–77.

40. Fred H.C. Openshaw, "The Benefit of Small School Systems as Percieved by the Staff, Students, and Schools of the Ten Smallest School Districts in Utah" (Ed. diss., Brigham Young University, 1976), 4.

41. Ibid., 5.

42. Ibid., 6.

43. McCune, *Juab County,* 76.

44. See George A. Sperry, et al., *Nephi's Centennial Jubilee.*

45. Worthington, et al., *They Left a Record,* 44.

46. Ibid.

47. Ibid.; "Graduating Exercises of the Nephi High School," 11 May 1900, pamphlet 13826, Utah State Historical Society.

48. Newell, *Mona and Its Pioneers,* 33, 34; McCune, *Juab County,* 143.

49. Stephensen, *Levan,* 14.

50. Ibid., 21.

51. Stephensen, *Levan,* 61.

52. Ibid., 12.

53. Ibid.

54. McCune, *Juab County,* 82; Stephensen, *Levan,* 19.

55. Polk, *Utah State Gazetteer, 1900,* 162.

56. McCune, *Juab County,* 83–84. McCune lists William M. Evans as the first chorister; however, Worthington, et al., *They Left a Record,* cites William Thorpe (1854), followed by David Webb (1855), and then William M. Evans (1860).

57. McCune, *Juab County,* 84.

58. Ibid., 84–87.

59. Worthington, et al., *They Left a Record,* 22–23.

60. Ibid., 23.

61. Ibid., 24.

62. McCune, *Juab County,* 102–3.

63. Ibid.

64. Newell, *Mona,* 32.

65. Stephensen, *Levan,* 5.

66. Ibid., 27.

67. Ibid., 31.

68. Ibid., 34.

69. McCune, *Juab County,* 109.

70. Worthington, et al., *They Left a Record,* 50.

71. Stephensen, *Levan,* 52, 61.

CHAPTER 5

THE TINTIC
MINING DISTRICT

The Tintic Mining District, located in Juab and Utah Counties, has been one of the most important mining areas in Utah and a key to the economic development of Juab County. Production from Tintic mines, in fact, was an important factor in the economy of the entire state. According to A. Paul Mogensen, geologist and past resident of Tintic, total production in the district has been equal to that of Park City and second only to the wealth extracted from Bingham Canyon. By 1976, total production of base and precious metals from the district was estimated at 16,654,377 tonnes, with a value of $568,620,003 at the time of production.[1] Tintic has also been important for geologists and mining engineers, who have surveyed its mineral wealth and geologic formations. The district is known throughout the world.

Early Development

Chief Tintic, a Ute sub-chief who resided with a small band of Indians in what is now the Tintic Valley, provided the name for this fabulously rich mining area. Tintic in the 1850s led resistence to the intrusions of cattlemen into Indian lands. Reportedly, after some of Tintic's band killed two herdsmen, Deputy Marshal Thomas S. Johnson proceeded to Cedar Valley, where Tintic was accosted, and, in the resulting fray, was shot in the hand. The posse followed him to Tintic Valley, but decided it too risky to follow the Native American leader any farther, and thus allowed him to escape. An article in the *Deseret News* of 5 March 1856 declared that, "Tintick, head chief of a disaffected band, and who was wounded in the skirmish near the south fort in Cedar county, is reported dead."[2] It was during this expedition of Johnson and his posse that the valley was first named "Tintic Valley."

The Tintic Mining District is located approximately seventy miles southwest of Salt Lake City, and lies on the eastern and western slopes of the East Tintic Mountains in Utah and Juab Counties. The East Tintic Mountains are bordered on the east by Dog Valley, Goshen Valley, and Cedar Valley and on the west by Tintic and Rush Valleys. Although the Tintic District includes several mines and one present ghost town which are in Utah County, the present study deals primarily with that portion of the district located in Juab County.

Mining in the area is thought to have begun in the late 1860s, perhaps spurred by successful claims having been discovered nearby in the Oquirrh Mountains and elsewhere by federal troops encouraged to prospect by their commander, Colonel Patrick Edward Connor, at Camp Douglas near Salt Lake City. Brigham Young generally counseled Mormons to shun prospecting and mining activities. According to one history,

> In 1869, Stephen Bliss Moore in company with Ed Peck, Joe Hyde and Sid Worsley discovered some silver claims in Utah. Ever ambitious and progressive, he organized a party to prospect a vast region now known as West Tintic. Returning from a hard and fruitless search, they were passing the Oquirrh [Tintic] range just as the sun was setting. Its rays fell upon a ledge which looked interesting, so they decided to camp there that night and explore the ledge the next morning. The result was the discovery of the "Sunbeam," which marked the beginning of mining in that district.
>
> One day during this trying time, Stephen met President

Jesse Knight's town of "Knightsville," located about one mile east of Eureka. (Utah State Historical Soceity)

Young and Joseph F. Smith in Goshen. President Young stopped and said to Stephen, "I hear you have been mining?" "Yes," answered Stephen. "Don't you know it is against my orders?" "Yes." "Well, what do you intend to do?" Stephen answered, "I intend to keep on mining." President Young paused a moment, then said, "Well, go ahead, and may God bless you."[3]

The Sunbeam Mine, located between what later became the towns of Silver City and Diamond, was the first mine discovered in the area and forged the beginning of the Tintic Mining District, officially organized on 13 December 1869. The men involved in the formation of the district were Joseph Hyde (president), W.J. Harris, Moroni Billingsly, E.M. Peck, Lewis R. Perry, S.W. Worsley, Stelin Colton, S.B. Moore, P.M. Wintz, S.J. Whitney, and Rollin Roberts.[4] Claims were staked and new mines begun, including the Black Dragon north of the Sunbeam on 3 January 1870, the Mammoth on 26 February 1870, and the Eureka Hill on 28 February 1870.

News of a new mining strike traveled like wildfire, attracting others to the area. Soon other mines were opened and operating. Among them were the Armstrong, Martha Washington, Shoebridge, Showers, and Swansea mines. Numerous miners came to prospect, hoping to strike it rich. By 1871 there were camps at Diamond, Silver City, Mammoth, and Eureka. Diamond, an early jewel in the Tintic area, received its name from the nearby white quartz crystals that sparkled like diamonds. The town became a boomtown in the 1870s, with a reported population of one thousand people; it boasted three hotels, five saloons, one post office, a Mormon church, and a Presbyterian or Methodist church.[5]

The first claim staked in Eureka, the Eureka Hill Mine, was owned by John Q. Packard, who hired Watson Nesbitt as superintendent. Nesbitt became a legendary for his fiery character and seemingly magical ability to locate ores. Packard eventually contributed Eureka Hill money to the building of the public library in Salt Lake City, which much later became the home for the Hansen Planetarium. Other mines followed in the Eureka area—the Bullion Beck, Blue Rock (later the Centennial-Eureka), and the Keystone (later the Gemini).

The West Tintic Mining District, located about thirty miles west of Eureka, began in 1871 when the Scotia mines were discovered. This area was a good producer or ore but was overshadowed by the production of the other mines in the district. One of its early entrepreneurs was Orrin Porter Rockwell, who had settled on a ranch at Cherry Creek. Rockwell was famed as a Mormon bodyguard and enforcer. His water rights at Cherry Creek were later sold to Samuel McIntyre's company.[6]

The early settlers of Tintic were primarily German, Irish, Welsh, and Cornish immigrants skilled in hard rock mining, many of whom had worked their way across the country at other mines before they reached the Tintic region. Thus, many of them had gained valuable mining experience; in fact, many of the early area methods of mining came from Germany and the Comstock Lode areas in California and Nevada, among them a method of timbering mines. Mining laws and practices also had been developed in California and transported to Utah.

A concern of mining operations was to ship only high grade ore and materials from the mines; therefore, getting the ore to a mill or smelter for further processing posed a problem. In the early years, some of the richest ore was transported from Tintic to San Francisco, California; Reno, Nevada; Argo and Pueblo, Colorado; Baltimore, Maryland; and even as far away as Swansea, Wales. It was hauled by wagons to the closest railhead, which was thirty-eight miles north at Stockton in Tooele County. In 1875 a terminus was established at York, at the northern tip of Juab County, and for two years it was the closest railroad to the Tintic District. Thousands of tons of ore were shipped to Salt Lake Valley smelters from this railhead.[7]

Several mills were built at various locations in the region, but none of them proved to be very successful. In 1871 a small mill and smelter was built at Homansville, in Utah County, about 2.5 miles east of Eureka. In 1872 the Crismon-Mammoth Mine had a mill at the Tintic Ranch, and in 1873 the Mammoth Copperopolis built a mill at Roseville. The Germania Smelting Company constructed a mill in Black Dragon Hollow, and another mill was built in Homansville by an Ohio Company called the Wyoming. In 1873, the Shoebridge, or Ely, Mill was developed six miles south of Diamond. It operated until 1879. From 1893 to 1895 the Eureka Hill, Bullion Beck, and Mammoth mines owners all built mills, as did the Sioux and Farrell Mine owners in Robinson. In 1905, mills were built by owners of the Godiva and Uncle Sam mines, and, in 1913, by the May Day, the Knight-Christensen, the Holt-Dern, and the Tintic Milling Company. The last attempt was made by the Chief Consolidated Mining Company from 1924 to 1926.[8]

In 1878 the Salt Lake and Western Railway was built from Lehi Junction down through Utah and Tooele Counties to a point about five miles southwest of Eureka, which became known as Ironton. A line was also run from there to Tintic Mills, where the McIntyre Brothers had constructed a mill and smelter complex for the ores from the Mammoth mines. With Ironton as the shipping point, the output of ore from the area nearly doubled. By 1882, a wye was installed, with the northeast leg going to Silver City and another leg going three miles south to Tintic Mills.[9]

In 1889 a branch was built up the canyon from Silver City Junction to Eureka, and this also was the year the Salt Lake and Western merged into the Oregon Short Line Railway. Numerous

Commercial block owned by well-known Eurekan, Minnie Lochwitz. (Tintic Historical Society)

short lines and spurs were extended to nearby mines, and, in 1892, a line was built up Ruby Hollow to the Northern Spy Mine. In 1893 another branch was built from Mammoth Junction to the Eureka Branch and into Mammoth, known at the time as Robinson.[10] In 1891 the Denver & Rio Grande Western Railroad constructed a line up Homansville Canyon to Homansville and on to Eureka, Mammoth, and Silver City. This gave Tintic two railroads, and by 1899 Tintic had become the leading mining center in the state in the value of its output. In 1906 the production of the district was valued at $8 million.[11]

J.A. Cunningham, in 1896–97, built a two-mile-long standard gauge line from Mammoth station to a switchback above the Mammoth Mill and then along the south and east sides of the valley to the mine. This was called the New East Tintic Railway and operated a twenty-one-ton shay engine called "Little Alice." The line was never profitable, but it was nearly impossible to get the ore down the steep grade, so the spur was kept going until the Mammoth Mine finally fazed out its operation in the 1930s.[12]

Settlements

After the Sunbeam Mine was staked in 1869, miners soon came to prospect for ore in the surrounding hills, and Diamond became the first settlement. As mentioned, quartz in the area glittered like diamonds; thus, the town and canyon where they were found became known respectively as Diamond and Crystal Canyon. Other mines soon were discovered and developed, including the Walker, Joe Bowers, Morning Glory, Rising Sun, and Showers. Unlike other settlements in Juab County, the first church organized was not Mormon, it was Presbyterian or Methodist, with a minister in charge by the name of Mathews. Later, the Church of Jesus Christ of Latter-day Saints did organize locally, with Frank Woodard named as first bishop.[13]

According to an 1879 directory, Diamond, "a town composed chiefly of miners," contained various businesses, including one operated by a woman. R.T. Course and R.A. Hill ran general merchandise establishments, and a Miss E. Dennis worked as a dressmaker. Joseph Murphy plied the trade of shoemaker, with Charles Poynter the local butcher and Simeon Stewart a blacksmith. Diamond supported a physician, surveyor, assayer, and John T. Thurmond, postmaster. Misses Lizzie Hills and E. Stewart taught school. By 1895 the town also boasted a weekly newspaper, the *Rock Mountain Husbandman*. The population reached between 900 and 1,000, but the mines soon had to be abandoned. Water, located at the 300-foot level, proved too expensive to pump.[14] The buildings gradually were moved or demolished for use in other settlements in the district, but the town would be revived briefly in the late 1890s.

In 1878, when the Salt Lake and Western Railroad extended into the Tintic area, it chose Ironton as its terminus. A later directory mentioned Ironton as "a station located on the Tintic branch of the O.S.L.R.R. [Oregon Short Line Railroad], in the northern part of Juab county, 49 miles from Lehi Junction and 77 from Salt Lake City."[15] A depot was built, along with a few dwellings and other railroad facilities. Ironton grew to be a fair-sized settlement, with a few saloons, restaurants, and a hotel. In the 1880s a new Union Pacific line was routed east of Ironton toward its meeting with the Utah

Southern extension railroad at Lynndyl, and the town subsequently declined.[16]

After the discovery of precious metals at the Black Dragon mine in 1870, the town of Silver City grew to become an early center of the Tintic region. The camp was located at the mouth of Dragon Canyon where several silver mines had been established; thus, Silver City seemed an appropriate name for the new town. Located between Diamond and Mammoth, the town developed more rapidly than either of the others, containing the telegraph, express, and recorder's offices for the entire district. The recorder of mining claims, S.B. Moore, and the assay office were both located there. In 1880 F.W. Lamb was assayer. A mail and stage line came from Goshen up past the Eureka Standard Mine, through Silver Pass and down Ruby Hollow to Silver City, then on to Diamond and Mammoth. A branch of the Western Telegraph was installed.[17]

During the late 1870s area miners began to hit water in some of the mines, while in others the mineral deposits seemed to be coming to an end. The Polk directory for 1879–80 illustrated how Silver City had dwindled, with only five business listings. However, new strikes were made after 1896 and Silver City experienced a rebirth. Buildings were constructed as fast as lumber could be obtained and workmen found to build them.[18] During 1896 George Paxman doubled his hotel's size; and John Leyshan erected a new facility on the site of the old Condon House Hotel. Postmaster James McLaughlin constructed an office, and J.D. Sullivan built his famous 16 to 1 Saloon, so named because the demand that the U.S. Treasury coin silver at a ratio to gold of sixteen to one was an important political issue of the time. The town even supported the *Silver City Star,* a weekly newspaper, which was published from 1897 to 1903.[19]

The Swansea and the Sunbeam Mines began to produce again and a Park City group formed the Junction Mining Company. A *Salt Lake Tribune* article of 1 January 1897 stated, "Ever since the early days of smelting in Utah it [the Dragon Iron Mine] has been the chief source of supply for iron fluxing material."[20] Jesse Knight, who was operating mines in Juab and Utah Counties, built the Utah Ore Sampling Company west of Silver City, where he planned to sample and smelt his own ore. He built a narrow-gauge railroad from the

Art Rowley prospects in the North Tintic Mining District. (Tintic Historical Society)

smelter to his mines, and he also built almost one hundred frame houses at the northwest end of Silver City. There were two rows of houses, all painted white. At this time, Silver City's population reached 1,500.[21] On 24 July 1908 Silver City celebrated Pioneer Day and "Smelter Day," a celebration that has been called the most festive held in the district.

Silver City's boom did not last long. Silver City peaked in 1908; by the late 1930s it was practically deserted. Freight rates soon fell and it was more profitable to ship the ore to Salt Lake Valley smelters. The smelter was dismantled and moved to Murray, where it continued to operate for many years.[22] Later, Jesse Knight and George H. Dern (who would become governor of Utah in the 1930s) operated what was known as the Tintic Milling Company on the same site. Work began on the construction of this mill in July 1915, and by March 1916 some milling work was being done. By April the mill had proven to be a success, and by January 1918 it was shipping two bullion cars a month.[23]

To the north and east of Silver City a group of small mines which later became the Mammoth Mine were staked and a claim filed on 26 February 1870 by Thomas G. Wimmer, William D. Wimmer, Robert Wimmer, Joseph W. Wright, John W. Moore, Sr., James J. Perry, W.S. Pace, J.S. Pace, George Patten, Charles Brewerton, George Bailey, Dave Saben, and David D. Tanner. In March another claim also was filed by Thomas Jenkins, Heber P. Kimball, and George and Charles Crismon. George Crismon began work on the mine.[24]

Meanwhile, William H. and Samuel McIntyre had become interested in the Tintic area because of its potential as a place to establish a cattle ranch. As mentioned, in 1871 they brought a herd of long-horn cattle from Texas and sold them at a good price, so they returned for more. In 1873 they traded 1,400 cattle to the Crismon brothers for a large interest in the Mammoth Mine. The proposition turned out to be a very good investment for the McIntyres, in part because during the following winter most of the Crismons' cattle froze.[25]

By the 1870s, British investors had invested extensively in Utah mining ventures, including the Mammoth Copperopolis, later the Ajax Mine, southwest of the Crismon-Mammoth. As a result of the national economic depression known as the Panic of 1873, the Mammoth Copperopolis company sustained a loss of $14,000 during 1873–74. It advertised in the *London Mining Review* and raised $84,000, which was used to build a mill in Roseville, six miles from the mine. The mill failed, however, resulting in the first labor strike in the Tintic District. On 12 January 1874 about fifty miners took control of the mine in an attempt to collect their back pay. At the same time, creditors took possession of all moveable property. The British investor, who reportedly had received the Copperopolis from Noah Armstrong in 1870, refused to grant more financial aid to the Crismons, thus forcing them to sell to the McIntyre brothers.[26]

By this time, Mammoth was becoming a typical mining town. Other mines such as the Black Jack, Victor, Grand Central, Ajax, and Lower Mammoth were opened. The miners and their families were coming to the area from mining towns in surrounding states and from other countries, searching for a better way of life and willing to work hard to acquire it. They built homes and hauled their water from Eureka. In the 1880s, a wooden pipeline was constructed from Jenny Lynn Spring, and water was collected in pails from its end near the town.[27]

George C. Robinson was hired to supervise the construction of the Mammoth Mill, and between 1893–95 a few cabins were built around the mill site. Robinson proceeded to lay out a townsite, which he named in his own honor. In 1895, as twenty-five to fifty new homes were added to Mammoth, twelve houses were built in Robinson. The Roberts brothers maintained a store in Robinson. John B. Roberts became postmaster, with W.B. Brimstone succeeding him in 1894. Joseph H. Nielson established the Robinson Meat Market. The Hotel Mammoth was built by the McIntyres and was operated by the Dix family.[28]

In 1892 Mammoth had a population of 300, with the following businesses listed: J.T. Donahue and Company, hotel, general merchandise, and saloon; Max Friedersdorff, general merchandise; L.E. Riter and Company, general merchandise; Taylor and Allen, saloon; and J.M. Wheeler, saloon.[29] In 1895–96, building lots were selling for up to thirty-five dollars; this rose to from $500 to $600 in 1896–97. At this time D.R. Beebe established a lumberyard, which later became the Tintic Lumber Company of Eureka. A two-story brick schoolhouse was built in the early 1890s to serve both Robinson and Mammoth. On 6 January 1896 a fire destroyed several residences as well as a saloon belonging to Hans J. Hassell and James Donahue.

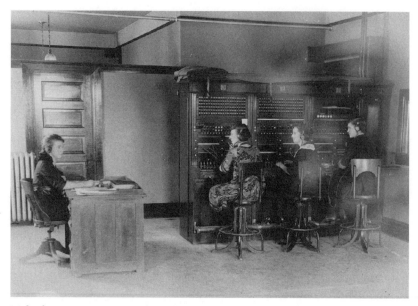

Telephone operators and personnel using equipment upstairs in the Pay Building, 48 North Main, Nephi, 1921. (Fred Chapman)

The saloon was rebuilt and the Mammoth Opera House constructed.[30]

The LDS church organized locally on 26 January 1890, with Lewis Stout as branch president and Edward D. Cox and John Mordise as counselors. On 25 May 1890 the branch was reorganized because of the death of Lewis Stout. Edward D. Cox was sustained as president, with John Mordis as first counselor and Henry Reed as second counselor. On 11 May 1895 the branch was reorganized again; George Hales became president, Edwin Cox first counselor, Moroni Stark second counselor, and George E. Debble clerk. A Sunday School was also organized at this time, with John Hopkins as superintendent, Albert Hagen as first assistant, and John Moredo as second assistant. A meetinghouse was built and the first meeting was held there on 15 March 1896. Juab Stake President William Paxman and Apostle George Teasdale attended. The building was dedicated on 22 November 1896 by Apostle Joseph F. Smith. Prior to this time, LDS church meetings had been held in a house rented from Albert Hagen.[31]

Mammoth also supported other institutions. A Congregational church was opened in the early 1890s, with a Reverend Foster in charge.[32] I.E. Diehl published a weekly newspaper, the *Mammoth Record*, from 1896 to 1930.[33] The paper truly acted as the lifeblood of the community, as Diehl recorded the daily happenings of Mammoth and Robinson. For many years, Mammoth had two post offices, one in what locals called Uppertown (Mammoth) and one in Lowertown (Robinson). In 1916 the offices were combined and located in Middletown. Margaret A. Brown was postmistress at that time.

In 1910 Mammoth City was incorporated. James Hutchinson became the first mayor, with I.E. Diehl as city recorder. Nineteen years later, on 29 November 1929, when the city was disincorporated, Albert Larsen was mayor and E.R. Wheelock was city recorder. During the summer of 1912 Mammoth experienced another fire, which destroyed the post office, confectionery, and a moving picture theater owned by McIntyre and McGee in Robinson. As a result, a volunteer fire department was organized.[34]

Eureka became the center of the Tintic Mining District. The Eureka Hill Mine, staked in February 1870, was the first of a group to be located in the Eureka area. As mentioned, John Q. Packard, with Watson Nesbitt, were among the first entrepreneurs in the area. Nesbitt, according to legend, fought actual battles over the Eureka Hill Mine. One raged between Watson and William Rose, who struck a rich vein of silver near the Eureka Hill. Surveys indicated that the claims overlapped, but the shrewd Nesbitt came out on top. He reportedly ruled the claim "by right of might."[35]

John Beck came to Eureka in 1871. After filing a claim in Diamond and selling it to the Fon-du-Lac Company of Michigan, he staked a claim at the bottom of Eureka Gulch and called it the Bullion Beck. Beck had come from Germany and when he staked his claim, he was referred to as "that crazy Dutchman." Up to this time, mineral deposits had been located higher in the hills and no one believed Beck could find anything where he was working. He hit ore at the 200-foot level, however, and the Bullion Beck Mine became one of Tintic's big producers. Beck was always willing to share his good fortune with those who were in need and eventually died a poor man. Reportedly, it was John Beck who, upon finding glittering silver ore clinging to the roots of some sagebrush, cried, "Eureka," meaning "I have found it!" Thus, Eureka received its name.[36]

By 1886 the Blue Rock (later the Centennial Eureka) Mine consisted of several claims in the Eureka Hill area, and it and the Gemini (old Keystone) Mine were producing. These two mines together with the Eureka Hill and the Bullion Beck became known as the "Big Four" and were Eureka's major producers.[37] Tintic in effect had become a network of mines. Business establishments and residential buildings were springing up everywhere. Eureka's business district developed at the bottom of Eureka Gulch, but homes were built wherever it was convenient to put them, a common practice in mining towns. Unlike the checkerboard-plot pattern of Mormon farming villages, such as those in east Juab, mining towns meandered around mountains and hills, adjusting to the contours of the land.

As Eureka assumed the role of commercial center for Tintic, business establishments congregated on its fledgling Main Street. In 1880 Eureka's businesses included the following: William Hatfield, general merchandise; Williams and Cusick, general merchandise, saloon, and billiards; and W.W. Mathews, saloon and billiards.[38] A post office was also established in 1880.

The early 1890s were a time of rapid growth for all of Tintic. During that time, an International Order of Odd Fellows (IOOF) hall was erected in Eureka, at a cost of $9,000; also, a two-story brick building was constructed by McCrystal and Company for $10,000. Additions were made to the Tomkins Eureka Hotel and the Hatfield House; improvements were also made at the Meyer's Hotel (Keystone) and at Anna Mark's store. The Pat Shea boardinghouse and the Beaumont Building were constructed, and the George Arthur Rice and Company Bank and other stores were established. Juab County constructed a courthouse in Eureka in 1891 to serve the county government needs of residents. Nephi, the county seat, also had a courthouse.[39]

Eureka quickly became the Tintic area's major political center, incorporating as a city on 8 November 1892. City designation meant the establishment of a local government, with ordinances and committees to enforce civic action. Hugo Deprezin was elected mayor; C.W. Clark, H.F. Fullride, Pat Donnelly, M.C. Sullivan, and W.D.

The cemetery is all that remains of the old town of Diamond, 1998. (Wayne Christiansen)

Meyers were councilmen; W.S. Shriver was treasurer, T.W. Blue recorder, and Gus J. Henroid marshal.[40]

As was the case in other communities, the need for local schools became evident from the outset. Eureka's first school was located on the west end of town in 1881, in the section commonly known as "Dutch Town," where those of German ancestry resided. Rudolph Van Bauer was the schoolmaster, assisted by a Miss Courtney and Miss Hattie Lawson. In 1884 John Q. Packard financed a two-story brick school building in the north-central part of town. In 1907 Eureka's first high school was built.[41] A private school would soon follow.

Father Lawrence Scanlan, only thirty years old when he came to Utah from Ireland in 1873, became the "pioneer" Catholic prelate of the Utah area. By this time, railroads and mining districts had attracted many immigrants who belonged to the Catholic faith, especially the Irish. However, these people were scattered throughout the vast Utah Territory. Father Scanlan is said to have once traveled 375 miles to Silver Springs by horseback and then gone on to Tintic Junction, where he lived for three weeks in a log cabin and slept on the floor. In December 1873 Scanlan traveled by stage to Lehi and then to Tintic. While there, he baptized several people in Silver City and Diamond.[42]

Eureka Catholics requested a resident priest in 1884, and Father Denis Kiely was sent in 1885. Land was purchased and St. Patrick's Church was erected in town; the name itself indicating the importance of Irish immigrants to the developing Catholic church in the Tintic area. Completed in time for Christmas services in December 1885, the building also doubled as a school. By 1886 Father Patrick O'Donahue was pastor of St. Patrick's Church and William Jo Bogan taught school from January to October of that year. Bogan also taught a night school for adults that was attended by miners and other citizens.[43]

Lawrence Scanlan was now bishop of the territorial diocese and, upon his official visit to Eureka in 1891, he found that the school was not large enough to accommodate the number of children attending. Under his leadership a new school was constructed. St. Joseph's School opened in 1891, with five Sisters of the Holy Cross who were brought from South Bend, Indiana, teaching the children. St. Patrick's Parish covered Silver City, Mammoth, Eureka, and Diamond. A convent for the sisters was established in 1912.[44]

In 1880 the Methodist church was organized in the area by W.A. Hunter, with G.F. Jane as presiding elder. The church extended to Nephi the same year, with the circuit named the "Nephi and Eureka."[45] On 18 June 1890 Dr. Thomas C. Iliff preached a sermon and immediately obtained $700 from the congregation toward the construction of a Methodist church building. This was followed by an appropriation of $525 from the regional mission conference of 1890. The building was built in the summer and fall of 1891. W.A. Hunter became the first pastor, followed by Dr. J.D. Gillian. During 1899 a four-room parsonage was added, and in 1918 a new parsonage was constructed. The church continues in service.[46]

Religion was important to Tintic residents. In addition to Catholics and Methodists, Eureka also attracted Lutheran, Baptist, and Episcopal populations. A level of tolerance developed in the area, where the people had to work together to survive.

The Church of Jesus Christ of Latter-day Saints had organized in

Eureka in November 1883, becoming more fully organized on 27 April 1884 at the office of the Bullion Beck Mine. John Beck served as presiding elder, with Henry Simons and Lorenz Fullenback as counselors. A Sunday School was organized the same day, with Henry Simons as superintendent and John R. Johnson and Adolph Van Bauer as assistants. The Mutual Improvement Association for young people was organized on 15 March 1891 under the direction of Peter Lowensock, president, and counselors Lorenz Fullenback and Samuel Freckelton. Also in 1891, Anna V. Loutensock became president of the Primary Association for children, with Christene Harrison and Elizabeth Siefert as her assistants. The women's Relief Society was organized on 13 November 1897, with Rhoda Heaton as president. On 15 June 1893 the Eureka LDS Branch was organized as the Eureka Ward of Juab LDS Stake by Apostle John Henry Smith. Peter Loutensock became the first bishop.[47]

Tintic remained part of the Juab Stake until May 1905, at which time it was joined to the Nebo Stake. On 22 April 1917 the Tintic LDS Stake was organized; it included Eureka, Knightsville (a town built and owned by Jesse Knight), Mammoth, and Silver City. Erastus Frank Birch of Silver City became the first stake president, with William John Adams of Eureka and Norman Dahle of Silver City as his counselors. On 2 April 1939 the Santaquin-Tintic LDS Stake was organized.

John Beck had financed the construction of the town's first LDS church building on a hill north of the Bullion Beck Mine. Ground was later purchased on the south side of Eureka's Main Street, with a larger Gothic style building constructed there in 1902. Upon its completion, Apostle Reed Smoot dedicated the edifice on 30 October 1904.[48] The three main religious buildings of Eureka—St. Patricks, the Methodist church, and the LDS meetinghouse—continue to stand as testaments to the religious commitment of Tintic's pioneers.

The American economy fell drastically because of the Panic of 1893, adversely affecting all of Utah. This, coupled with the repeal of the Sherman Silver Purchase Act of 1890, which had required the federal treasury to purchase 4.5 million ounces of silver every month, caused the price of silver to drop.[49] Also, because of the troubles, a resulting miners' strike crippled Tintic. As one historian wrote:

house at Joy.
Sam Hagens

Sam Hagens numbered as one of few residents at Joy. (Ray Spor)

Declining lead and silver prices and an apparent victory over labor by the Coeur d'Alene Mine Owners Association spurred western mine owners to launch an attack on wages and unions in the winter of 1892–1893. The Bullion Beck of Eureka initiated the attack in Tintic. The mine was closed in early February and 200 men were out of work. The company offered to pay $2.50 per day until silver reached 95 cents an ounce, then after one month the $3.00 a day wage would be restored. The Eureka Miners' Union, established in the late 1880's, countered by proposing a $2.75 per day wage and $3.00 restored when silver was 90 cents an ounce. A compromise failed to materialize, and the strike followed with both sides adamant with regard to their respective positions. [50]

The Bullion Beck Mine's board of directors at the time consisted of Moses Thatcher, president; John Beck, vice-president; William B. Preston, treasurer; A.E. Hyde, general manager; and W.J. Beattie, secretary. Mormon leader George Q. Cannon was also a member of the board. John Duggan represented the Eureka Miners' Union. In February, the Eureka miners proposed a wage scale based on a sliding scale tied to silver prices. Hyde refused the offer, looking to utilize strikebreakers to work the mines. At that time, most of the mines maintained a boarding house and a company store which they expected their employees to patronize. This also became an issue along with the wages.[51]

On 7 March the Bullion Beck opened with about forty miners, most of them non-union. Union men met the workers' train at the mine and persuaded the strikebreakers not to go to work. On 10 March a group of about forty women, under the direction of Miss Annie Kelly, marched to the Beck mine and paraded to show their disapproval of the opening of the mine. By mid-March United States marshals and special marshals had been requested by the Beck mine directors. There was some controversy and some arrests, but, as one historian expressed, "For a mining town experiencing a strike, the number of arrests for violence was surprisingly low."[52]

The strike was lost by the miners, and labor troubles dragged on until the end of the year. The Panic of 1893 had caused almost all the mines to close, and by July only the Eureka Hill continued in operation. The Mammoth Mine opened in May 1893 with a small crew, and by the end of the year a few other mines were opening. Trials and tribulation continued to haunt the district, however. On 10 July 1893 a fire began on Main Street in a saloon and lodging house belonging to Minnie Lockwitz, soon spreading east and west along both sides of the street. The loss of property was estimated at $37,000. After this, Eureka developed a more stringent fire code—buildings were to be constructed of stone or brick or clad with metal sheeting.[53] A flood caused by heavy rains descended upon Eureka on 13 July 1896, inflicting heavy damage and causing the deaths of two people. Despite all this, Eureka survived as the social and economic center of the Tintic Mining District. By 1890 the city's population numbered 1,733.

Jesse Knight came to Tintic in 1896 with no apparent knowledge about mining, just an acute interest in it. When he began to work his claim, an engineer reportedly laughed and told him, "humbug." But Knight continued and eventually became one of the most wealthy of Tintic's mine owners. He called his mine the Humbug. Knight located other mines in east Tintic, including the Uncle Sam, Iron Blossom, Black Jack, Dragon, and Star.[54] His enterprises later would be of signal importance in many facets of the district.

"Uncle Jesse," as Knight was called affectionately, started the town of Knightsville about two miles east of Eureka. He began by building twenty homes; within a short period of time, there were sixty-five homes, two boarding houses, a church (which was also used as a schoolhouse), a post office, general and dry-goods stores, a livery stable, and a brick schoolhouse—but no saloons. Reportedly, Knightsville was the only "saloon free" mining town in the West; however, Eureka with its many saloons was but a short distance away.

Knight gained a reputation for looking after his workers. The year after the school was started, a notice was received that there were not enough schoolchildren in the area to qualify for funds from county taxes, so Knight journeyed to Diamond and hired James Higginson, whose family consisted of a wife and eight children. This increased the school enrollment to a point that the town was entitled to county school funds.[55] Knight was a devout Latter-day Saint, and his mining operation was the first to give mine workers a day off on Sunday. He did expect the miners to attend church and to abstain from the use of liquor and tobacco. He also paid his workers twenty-five cents per day more to compensate for the day of work lost. When the LDS church was organized in Knightsville, the first bishop was William McCullough, with Andrew Madsen and Charles Reese as his counselors. James B. Whitehead was superintendent of the Sunday School, and his wife, Julia W. Whitehead, was president of the Primary. Perry B. Fuller became president of the Mutual Improvement Association, and Mrs. Andrew Madsen was president of the Relief Society.[56]

Until 1898, when the Juab County boundary line was surveyed and found to be on the eastern side of Knightsville, area residents paid taxes to Utah County. In 1899 they began paying taxes to Juab

County.[57] Knightsville's population reached 1,000 citizens by 1907. However, in about 1915 ore from the mines began to decline, and by 1924 only one or two mines remained in operation. By 1940 they were all closed and nearly all of the residents had moved away, most structures also having been dismantled and moved by that time.[58]

From 1894 to the turn of the century the Tintic Mining District grew and prospered, helping the entire county to prosper. People who lived in valley towns in both Utah and Juab Counties found Tintic an outlet for their farm produce and goods. The mines in the district were improved and the population skyrocketed. Tintic promised to be one of Utah's most important mining areas. In fact, mining people were so optimistic that the *Salt Lake Mining Review* in June 1899 asserted,

> The present high price of lead and copper, together with the boom in gold mining and the many new mines opened to production in the district, have easily rendered Tintic one of the foremost districts in America. . . . It has a very large area yet undeveloped and offers to the miner, capitalist or speculator a magnificent field for investment . . . and today few spots of the earth are more promising to old or young in the mining field than Tintic.[59]

Thus, the dawn of the twentieth century commenced on a high note of confidence, enthusiasm, and encouragement regarding the Tintic Mining District—continued prosperity seemed at hand.

ENDNOTES

1. Philip F. Notarianni, *Faith, Hope, & Prosperity: The Tintic Mining District* (Eureka, Utah: Tintic Historical Society, 1982), vii.

2. Peter Gottfredson, *Indian Depredations in Utah* (Salt Lake City: Skelton Publishing, 1919), 100–1.

3. Kate B. Carter, *Heart Throbs of the West*, 2:10. There are several different versions of the discovery of the Sunbeam mine; see Notarianni, *Faith, Hope, & Prosperity*, 14, and Kate B. Carter, *Our Pioneer Heritage*, 7:101.

4. Notarianni, *Faith, Hope, & Prosperity*, 14.

5. Alice P. McCune, *History of Juab County*, 233–35.

6. Notarianni, *Faith, Hope, & Prosperity*, 21.

7. McCune, *Juab County*, 172; Stephen L. Carr, *Utah Ghost Towns*, 99.

8. McCune, *Juab County*, 172, 173–74.

9. Stephen L. Carr and Robert W. Edwards, *Utah Ghost Rails,* 139.

10. Ibid.

11. McCune, *Juab County,* 176.

12. Carr and Edwards, *Utah Ghost Rails,* 140, 142.

13. McCune, *Juab County,* 134.

14. *Utah Directory, 1879–80,* 357; Carr, *Utah Ghost Towns,* 94.

15. *Utah Directory, 1900,* 119.

16. Carr, *Utah Ghost Towns,* 94.

17. See McCune, *Juab County,* 227; and Carr, *Utah Ghost Towns,* 90.

18. *Utah Directory, 1879–80,* 358; Notarianni, *Faith, Hope, & Prosperity,* 52.

19. Notarianni, *Faith, Hope, & Prosperity,* 52; J. Cecil Alter, *Early Utah Journalism,* 390.

20. Notarianni, *Faith, Hope, & Prosperity,* 53.

21. McCune, *Juab County,* 229.

22. Carr, *Utah Ghost Towns,* 90.

23. Notarianni, *Faith, Hope, & Prosperity,* 104.

24. Ibid., 16.

25. Sherri Scoville, "Samuel H. McIntyre: Founder and Builder in Utah History," copy courtesy of E. Steele McIntyre, Eureka, Utah.

26. Notarianni, *Faith, Hope, & Prosperity,* 16.

27. Ibid., 17.

28. Ibid., 48.

29. Ibid., 35.

30. Ibid., 48.

31. "Mammoth Ward Records to 1898," and " Mammoth Historical Records 1890 to 1896," LDS Genealogical Library, Salt Lake City.

32. McCune, *Juab County,* 222.

33. Alter, *Early Utah Journalism,* 386.

34. McCune, *Juab County,* 224; Notarianni, *Faith, Hope, & Prosperity,* 97.

35. Notarianni, *Faith, Hope, & Prosperity,* 17–18; McCune, *Juab County,* 190.

36. See *Eureka Reporter,* 19 July 1996.

37. Notarianni, *Faith, Hope, & Prosperity,* 19.

38. Ibid., 26.

39. Ibid., 48.

40. McCune, *Juab County,* 194.

41. Ibid., 195. Notarianni, *Faith, Hope, & Prosperity*, states that the second school was built in 1896.

42. Bernice Maher Mooney, *Salt of the Earth: The History of the Catholic Church in Utah, 1776–1987* (Salt Lake City: Intermountain Catholic Press, 1992), 54, 83.

43. Ibid.

44. Ibid., 83, 85.

45. McCune, *Juab County*, 198–99.

46. Notariani, *Faith, Hope, & Prosperity*, 66.

47. McCune, *Juab County*, 196–97; "Mammoth Historical Records 1890 to 1896."

48. McCune, *Juab County*, 197.

49. Notarianni, *Faith, Hope, & Prosperity*, 39.

50. Ibid.

51. Ibid.

52. Ibid. For a more detailed account of the strike see pp. 39–43; and Paul A. Frisch, "Labor Conflict at Eureka, 1886–97," *Utah Historical Quarterly* 40 (Spring 1981): 145–56.

53. Notarianni, *Faith, Hope, & Prosperity*, 43.

54. Carr, *Utah Ghost Towns*, 95.

55. McCune, *Juab County*, 238.

56. Ibid.

57. Ibid., 241.

58. Carr, *Utah Ghost Towns*, 96.

59. *Salt Lake Mining Review*, 30 June 1899.

CHAPTER 6

TINTIC AND JUAB ENTER
THE TWENTIETH CENTURY

Juab County entered the twentieth century as the sixth most populous county in Utah, with 10,082 people. It boasted two thriving cities in Eureka and Nephi, with 3,085 and 2,203 inhabitants, respectively. Both mining and agriculture were generally prospering—a trend that would continue for at least twenty years. In fact, the county had almost doubled in population from its 1890 census count of 5,582 people—the largest rate of gain in the territory (and new state), with the exception of that experienced by Uintah County during the period.[1]

The Tintic District

Tintic, fresh from the prosperity that has been called the "Rainbow Era" of the 1880s and 1890s, launched into the new century at a pinnacle of prosperity. The *Salt Lake Mining Review*, in its review of Tintic, stated,

> The largest camp in the district is Eureka, which is now one of the most progressive and prosperous mining towns in this western country. It is here that the greatest number of producing and pay-

Majestic Mt. Nebo looking east from narrow guage railroad grade near Silver City, 1998. (Wayne Christiansen)

ing mines are located . . . it boasts of nearly every metropolitan advantage and is a little city instead of an isolated mining camp. . . . Mammoth, also, has kept pace with the times, and while not as large as Eureka, enjoys about the same facilities [including two railroads].[2]

While optimism reigned supreme, the years after 1900 were characterized by cyclical patterns of upturns and downswings.

Both commercial and social activity were significant measures of the local conditions. Businesses abounded in the towns of Tintic. The George Arthur Rice Bank in Eureka had failed in 1897; but in 1898 McCornick and Company of Salt Lake City closed its bank in Mercur, moving the firm to Eureka. By 1904 the bank was firmly established, with Frank D. Kimball as cashier.[3] The telephone came to Utah in 1879 and communities from Logan to Eureka soon were linked together by the Rocky Mountain Bell Telephone Company. In February 1895 the Eureka Electric Light Company was granted a franchise to supply electricity to the area.[4]

Eureka's population by 1900 had grown to 3,085 residents, over 800 more than were in Nephi, and commercial and business activity

Early 1870s photograph of Diamond, Tintic Mining District. (Tintic Historical Society)

had grown comparably. By 1903–04 there were some ninety businesses in Eureka; also, Mammoth claimed fifteen business establishments, Robinson had twenty-seven, Silver City eighteen, and Diamond three. These included mining company offices, general mercantiles, meat markets, confectioneries, bakeries, saloons, restaurants, hotels, furniture stores, milliners, tailor shops, cobblers, men's furnishing stores, barbers, jewelers, photographers, laundries, druggists, utility offices, telegraph and freight agencies, undertakers, newspapers, midwives, blacksmiths, tinners, livery stables, banks, doctors, and lawyers.[5]

James Cash Penney established his second in a chain of Golden Rule stores in Eureka. Penney, labeled as one of the great "merchant princes" of the century, expanded into Utah in 1909. With the Eureka store, Penney created a base from which he recruited for his national chain. Earl C. Sams, who assisted in creating the Eureka Golden Rule store, succeeded Penney as president of the company in 1917. In fact, stores in the chain were actually opened out of the Eureka store, where managers and other staff were trained by Sams. A.W. Hughes, a manager-partner of the Eureka store in 1923–24, later became the third president of J.C. Penney Company. Some other establishments opened in Eureka also later expanded to other Utah cities.

W.F. Shriver, with his brother F.L. Shriver, opened a menswear store; Joseph Worthlin and John R. Morgan operated a meat market in Eureka in 1903. At Mammoth, the Miner's Supply was owned by David Keith. D.C. Forsey opened a general merchandise store.[6] Peddlers from the valley towns were taking their fresh fruits and vegetables to Tintic to sell. The Tintic merchants resented this, and on 26 December 1902 an article in the *Eureka Reporter* asked, "Is it any wonder that business is somewhat slow with the merchants of Eureka?" However, in spite of the ordinances passed and the license fees charged, the peddlers continued a presence into the early 1930s.[7]

Local newspapers exerted an influence on Tintic residents. As in Nephi, the local press served as the main source of news, as they editorialized, sold advertisements, and kept residents aware of local happenings. Eureka had an especially colorful series of newspapers, beginning with the *Eureka Chief,* which dated from 18 October 1889, with E.C. Higgins as editor and publisher. It was eventually purchased and consolidated with the *Tintic Miner.* The first publication of the *Tintic Miner* was on 1 May 1891, with C.F. and E.H. Rathbone listed as publishers. On 11 March 1893 the *Spanish Fork Sun* quoted the *Brigham City Report* as stating, "Newman A. Mix, formerly of the *Tooele Times,* has assumed charge of the *Eureka Miner.*" C.F. Spillman, in an editorial in the *Tintic Miner* on 19 December 1898, mentioned that he purchased the *Miner* from Mix on 11 August 1894. The *American Newspaper Directory* for 1896 and 1898 listed Fred Nelson as editor and publisher.[8] In the directory for 1898, the paper was credited as follows:

> *The Eureka Democrat,* Fridays, 4 pages, 15 x 22, established 1894, Charles P. Diehl, Editor and Publisher. In 1898 the Democrat lists James N. Lauder, Editor; Charles P. Diehl, Publisher, circulation, smallest edition within a year, not less than 400. Advertisers will take notice that this is the only paper in Eureka to which this Directory accords a circulation in actual figures and guarantees the

The "Horseless Carriage" era invades Nephi. (Fred Chapman)

accuracy of the rating by a reward of $100, payable to the first person who successfully assails it.[9]

The *Utah Editor and Printer,* a magazine-type publication, was launched by Charles P. and Isaac E. Diehl. It was mentioned in the *Wasatch Wave* in July 1897, and sold for one dollar per year; but it evidently did not last very long.[10] The *Juab County Republican* commenced in 1894 with Charles S. King as editor and William C. Dewar as manager. This newspaper ran more or less continuously until 1900.

The *Eureka Reporter* became the most important weekly newspaper in Tintic. It first appeared about 1 November 1900. The earliest number found of the paper states, "The Reporter Publishing Company, J.C. Sullivan, President, P.J. Donnelley, Vice President, Hans J. Hassell, Treasurer, Charles E. Huish, Secretary." The de facto editor, publisher, and proprietor was Huish; the other names were used only for political and business prestige. Beginning with the issue of 20 November 1903, the paper's name was shortened to the *Eureka Reporter.* Editor Huish quipped that it was "weakly" enough without calling attention to the fact. Huish continued in full charge of the

Showers & Bowers "inclined shaft headframe," near Diamond, 1998. (Wayne Christiansen)

newspaper for nearly thirty-two years. On 28 April 1932 the masthead read "C.E. Huish, editor, C.E. Rife, manager." On 5 May 1932, however, it read, "C.E. Rife, J. Vern Rife, publishers."[11]

The language used in the early local papers proved most entertaining. Examples follow:

> Another old timer of the Tintic district has taken his chamber in the silent halls of death. . . .
>
> An Eastern editor refuses to publish obituary notices of people who while living did not subscribe for his paper, and says, "people who do not take their home paper are dead anyhow and their mere passing away is of no news value."

The *Reporter* and *Mammoth Record* often jousted. One good-humored entry from the former stated,

> The *Mammoth Record* is authority for the statement that there were twenty-five fights in Eureka on Christmas Day. This paper has made a careful canvass of the situation and we are under the necessity of calling the *Record* editor down for exaggerating the immorality of the camp. There were but twenty-four fights here on that day.[12]

Silver City, the early center of the Tintic Mining District. (Utah State Historical Society)

C.E. Rife exemplified local publishers of the era. According to information supplied by his son Rusty, Rife was hired by Huish to operate and teach others how to operate a new typesetting machine purchased by the paper. Rife refused to come to Eureka for only a salary, and so was sold a one-third interest in the newspaper. Shortly after, Rife brought his brother Vern to Eureka to learn the trade and they eventually purchased the remaining two-thirds interest in the newspaper. Several years later C.E. Rife bought his brother's share.

The social life in Tintic continued to revolve around the local churches and fraternal organizations. In the early 1900s, Eureka, as mentioned, had Catholic, Methodist, Lutheran, Baptist, Episcopalian and LDS churches; Mammoth housed a LDS and a Congregational church; Diamond boasted both LDS and Methodist churches; and Silver City had a LDS church. The Mormons in Eureka added a social hall to the east side of their chapel in 1909, where the Mutual Improvement Association and the Relief Society auxiliaries held dances, plays, and other activities. Catholic organizations included the Knights of Robert Emmet, the Blessed Virgin Mary Society of St. Patrick's Church, and later the Knights of Columbus.[13]

Numerous fraternal organizations contributed to Tintic's social life by providing entertainment and association with others who had

William Howard's Nephi home was constructed using hand-chiseled red sandstone from Andrews Canyon. (Fred Chapman)

similar interests. These organizations included: the Godiva Lodge No. 8, Knights of Pythius; Tintic Lodge No. 9, Free and Accepted Masons, organized 12 January 1892; Keystone Encampment No. 8, Independent Order of Odd Fellows; Eureka Lodge No. 2, IOOF; Court Eureka No. 8503, Ancient Order of Foresters of America; Oquirrh Lodge No. 19, Ancient Order of United Workmen; and Columbia Lodge No. 12, Daughters of Rebekah.[14] After the beginning of the century other organizations were established, including the Eureka Camp No. 451, Woodmen of the World; Twentieth Century Circle No. 316, Women of Woodcraft; Court Gladstone No. 6, Foresters of America; Tintic Hive No. 5, Ladies of the Macabees; Evening Star Lodge No. 7, Degree of Honor Ancient Order of United Workmen; Tintic Lodge No. 711, Benevolent and Protective Order of Elks. The Elks organized on 20 June 1901, the second Elks lodge in Utah. The Eureka Miners' Union Local No. 151 of the Western Federation of Miners was reorganized on 8 February 1902, with fifty charter members.[15]

The activities of the lodges were listed in the *Eureka Reporter*

Osborne Boarding House, Silver City. (Tintic Historical Society)

under the heading "Secret Societies." They not only provided entertainment for their own members but also for others in the Tintic communities. Among the entertainments sponsored were plays and dances. It is interesting to note that they helped with civic improvements; for example, in the *Eureka Reporter* of 29 May 1903 an article stated that, "The work of putting the pipe line into the city cemetery was completed Tuesday afternoon. The cost will be $325, a portion of which has already been subscribed by the secret societies of the camp. The rest will be paid by the city."

In 1891 the Odd Fellows built a hall which served as an opera house and gathering place for other organizations in Eureka. In 1907 the Miners' Union Hall was completed. This two-story concrete block structure cost $14,000 and also housed other fraternal orders on the upper floor and commercial establishments on the lower level. The J.C. Penney Company store was located there from 1907 into the mid-1930s.[16]

In October 1909 the Eureka Public Library was built, with dedication ceremonies held on 13 October of that year. The library committee had contacted philanthropist Andrew Carnegie, who was well known for his contributions to such projects and during his life helped to finance some 2,000 public libraries throughout the United

Railroad depot at Silver City, ca. 1925, functioned as the life line for the town. (Tintic Historical Society)

States. Carnegie's library foundation furnished $11,000 and the city added $6,200 to finance the project. A banquet and program was also held in which $400 was collected for the purchase of books.[17]

Sports and sporting events captured the interest and imagination of Tintic residents. In 1904 the people of Eureka selected a board of directors to form a corporation for a baseball team. Enough stock was sold to the businessmen of the area to "guarantee the success of the venture." This included funding for fencing, improving the grounds, and erecting a grandstand for spectators.[18] Mammoth and Silver City also had baseball teams. The *Reporter* published a regular sports column that reported the results of baseball and football games and also of boxing matches and "socker" ball scores.

Life in the district was busy, as both work and social life flourished at the turn of the century. On 15 May 1903 the following article appeared in the *Eureka Weekly Reporter*:

> With the amount of work which is being done at the Tintic mines, this summer should be a very prosperous one for the district. Silver, lead and copper, three metals which predominate in the mines of Tintic, are bringing good prices and besides the work at the older properties a good deal of prospecting is being done. . . .

There are less idle mine[s] in the camp than at any time during the past four years and last week we understand two or three mines were unable to secure miners enough to carry out the work which they had mapped out. Again we say this ought to be a prosperous year for the people of Eureka, Mammoth and Silver City.

Tintic's economy fluctuated according to the price of precious metals, the cost of shipping and smelting, and the fact that some of the mines struck water that was too expensive to pump it out. New smelters were built at the Uncle Sam and the May Day Mines, but when it became more profitable to ship the ore to the Salt Lake Valley to be smelted, the smelters were closed, including the modern mill that Jesse Knight had built in Silver City, which was only used for about a year.

By 1909 Tintic mines had gained a national reputation touted by many mining advocates. Leroy A. Palmer, a prominent mining writer, confessed that while most attention was focused on Nevada, "the fact often escapes our notice that almost at our door we have their equal," referring to the Tintic District. In another article, he stated succinctly,

If you have a mine anywhere in the country and you don't like the location, move it to Tintic. No matter what kind of a proposition it is, if you can get it in this district it will command attention, for this section seems to be the long odds favorite in Utah's list of mining districts. A visit to the local stock exchange will almost convince one that Tintic is the only place on the map where something is doing all the time.[19]

Walter Fitch, who had purchased shares in the Little Chief Mining Company, incorporated his holdings into the Chief Consolidated Mining Company in 1909. Fitch organized the Eureka City Mining Company for the purpose of prospecting under the actual townsite. He offered 1,000 shares of stock for the mineral rights to one acre of ground, and was able to purchase a good share of the town property. By 1910 the Chief Consolidated and the Eureka Mining Company were consolidated. The resulting Chief Consolidated Mining Company became one of Tintic's most profitable ventures.[20]

Just prior to the turn of the century most people who immi-

Silver City Post Office, 1935. (Tintic Historical Society)

grated to Utah arrived from the northern European countries. However, when the railroad and mining industries began expanding, Utah experienced a growth in the number of immigrants from southern and eastern Europe and the Middle East. This influx added diversity to the population of Juab County. United States census reports in 1900 of "foreign-born" listings included 164 Finns and 72 Italians, while the 1910 count registered 50 Austrians, 237 Finns, 22 Greeks, and 70 Italians in the area. Earlier, some Chinese railroad workers who had completed their work on the transcontinental railroad came to the newborn Tintic district. Sing Chung operated a Chinese and Japanese goods business on upper Main Street in Eureka and also advertised himself as an agent for Chinese cooks and laborers, "furnished at short notice." The *Eureka Reporter* ran ads for a Chinese laundry and reported fights and other acts involving Chinese residents which aroused complaints. Overt racism and ethnic clannishness were features of the times in Tintic as elsewhere in the county, state, and nation. Another *Reporter* article observed in 1903,

> The Chinese gambling fraternity of the camp have been "hitting" the local gambling houses pretty strong during the past week. The

One of several courthouses built by Juab County to service Tintic's mining towns, 1935. (Tintic Historical Society)

> Chinks are past masters in the profession of gambling—their favorite game being faro—and it is stated a few of the Celestials have won in the neighborhood of $2,000 from the local gamblers during the past few days. As this coin is all sent to China it is out of circulation for some time to come.[21]

This sentiment, and preoccupation about money being sent to homelands, formed part of the national concern over immigration of the era.

Concerns about the influx of southern and eastern Europeans reached a peak during the 1908–1912 period in Tintic. Italians had arrived in Tintic earlier in the century, mostly in small numbers; however, with the increased smelter activity after 1910, larger numbers of Greeks and South Slavic immigrants were brought in as workers by smelter operators. An article describing a killing in Silver City involving two Croatians illustrates local sentiment.

> The people of Silver City are pretty well stirred up over the affair and some of them blame the mine and smelter superintendents for hiring Greeks and Austrians, who are undesireable [sic] citizens. Over at Bingham these alien laborers have caused so much trouble that an effort is no being made to drive them out of the camp.

Silver City Public School, ca. 1920s. (Tintic Historical Society)

> Those who have the best interest of Bingham at heart are trying to make it a "white man's camp." Why don't the people of Silver City do likewise.[22]

A Silver City resident of the time penned the following:

> Before the smelter was completed a boat load of Turkish people [Greeks] was imported for cheap labor which of course caused contention among the working people, these Turks were housed in large rooming and boarding houses near the smelter and much to them selves and a good thing because these people were considered very dangerous and most of them carried long knives in the side sash around their waist and we kids were admonished to stay away from that part of town or we would be butchered and eaten.[23]

A deep apprehension continued. A 1912 article in the *Reporter* asked, "Is Eureka To Be 'Bohunk' Town?" The article continued,

> Their presence [South Slavs] in a mining town, or any other town for that matter, adds nothing to its dignity, its wealth or its importance. . . . For the first time in the history of Eureka the "bohunks"

Jesse Knight's company houses, servicing Knight's Smelter at Silver City, ca. 1920s. (Tintic Historical Society)

> have got a foothold here, over one hundred of them being at work
> at the present time. What does it mean? Where is it going to end?[24]

This work force moved with job opportunities, and the sporadic smelter activity in Tintic meant that defined ethnic communities did not really develop in the area. Many of these immigrants had come with the hope of earning enough to support themselves and their families and then return to their homelands. However, once they became aware of the opportunities available, many decided to remain in Utah and tried to accommodate to the existing social and cultural environment. Eureka, and the entire Tintic area, primarily still contained people from the northern European countries, resulting in a rather homogenous social situation that also helped inhibit the formation of solid ethnic communities of southern and eastern Europeans.[25]

In 1902 a boardinghouse in Robinson, built in 1893, was converted to the Tintic Hospital, originally briefly operated by Doctors Mott, Townsend, and Stephens. Dr. Steele Bailey and Dr. Charles Harvelle later purchased the structure. Dr. Steele Bailey, Jr., joined his father and brother-in-law in 1904, and continued to operate the hospital until 1933, when he moved to Eureka. The services rendered by

"Uncle" Jesse Knight, Tintic entrepreneur "extraordinaire." (Utah State Historical Society)

area doctors to the people of the district during the influenza epidemic of 1918 were long remembered, as were the numerous emergency treatments given to miners and their families in the district. The hospital building was destroyed in 1935.[26]

Mining towns were especially susceptible to disasters and emergencies. Fires were a recurring problem for mining communities. In 1912, flames destroyed the post office, confectionary, and a motion picture theater in Mammoth. The city council immediately authorized the organization of a volunteer fire department, and such volunteer firefighting groups provided vital services to many communities.[27]

Social life in Tintic during the early years of the twentieth cen-

Mammoth Mill towers over the town of Robinson, ca. 1905. (Tintic Historical Society)

tury continued along similar lines as in previous years, although ladies clubs were more frequently organized and became increasingly popular. By 1911 the Entre Nous Literary Club met on a regular basis. This group was composed of women who met in private homes to review books and plays as well as to gather for teas and dinners. Some groups were not just social, having political interests. In 1910, Mrs. Emma Langdon, a special organizer and labor activist for the Western Federation of Miners, had journeyed from Colorado to organize the Eureka Auxiliary No. 3, comprised of women relatives of union men. Langdon was also expected to establish a branch at Mammoth, but no evidence of it has been found.[28]

Dancing had always been a favorite social activity. The Elks Pavilion and Finn Hall in Eureka both became favored dancing places. Saloons appealed to a broad spectrum of working men. One remembered incident occurred at a saloon frequented by Finnish miners in Eureka. The Finns of Eureka possessed a reputation for

Mammoth Beanery (boarding house), ca. 1910. (Utah State Historical Society)

toughness and drinking prowess, and Irish miners exhibited a persistence in testing such prowess. Reportedly, the local Finns became fed up with the situation and wired to the Bingham mining area to summon a massive countryman. The Finn arrived in Eureka and "taught the Irish boys a lesson," also having "chewed up" a whiskey glass to help show his prowess.

An opera house existed in Eureka, operated by the Odd Fellows, and in Mammoth Earl McIntyre managed the Hassell Opera House. Later there were also movie theaters, such as the Crescent in Eureka, and traveling shows, which were performed under large tents and referred to as "tent shows."[29] Local bands and music operated in part as boosters for many cities and towns. Owen Humphrey had organized and led the Robinson Juvenile Band in 1903. John Ivey, Frank Morley, John Dooly, and Joseph Phillips comprised the Eureka Quartette. Isaac B. Darton formed Darton's Orchestra. In November 1903 a new group entered the area, getting this response from the *Reporter:* "A good band has a wonderful effect in advertising a town and it is to be hoped that Eureka will never be without one again."

Mammoth shaft house and glory hole, 1998. (Wayne Christiansen)

Music was both a release and a means of socializing in a time prior to More "packaged" and imported entertainment. The Eureka Union Band entered the scene in 1904, comprised of twenty-one members and managed by Henry Matsch. One historian wrote that,

> Such musical groups played at dances, parades, and celebrations and basically provided the communities with a service essential to the life-style of the time. Waltzes flowing at the Elks Pavilion in Eureka captivated hundreds of participants as many single miners scurried to select their partners. It is said that the pavilion's hardwood floor bounced and flexed with each rhythmic tone as both music and dancers abounded at each social event.[30]

The Eureka Juvenile Band entered the scene in the early 1910s, comprised of some twenty-five members. Maynard Griggs remembered that a Mr. Ludlow purchased some used horns, and each member paid $12.50 for an instrument. Griggs figured that he wanted his "money's worth," so he selected a huge E-flat horn. The band, which specialized in Sousa marches, paraded up and down Main Street on paydays. "Miners were paid in gold," stated Griggs, who recalled that

View of Eureka, looking east, ca. 1910. (Tintic Historical Society)

his large horn was a receptacle for coins tossed by workers as the band marched by.[31]

Growth continued in the Tintic district. By 1912 Eureka's population was about 4,000; Mammoth had 1,700 inhabitants; and Silver City had 300. Eureka contained 112 businesses, Mammoth fifty-four, and Silver City eight. Merchants organized in attempts to boost their businesses. The Tintic Merchants' Association in 1908 had attempted to stop a "notorious dead beat" who secured credit but did not pay and then acquired credit at another establishment. By 1918, a Retail Merchants' Association existed, with William F. Shriver as manager. Credit problems continued, especially when men were out of work and increased credit was sought.[32]

Growth spawned the need for new schools. In 1912 Eureka constructed a new high school, designed by the architectural firm of Irving and Goodfellow, designers of many Utah schools. At that time, the schools in Tintic were part of the Juab School District, which proved inconvenient because of the distance between the two areas, which in those days was a three-hour trip one way between Nephi

Eureka Cleaning Company became one of many Tintic businesses named after the city in which it stood. (Tintic Historical Society)

and Eureka. The people must have been relieved in 1915 when Governor William Spry recommended "mandatory reorganization and removal of the barrier against reorganization in the counties with small school population."[33] Under this ruling Juab County became divided into the Juab and Tintic school districts.

The Tintic School District also included the schools in the western part of Juab County. The *Eureka Reporter* on 17 April 1903 stated that, "Salt Creek, a small settlement near Fish Springs in West Juab will have school next winter. There are 37 children." According to school district records, in 1913 there was a school in Callao, and in 1914 the school board voted to establish a school in Trout Creek.

According to articles in the *Eureka Reporter,* between 1912 and 1917 the mines were producing well and the Tintic area's economy was booming. During this time labor unions were organized but did not cause much unrest. Most of the union members were active in local politics and were accepted by the communities.[34] An article that

John McCrystal's General Merchandise provided goods for miners from the Gemini, ca. 1890s. (Tintic Historical Society)

appeared in 1912 in the *Intermountain Worker* offered a good description of the labor situation in Tintic.

> Organized only ten years ago, in 1902, with 25 members, Tintic District Miners Union has grown to a militant body of united workers numbering 800 paid up and active members. Four-fifths of its members are married men citizens of character and responsibility, well read and intelligent men and sturdy pillars of the community. The majority of them are American born.[35]

In 1912, for a six-day week, muckers (those who shoveled ore) were paid $2.75 per day, miners $3.00, and machine and timbermen $3.25. By October, wages were raised to $3.00 for muckers, miners were paid $3.25, and machine and timbermen $3.50.[36]

Labor-management relations were generally good. In 1917 the more militant Industrial Workers of the World (IWW), or "Wobblys," as they were called, came to Tintic and aggressively tried to recruit members. They were coldly received and were unable to make any progress. Press reports stated,

> there is no place in this peaceful community for I.W.W. agitators. We have an excellent labor organization here with a membership

McCrystal offered a diversity of supplies. (Tintic Historical Society)

> that includes come of the best people in the district, men who will
> always counsel their more radical brothers against rash acts. This
> organization has money invested here—has been an important
> factor in the district's growth—and prominent members of this
> union tell us that they discount any chance [of] the organization
> here of the I.W.W.[37]

Longtime Tintic resident Carl Fields recalled in 1976 that the
Wobblies were told "to get the hell out of town."

Labor issues were important, however. During the World War I
era, local mine owners initiated a card system for employment in
Tintic mines. Operators organized the Tintic Mines Information
Bureau, and men seeking employment at any of the mines in the district were first compelled to secure a "rustling card," issued at the
bureau's office. Owners explained that the move served as a means of
securing the "best class of labor." It doubtless was also used to counter
Wobbly or other radical labor activity in the area. At this time, wages
were raised to $4.50 a day for miners and $4.00 for muckers. Most
other workers were also given raises.[38]

In the spring of 1918, local miners again began to voice dissatis-

McCrystal home on lower southwest side of Eureka, ca. 1890s. (John Schmidt)

faction with their working conditions. They were unhappy with the rustling card system and with wages, and they also desired semi-monthly paydays. By June most of the mines had granted the semi-monthly payday; by July wages had been raised to $5.25 per day for miners and $4.75 for muckers.[39]

During this time, mine leasing became a profitable endeavor for some and gave miners a chance to share in the mine profits. Considered a development of the Chief Consolidated Mining Company, this system involved the leasing of a block of ground within a mine, for which a royalty payment was made to the mine owners. In 1915 hundreds of lessors were reportedly doing very well at the Gemini, Chief, May Day, Eureka Hill, Bullion Beck, Yankee, Beck Tunnel, and Colorado Mines.[40]

By 1910 dry farming in the Tintic Valley was becoming a successful venture. Dry farming was susceptible to changes in weather and to marketplace demands. Some of the ventures proved somewhat successful, and the *Reporter* quipped in headlines, that Tintic "Produces Some Things Besides Metals."[41]

Farm property in eastern Juab County was selling for about $150 to $250 per acre at this time. In 1910 Dode Wing of Springville secured 1,000 acres in the Tintic Valley and was clearing it, and Gus J. Henroid and Herbert Hopes had about 100 acres and purchased a machine to clear the brush so they could plant in the fall. In 1911 the *Reporter* added,

> Professor J.C. Hogenson came to investigate the resources of dry farming in this area. The soil is rich and deep with sage brush and this is a good sign of good land. Professor Hogenson said that two possible drawbacks are low rainfall and high altitude. The annual rainfall is 10 inches and the altitude is 6,000 ft. The residents were anxious to have a demonstration farm established here. Professor Hogenson said he would talk to the College Authorities.[42]

According to sources, large crops were produced in 1912. Hans J. Hassell and Samuel McIntyre, Jr., of Mammoth operated one of the area's largest dry farms. The operation was located in Juab and Tooele Counties, about fifteen miles west of Eureka. The 1912 yield was placed at 12,500 bushels of wheat. With the success of this crop, the *Reporter* advertised the opportunities in dry farming and wrote of its importance.[43]

The farm operated by Jesse Knight became one of the largest in the Tintic area. Located just west of Eureka, the Knight farm was begun in about 1914. In August 1914 the farm yielded sixty bushels of wheat per acre, the best to date in the Tintic area. In June 1915, Knight began construction on a concrete grain elevator near Tintic Junction. This structure was erected by his company, the Union Grain and Elevator Company, headed by J. William Knight. The cost was estimated at $15,000.[44] The farm was described for sale as 2,640 acres of land with 1,240 acres under cultivation, all fenced and cross-fenced. There was a house and sheds, water system, including title to Jenny Lind Springs, and the 50,000-bushel concrete elevator"[45] By 1918 W.L. Creer was operating the farm, and in 1921 a three-year lease was given to Vet Whiting of Mammoth.

Mona's school displays the date of its construction, 1907. (Beth Yates)

The Tintic Valley National Land Loan Association came into existence in 1917 as a way of aiding local farmers. However, later farmers, primarily from Nephi, would have more consistent success working the dry farms of the Tintic Valley.[46] In 1917, twenty carloads of wheat were shipped from dry farms in Tintic Valley. California wheat buyers contracted for nearly all of the wheat raised. The grain brought from $1.78 to $1.90 a bushel delivered on the cars, and it was estimated that the area dry farms produced about twenty carloads, or about 35,000 to 40,000 bushels. In August 1918 the Knight farm harvested an estimated 12,000 to 15,000 bushels of wheat.[47]

East Juab County

Dry Farming. The Levan Ridge between Nephi and Levan comprises about 40,000 acres of land with a gentle slope to the northwest. In 1897 Stephen Boswell and his brother-in-law Henry Garrett filed on homesteads of 160 acres on Levan Ridge, and they began to live on their farms in the spring of 1898. At this time the Ridge was covered with western wheatgrass and rabbitbrush and was used by the settlers in both Nephi and Levan for livestock grazing. When Boswell

St. Patrick's church, constructed in 1885, remains among the oldest Catholic churches in Utah, 1998. (Wayne Christiansen)

and Garrett began to fence their property, according to one account, "it brought forth a roar of protest from the settlers in both Nephi and Levan because they had lost some of their cattle range."[48] Because Boswell and Garrett planned to dry farm their land, they were ridiculed for what was considered a foolish undertaking. Their efforts were later described:

> The first year that the northwest one-fourth was planted to wheat the rabbits ate all but a few acres. This was cut and shocked up, then the rabbits ate the grain in the shocks. Not one bushel was realized. The second year they raised 600 bushels which was about 40 bushels per acre. During the third year the false chintz bugs were serious and took a high percentage of the crop.[49]

The farmers also tried to dry farm alfalfa and in good years could raise about a ton of first crop per acre.

Utah state senator George C. Whitmore of Nephi introduced a bill into the Utah Legislature and secured an appropriation for experimental work with dry land crops. In 1903 the Nephi Experiment Farm was established on the Levan Ridge. According to an article in the *Nephi Record,* dated 14 August 1903,

> Engineer L.C. Laughflin of the Experiment Staff at Logan finished surveying the new Juab County experiment farm on last Saturday. According to the survey the entire forty acres is to be surrounded by a splendid road one rod in width, and four streets 13 ft. wide to extend across the farm north to south. The farm is sub-divided into 170 equal parts, or plats, containing 72 x 121 feet and each surrounded by a nice walk so that it is possible to walk anywhere about the farm without treading upon the cultivated soil.
>
> An elegant woven wire fence which encloses the whole area has just been completed. It is one of the most ornamental and serviceable fences in this section. A force of carpenters will commence work on the new building about the first of the week. This is to consist of an office, machine shed, and stable, all enclosed under one roof.
>
> Foreman Stephen Boswell has most of the land plowed and in perfect condition for seeding, which is to commence tomorrow and be kept up at regular intervals, as directed by Professor Merrill

Mining towns attracted many different religious groups. Eureka Episcopal
Church on Leadville Row. (Tintic Historical Society)

of the Agricultural College. Mr. Boswell has just received a nice list
of farm implements, consisting of disc and mould-board plows,
press drills, cultivators, etc. with instructions that other machinery
will be supplied as needed.

In 1905 the Experiment Station produced its first dry land crop.
From then until 1907 the station was operated as one of several
"County Farms" located at various points in the state. During the
years following 1905, others planted and grew dry land crops in Juab
County, including farmers in and around Levan and Mona.
According to a report of the time,

> The Levan Ridge, stretching from east to west through Juab
> Valley and covering several square miles is practically a solid, well
> cultivated field, and about half of that land produced this year over
> 80,000 bushels of high grade wheat, the latter averaging in the
> neighborhood of 25 bushels per acre. Grace Brothers, Broadheads,
> Boswell, and several other farmers reported yields better than 30
> bushels while the 40 bushel mark has been closely approached.
>
> On the west of Nephi, in the Dog Valley, a great deal of work
> has been and is being done. To the west of this valley, Ferner Valley

is being rapidly developed and still further west, in the Tintic District, crops on new land this year were reported as yielding as high as 17 bushels, and dry farming is quite a new thing in Tintic.It has been proved beyond a doubt that dry-farming is a success in east Juab and indications are very favorable in other sections."[50]

Agriculture. David Broadhead's farm produced peaches, corn, and peas, and as much as 100 bushels of potatoes per acre were produced without water. Irrigated land reportedly produced as much as twenty to thirty bushels of apples per tree, and other fruits, such as apricots, cherries, watermelons, cantaloupes, and other garden produce were raised in abundance.[51]

A good share of the ground in the eastern Juab County area was planted to alfalfa, and growers were able to grow three good crops per year. Most of this was used locally, being fed to cattle or sold to herders. Many of the farmers raised alfalfa (lucerne) seed. According to an account of 1912 by Jacob Coleman, "The Juab development Co. in the south end of the county, on a conservative estimate will realize $15,000 to $20,000 from their 200 acres of lucerne seed."[52]

Raising cattle, hogs, and other domesticated animals grew into successful businesses throughout Juab County. The above source noted that,

> Experiments demonstrating that alfalfa is one of the best hog feeds known is causing scores of farmers to launch out in this industry. The Utah Arid Farm Co. in Dog Valley have nearly five hundred head; Grace Bros. and Mendenhall are going into the business on a large scale, besides many others. And the fact that fifty dollars for the meat of one hog has been received by several growers, is causing the people here to realize that fortunes are in sight for the coming hog raisers of Juab County.

Coleman noted that stock raising and shipping were among the most important industries of Juab County:

> There are a large number of resident cattle dealers who purchase thousands of range cattle every year from all parts of the state, drive them here, pasture them on the grazing lands of the Forest Reserve, and in the fall fatten them on the grain and alfalfa produced here, then ship them to California and the eastern markets.

The railroad records show that Nephi is one of the greatest live-stock centers in the state, and thousands of dollars are in this way distributed annually among the Nephi farmers.[53]

With plenty of feed for dairy cows, the Nephi Creamery flourished. Farmers from both Mona and Levan brought dairy products there. Almost every family had chickens, and eggs which were not consumed by the family often were bartered for groceries.

Because of the Mills area's alkaline soil, farming was not too profitable there, so many settlers soon turned to raising livestock. Aberdine angus cattle were brought to Mills by George E. Howard and James E. Andrews in 1914. The Howard family and Will and Willard Ockey even attempted to raise angora goats, but the animals' wool did not grow very long or thick.

Industry. In 1909 a modern metal building was erected at the Nephi gypsum mill. Gypsum was also discovered at the mouth of Chicken Creek, near Levan. In 1906 W.J. Robinson asked the local irrigation company for permission to use water from Chicken Creek to provide power to operate a plaster mill. At first this request was denied, but the following year Robinson was granted permission to use the water. He began construction of the mill, built a reservoir, and sent workers into the canyon to clean out the springs. This increased the flow of water considerably.[54]

Civic Developments. In a special meeting of the Nephi City Council held on 27 September 1902, Mayor Isaac H. Grace was authorized to employ F.C. Kelsey to survey, plan, and make specifications for the construction of a race in the canyon to bring water to a proposed electric power plant. The council minutes of 17 April 1903 record that approval was given to borrow money from the First National Bank of Nephi to construct the canal. By June the canal was complete, and Stanley Crawford had presented plans to the city council for a powerhouse.[55]

On 7 August 1903 plans were made to put electric lights on Main and Depot Streets and at the intersection of Hague and School Streets. T.H. Carter was appointed local Supervisor of Electricity. It was soon apparent that the plant did not generate enough electricity to supply the demand, so in 1910 it was enlarged.

1910s cattle drive up Eureka Main Street. (Tintic Historical Society)

By 1910, Nephi's population had grown to 2,759. The town's businesses also continued to increase. One source lists some of these early businesses and merchants:

The Co-op Store, owned and operated by citizens of the town; Excelsior Mercantile; Charles Foote and Sons; Reed and Bryan; Cazier Brothers Clothing Store; James W. Paxman Shoe Store;

Edward Williams, Tailor; Cartwright Bakery; Ostler and Allen, Harness Shop; Reid's Harness Shop; Hyde and Whitmore Mercantile Establishment; Frank's Clothing Store; National Dollar Store; Sells Furniture Store; two millinery stores owned by Miss Mary Morgan and Mrs. Harriet Wheeler; two barber shops operated by Harry McCune and William Jenkins; and many others.[56]

Henry Goldsbrough owned a hotel and maintained a "Sample Room" where traveling salesmen could display their samples to the merchants of Nephi. Often he made beds on the floor in order to accommodate all of his guests. By 1912, business directories also listed the Forrest Hotel, operated by E.R. Forrest, as having "good sample rooms"; and accommodations were also available at the Union Hotel, with Mrs. C.R. Foote proprietor, and at an establishment owned by Lizzie Henriod.[57]

The *Juab County Times,* with its first issue dated 15 October 1919, was edited and managed by Jacob Coleman. In 1912 J.M. Christensen purchased a half-interest in the *Times* from Coleman, becoming editor; and in 1913 A.B. Gibson, who since 1909 at the age of fifteen had worked as a printer, purchased Coleman's remaining half-interest, becoming the paper's manager. The two operated the *Times* until 1 April 1917 when the paper was consolidated with the *Nephi City News,* which started on 1 May 1916 by Dennis Wood and R.J. Henroid. It thus became the *Times News* and began its long service to the community and region.[58]

By 1910 Mona's population was 400. A large brick school building, built in 1907, stood on the west side of Main Street until the schools were consolidated and Mona's students were sent to Nephi.

Levan became an incorporated town on 8 October 1906. At this time Levan's first municipal election was held and John A. Morgan became president of the town board. In 1899 a one-story brick schoolhouse was built in Levan, and in 1912 the building was enlarged. This building was large enough to accommodate the elementary grades and two high school grades. Those students who wished to continue their education went to classes in Nephi.

In January 1902 plans were made to build a new Mormon chapel in Levan; Andrew Jacobsen of Nephi was to be the building supervisor. Material was assembled, and the cornerstone was laid. Almost every able-bodied person worked on the building. The building was completed and the area LDS stake conference held in it on 30 and 31 October 1909. The cost of the new chapel was $16,124.09. Of this amount, $4,225.24 was paid by the general church; most of the remainder was contributed by the members of the ward.[59]

The Nephi (Center) Ward was organized in 1914, with Thomas Bailey as bishop, Parley P. Christensen as first counselor, and John C. Hall as second counselor. The Juab Tabernacle served as the chapel for the Nephi Ward at this time.

Schools. In 1911 Ivan C. Dalby at the age of twenty-two, became the Juab County Superintendent of Schools. Students who wanted to attend high school had to travel to Nephi. Trustee John A. Morgan unsuccessfully petitioned the Juab School Board for a full high school in Levan. On 3 June 1912 the board established a branch high school in Levan offering the first two years of prescribed curriculum.

According to a story in the *Times News* on 12 October 1912, "most of the school boards are providing ways for students of smaller towns to get to school, either by wagon, autos, or train. The few students going to High School from Mona and Levan are planning on staying in Nephi. Levan students are given 40 cents more per week to pay for room and board. This is unjust. It costs just as much for room and board for a Mona student as it does for a Levan student," the writer complained. A.J. Izatt and Ethel Erdman were hired and taught English, geometry, ancient history, general science, physiology, agriculture, home economics, and music. In 1920 a school bus was purchased to transport Levan students to Nephi to complete their high school requirements.[60]

In 1914 Governor William Spry was notified of the serious legal problems which began to emerge because of the existence of overlapping school districts. Utah Attorney General George C. Barnes urged that many small high school and elementary school districts be eliminated and that county school districts be mandated in all counties in the state.[61] Juab County was divided into the Juab and Tintic school districts.

In 1916 Utah elected Simon Bamberger governor and Democrats gained control of both houses of the Utah State Legislature. They then passed legislation which proved important to both agriculture and mining. A public utilities commission was established to regulate the railroads and other utilities such as gas, electricity, telephone, and water. The legislators also passed the most stringent workman's compensation law in the nation and declared labor unions to be lawful organizations, limiting the use of injunctions in labor disputes. They also established regulations governing water rights and irrigation districts, and they passed a statewide prohibition law that took effect on 1 August 1917.[62] Although not all the measures were universally popular in the state or in Juab County with its farming and mining and Mormon and gentile (non-Mormon) groups, all people in the county hoped for the end of the world war in which the United States was then engaged and a continuation of the prosperity or improving conditions most of them enjoyed.

ENDNOTES

1. Allan Kent Powell, ed., *Utah History Encyclopedia,* 431–38.

2. *Salt Lake Mining Review,* 30 April 1900.

3. Philip Notarianni, *Faith, Hope, & Prosperity, The Tintic Mining District,* 72.

4. Alice P. McCune, *History of Juab County,* 213.

5. Notarianni, *Faith, Hope, & Prosperity,* 70.

6. Ibid., 72.

7. The author remembers climbing on the side of the trucks while women chose the fruit they would later can for winter.

8. J. Cecil Alter, *Early Utah Journalism,* 70, 73.

9. Ibid., 71.

10. Ibid., 71–72.

11. Ibid., 72.

12. Notarianni, *Faith, Hope, & Prosperity,* 80.

13. Ibid., 75.

14. Ibid., 67.

15. Ibid., 74–75.

16. Ibid., 76.

17. McCune, *Juab County,* 200; *Eureka Reporter,* 15 October 1909. The *Eureka Reporter,* 15 October 1909, lists the total cost as $16,000.

18. *Eureka Reporter,* 15 April 1904.

19. *Salt Lake Mining Review,* 30 March 1909, 30 July 1909. See also Notarianni, *Faith, Hope, & Prosperity,* 89.

20. Notarianni, *Faith, Hope, & Prosperity,* 87.

21. *Eureka Reporter,* 23 January 1903.

22. *Eureka Reporter,* 9 July 1909.

23. Unpublished manuscript, Tintic Mining Museum, Eureka, Utah, no author named.

24. *Eureka Reporter,* 11 October 1912.

25. Richard D. Poll, et al., *Utah's History,* 151–52. Also see Notarianni, *Faith, Hope, & Prosperity,* 93–94.

26. *Provo Herald,* 1 October 1974. In 1974 a stone marker identifying the site of the hospital was erected and unveiled by the Tintic Historical Society.

27. Notarianni, *Faith, Hope, & Prosperity,* 97.

28. Ibid., 95.

29. Ibid., 95–96. The author, Pearl Wilson, recalls attending tent shows with her family when she was in her pre-teen years.

30. Notarianni, *Faith, Hope, & Prosperity,* 75.

31. Ibid., 95.

32. Ibid., 94–95.

33. Fred Openshaw, "The Benefits of Small School Systems . . . of the Ten Smallest School Districts in Utah," 6.

34. Notarianni, *Faith, Hope, & Prosperity,* 100.

35. Reprinted in the *Eureka Reporter,* 28 June 1912.

36. Notarianni, *Faith, Hope, & Prosperity,* 100.

37. Quoted in ibid.

38. Ibid., 102.

39. *Eureka Reporter,* 29 March 1917, 18 July 1918.

40. Notarianni, *Faith, Hope, & Prosperity,* 106.

41. *Eureka Reporter,* 22 June 1917.

42. *Eureka Reporter,* 25 March 1910, 1 September 1911.

43. *Eureka Reporter,* 19 July 1912, 9 August 1912.

44. *Eureka Reporter,* 21 August 1914, 9 July 1915, 18 July 1915.

45. "Papers of the Knight Investment Company," manuscript 278, Special Collections, Harold B. Lee Library, Brigham Young University, Provo, Utah.

46. Notarianni, *Faith, Hope, & Prosperity,* 111.

47. *Eureka Reporter,* 2 August 1918.

48. Stephen R. Boswell, *History of Dry Farming on the Levan Ridge,* 4, Special Collections and Archives, Utah State University, Logan.

49. Ibid., 5.

50. Philip V. Cardon, "Juab County-The Birthplace of Dry Farming," *The Arrowhead* [no date or page number able to relocated by the author]. For related material see the following: Philip V. Cardon, "Minor Dry Land Crops at the Nephi Experiment Farm," *Utah Agricultural College Experiment Station Bulletin 132* (1914); and Philip V. Cardon, "Tillage and Rotation Experiments at Nephi, Utah," *Bulletin of the U.S. Department of Agriculture 157* (Contribution from the Bureau of Plant Industry, January 21, 1915). Sources are pamphlets 11410 and 3038, respectively, located at the Utah State Historical Society.

51. Jacob Coleman, "Nephi," *The Arrowhead,* October 1912, 19.

52. Ibid., 20.

53. Ibid.

54. Maurine Stephensen, *A History of Levan,* 70.

55. Keith N. Worthington, Sadie H. Greenhalgh, and Fred Chapman, *They Left a Record. A Comprehensive History of Nephi, Utah, 1851–1978,* 84.

56. McCune, *Juab County,* 113–14.

57. Ibid., 114–15; *Utah State Gazetteer and Business Directory, 1912–1913* (Salt Lake City: R.L. Polk & Co.), 154–56.

58. Alter, *Early Utah Journalism,* 142.

59. Stephensen, *Levan,* 66.

60. Ibid., 77–79.

61. Openshaw, "Small School Systems," 6.

62. Poll, et al., *Utah's History,* 423–24.

CHAPTER 7

WORLD WAR I AND
THE ROARING TWENTIES

During the second decade of the twentieth century both mining and agriculture in Utah generally prospered. This development was attributed to the growth of industrial and urban centers and to World War I, which created a demand for metals and agricultural products. An article in the *Eureka Reporter* of 5 January 1917 stated, "Twenty-two Utah mines paid over $24,000,000 in dividends in 1916; ten of the twenty-two dividend payers are Tintic properties. This is only one of the reasons why Tintic leads all other districts, and why our district has such a bright future." After the conclusion of World War I, the 1920s also brought a sense of optimism toward the future in many county residents.

The agricultural industry prospered during the war period and farm ground was improved in most of Utah. The only counties in which the farms did not increase at the time were Grand, Juab, Morgan, and Wasatch.[1] However, during this period, as mentioned, ranching did grow in west Juab. In 1917, a large group of farmers and other taxpayers met with the Juab County Commission and presented a petition requesting the commissioners to enter into a con-

Parades brought out the entire community. Parade up Eureka Main Street, 1906. (Tintic Historical Society)

tract with the United States through the Utah Agricultural College for the appointment of a county agricultural agent and that the commissioners appropriate the sum of $500 to apply toward the wages of the agent. In the meeting of 12 April 1918 the matter had been acted upon—they would have an agricultural agent.[2]

Prohibition

The Nephi *Times News* repeatedly urged the people of Juab County to support prohibition of alcoholic beverages, and repeated attempts were made at local and state levels to enact prohibition ordinances. In 1911 the *Eureka Reporter,* in regard to proposed new laws regulating the operation of saloons, published the following announcement: "On 26 June the people of all incorporated cities must vote and decide whether their respective cities are to be wet or

Interior of McCornick Bank, Eureka. (Tintic Historical Society)

dry." Another article had appeared in June quoting Rev. Elmer I. Goshen, pastor of the First Congregational Church in Salt Lake City, who provided numerous reasons why he believed prohibition would not "prohibit," stating in part,

> If you do away with the saloon, you must supply something in its place. . . . Well regulated saloons are not half so degrading as dives and whenever the saloons are closed the dives take their places. . . . A dry town will mean heavier taxes, empty business blocks, . . . and possibly an increase in drunkenness.

The article reminded the people to vote, saying that it was up to them whether Eureka would have well-regulated saloons operated by men who had the welfare of the city at heart, or dives. The well-regulated saloon would be the least injurious of the two.[3] Eureka, Silver City, and Mammoth voted to stay "wet"; Goshen, Nephi, Mona, Levan, Payson, Spanish Fork, Provo, and most other Utah towns went "dry." Park City, Bingham, and Ogden were among the few Utah towns voting wet.[4]

In 1915 Utah legislators voted for statewide prohibition, but Governor William Spry pocket-vetoed the bill. In October 1916 the *Times News* published an article urging people to vote for candidates

Eureka City Hall was designed by John J. Pilgerrim and constructed in 1899. The city built the Eureka Public Library with funds from philanthropist Andrew Carnegie in 1909. (Tintic Historical Society)

who would support prohibition. The article stated that it had been an issue since the summer of 1908 and had suffered through three stiff campaigns, with most of the people in the state in favor of it. When Simon Bamberger became Utah's governor in 1916 he instituted much legislation in favor of labor and agriculture, but one piece of legislation passed by the legislature provided for statewide prohibition after 1 August 1917, something not viewed favorably by most residents of the Tintic region. With the subsequent passage of the Eighteenth Amendment to the U.S. Constitution instituting national prohibition, all Americans who drank broke the law until the amendment was repealed in the early 1930s. Stills and bootlegging flourished throughout the nation, including Juab County, where some residents made their own liquor in backyard stills or supported the illegal trade in alcoholic beverages. Due to the illegal nature of such activity, documentation of its extent is non-existent; however, a perusal of Utah papers of the period reveals numerous articles on such illegal activity and law enforcement efforts to combat it.

Eureka High School Girl's Basketball Team, ca. 1910. (Tintic Historical Society)

World War I and the Influenza Epidemic—1914–1919

The declaration of war against Germany by the United States on 6 April 1917 in the long term perhaps influenced the lives of people in Utah more than any other event to that time. On 28 June 1914 Archduke Franz Ferdinand, heir to the throne of Austria-Hungary, and his wife were killed in Sarajevo, Bosnia, initiating a series of events that soon embroiled most of the nations of Europe in what has become known as World War I. The United States attempted to stay out of the war, although the sympathies of most Americans were with the Allied forces led by Britain and France against the Central Powers led by Germany.

German submarine warfare provoked American ire as it resulted in the loss of American lives, and the nation gradually prepared for war. On 26 February 1917 President Woodrow Wilson went before Congress and asked that diplomatic relations with Germany be severed. On 4 April he again appeared before Congress and asked that

Tintic High School's Football Team, 1919. (Tintic Historical Society)

war be declared against Germany. The Senate passed the war declaration on 4 April, and the House of Representatives passed it on 6
April.

Utah's territorial militia, the Nauvoo Legion, had been abolished
in the move toward statehood, and a unit of the National Guard had
been organized in the territory in 1894.[5] Many Utah men served with
enthusiasm in the Spanish-American War at the turn of the century;
however, by 1906 the enthusiasm for military service had waned;
membership in the volunteer National Guard had dropped from
1,012 men in 1894 to 363 officers and men. In 1916 enlisted guards-
men were paid 25 percent of the initial pay of enlisted men of corre-
sponding rank in regular military service.[6]

When war was declared, Juab County responded with enthusiasm to every request that was made. Patriotic gatherings were held
and young men volunteered for military service. On 13 April 1917
the *Eureka Reporter* stated,

Over at Mammoth they have the proper kind of patriotism. This

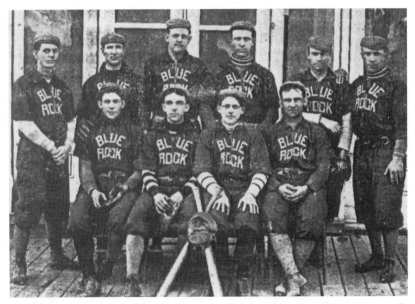

Baseball proved to be a most enthusiastically supported sport in many Utah towns. The Blue Rock Mine (Centennial Eureka) sponsored an impressive team in 1904. (Tintic Historical Society)

prosperous mining camp can boast of the largest bunch of recruits of any city in the state, population considered. . . . On Friday evening of last week twenty-eight young men announced their willingness to serve their country and the following day they departed for Provo, but they were later sent to Salt Lake where they were examined and sworn in.

By 8 June 1917 Juab County had registered 1,144 men for military service. "Eureka the metropolis of Tintic registered 597—more than one-half of the total registration of the county," it was reported.[7] Almost every newspaper on both sides of the county contained a list of men who were leaving to serve their country. On 3 October, forty-seven men from Juab County gathered in Nephi, where they were entertained with a dinner, free movie, and rooms at the Forrest Hotel. Included were men from most of the towns in the county. On the morning of 4 October they stood for roll call and then left on a train for training camp at American Lake, Washington.[8]

Women in Utah also served in many capacities. They helped the

Eureka's Finn Hall provided entertainment for both the Swedish Finn community and the entire town. (Tintic Historical Society)

Red Cross, served as nurses, and filled positions formerly held by men, among other tasks. They also served as telephone operators, secretaries, and in many other capacities.[9] Among the women who served actively in the war was Maud Fitch of Eureka. According to a report in the local paper,

> Miss Maude Fitch, daughter of Mr. & Mrs. Walter Fitch, Sr. of this city has the honor of being the first Utah woman to receive signal recognition from the French government for gallantry and bravery at the front. Miss Fitch is an ambulance driver in the Hackett-Lowther unit, attached to a division under the tricolor. The young lady was one of six selected for special recognition and was awarded the French war cross [*croix de guerre*] and the bronze star. While in Paris awaiting the arrival of her specially constructed and equipped car, purchased at her own expense, the young lady engaged in relief work, assisting in caring for the refugees of the war zone. . . . Miss Fitch was among six other Utah women who were honored.[10]

Maud Fitch wrote letters that form a record of her involvement. While waiting for a permanent assignment, she had sought a tempo-

Ladies Club of Eureka standing in front of the town's Carnegie Library. (Tintic Historical Society)

rary job with the Red Cross. In April 1917, while awaiting word, she enthusiastically wrote her family in Eureka,

> If they should . . . we will get into action AT ONCE—the magic of those two words! And to think at last I shall get into the very vortex of the greatest conflict in the history of the world. I can't think what it will mean. If only I shall have the right stuff in me to benefit by it—to go into it and come out with one's soul and heart all fire tried!

Though many initially thought war grand, few kept that illusion long on the battlefields. Maud Fitch did not get into battle, but in May she wrote that she had joined the "only Unit directly under the Military and we move with the [French Third] Army and under a French Lieutenant."[11] She chronicled her personal experiences of the war. In driving five wounded soldiers to a hospital, she recounted, "It got pit black and the roads were filled—packed tight with sometimes three streams of advancing troops, cavalry and camions." After her return from this foray, she "breakfasted on nothing and washed some layers of dust off, then strolled about the hills with the guns at the front hammering in our ears."[12] The overall experience proved remarkable to Fitch, and her letters home to Eureka provide a unique firsthand account of an American nurse in action during World War I.

The war experience was not viewed as favorably by many soldiers who suffered, were wounded, or died in the conflict. At least eleven men from Juab County died from wounds or other causes during service with the military. Dozens of others were wounded, and the lives of all were changed. Families of service men and women were also greatly affected by the war, doing what they could to support their loved ones in the conflict.[13]

The people of Utah bought Liberty Bonds and war savings stamps to help finance the war effort. The Red Cross had a chapter in practically every town in the state and women worked to produce knitted socks, sweaters, washcloths, and shoulder wraps. They also made operating caps, operating gowns, pillow cases, dish towels, bed-shirts, and pajamas. The Junior Red Cross also participated in these projects. Surgical dressings and gauze bandages were made and sent to hospitals. The Red Cross also collected used clothing, which was sent overseas to needy people in the war zones. Juab County residents vigorously participated in all of these activities. According to one local history,

> East Juab County, comprising the towns of Nephi, Mona, Levan, and Mills went over the top by the first week, over subscribing to their allotment of Liberty Loans by several thousand dollars. The amount apportioned to East Juab County was $45,000. Nephi alone subscribed to this amount by the end of the week. They were also one of the first ones to receive their honor flag for selling their allotment of Liberty Loans.[14]

Nephi City invested $2,000 of its funds into United States bonds. The investment was to be divided equally between the Nephi National Bank and the First National Bank of Nephi. On 20 September 1918 city officials authorized another purchase of $500.[15] Later, on 5 June 1922 Battery E of Nephi was mustered into the Utah National Guard, with Captain Thomas O. Durham in command. Fifty five men

Architect Irving Goodfellow designed the Tintic High School, 1912. (Tintic Historical Society)

enlisted for a period of three years.[16] The city equipment building, formerly used as the high school, was leased to them for meetings.

Early in 1918 a worldwide influenza epidemic of the Spanish Flu hit Utah. By 10 October the situation was bad enough that the state health officer banned all public meetings. One-half million people died from the epidemic in the United States; untold millions died throughout the world. When the war ended on 11 November 1918 the people of the county, state, and nation celebrated in spite of the quarantines and prohibitions against gathering in crowds, and the epidemic became worse.

Twila Peck recalled the outbreak in Tintic. Her father was stricken and her mother nursed him back to health. Other family members escaped, but she remembered looking through a neighbor's window and seeing a young mother with her infant, both laid out in the living room awaiting burial. "We had to play by ourselves, and if we went anywhere, we wore a mask," she recalled.[17] Dr. Steele Bailey, Jr., of Mammoth instituted a strict quarantine. One resident recalled that in the A.N. Wallace furniture store and mortuary, bodies were so numerous and space so limited that the undertaker was forced to place bodies on tabletops or wherever room could be found. It was claimed that hundreds died in Tintic District alone.[18]

Walter Fitch developed the Chief Consolidated Mining Company into one of Tintic's top producers. (Tintic Historical Society)

Although an accurate death toll from the epidemic in the county was not done, many died from the flu in both 1918 and 1919 in Juab County as elsewhere in the state and nation, making it the worst health epidemic in the county's history. Families were ravaged, and the epidemic brought out both the best and worst in people, as some sacriced greatly to help their neighbors while others isolated themselves for fear of contamination. The county's medical practitioners generally performed heroically in the crisis, assisted by hundreds of others who anonymously helped their fellow residents in uncounted ways.

Developments Throughout the County

The population of Juab County was recorded as 9,871 in 1920, a drop of almost 900 from the all-time high recorded ten years previously of 10,702. Still the figure was close to that of the turn of the century, when the county had almost doubled in population in ten years. Since the farming communities of east Juab stayed relatively stable due to their agricultural economies, the population indicated

Steam locomotive at the Knight Smelter, Silver City. (Tintic Historical Society)

that the more volatile mining and industrial sections of the county were remaining generally active and prosperous. Eureka, in fact, with 3,608 inhabitants, not only remained the county's largest town but reached its highest census figure ever. However, the population decline of the county was echoed later by Eureka, and continued in both throughout much of the twentieth century. Juab still was a mid-sized county, but other counties were beginning to surpass it in population, reducing its ranking from the previous decades.

Smaller municipalities attempted to organize some political structure during this time. On 13 December 1919, at the request of the residents of Callao, Trout Creek, and Fish Springs, a precinct was organized and S.F. Falkenburgh was appointed as justice of the peace; Joseph W. Sabey became constable. Prior to this time, the closest law officers were at Mammoth and Eureka.[19]

Before the entrance of the United States into the world war, demand for metal and agricultural products had increased. By the time the U.S. entered the war, the mines had not only supplied metals for the production of munitions and armament but stockpiled a supply which would last beyond the end of the war. Because ship traffic was curtailed, favorable freight rates were advantageous for Utah products, both mineral and agricultural. But at the end of the war both categories were left with a surplus. When the war ended, the mining industry felt the impact first. Early in 1921 the *Salt Lake Tribune* reported that the past year had been the most "trying that the mines of this Tintic District had weathered through in a great many years." But 1921 was to be even worse.[20]

Copper had been in great demand during the war and had been mined extensively and stockpiled. Therefore, copper producers were hard hit when the demand for most minerals plunged. Price supports enacted with the Pitman Silver Act of 1918 assisted the silver, lead, and zinc industries; however, even with that subsidy, the price of silver began to decline in the spring of 1920.[21] The mining industry, by laying off some workers and lowering wages, did adjust in Juab County as elsewhere during the decade.

Mining and milling activity proceeded during the 1920s. By 1922 the Chief Consolidated Mining Company had become the largest silver producer in the United States. In 1923 it was Juab County's largest taxpayer—$197,000. In 1924 the company built its own mill; a flotation mill that processed ore from the company's property in Eureka as well as from the old Eureka Hill mill dump. The American Smelting and Refining Company began buying and shipping ore from old mine dumps. It paid the Mammoth Mining Company $100,000 for 200,000 tons of ore and also bought the dumps from the Bullion Beck Mine and the old Tintic Mill. The American Institute of Mining and Metallurgical Engineers announced in 1925 that, "With a total value to date of well over $200,000,000.00 for its ore production, the Tintic mining district . . . ranks as one of the three main ore producing areas of Utah. In it are located the biggest silver mines of the country."[22] In 1925 the International Smelting and Refining Company acquired the Yankee Consolidated Mine, and by 1929 it also had the North Lily and the Knight properties.[23]

The agricultural sector also had to adjust to fluctuating prices. In 1919 wheat had sold for between $3.35 and $3.50 per bushel; but by 1921, with greater production in Europe and reduced domestic demand, it was selling for $.98. Other agricultural prices also had

Knight's Tintic Smelter employed workers from southern and eastern Europe. (Tintic Historical Society)

fallen. Many farmers chose to store their produce, hoping that it would increase in value.[24] Farmers had generally reacted to the good times by buying more machinery and land to increase production, often overextending their finances in the process, which were dependent upon continuing good times. The agricultural recession that developed in the 1920s resulted in many losing all that they had; others were forced to cut back and struggled to survive. Unfortunately, the Great Depression that followed led to increased troubles for most farmers and new troubles for almost all Americans.

During the 1920s many Americans prospered, or at least were determined to enjoy life after the horrors of war. The "Roaring Twenties," as the decade was called, saw the spread of recent inventions such as radio and motion pictures, both of which caught the public's fancy in a big way. By 1920 both Nephi and Eureka had two movie theaters, and the movies with their famous actors and actresses were advertised in the local papers much as they are today. The war had made it necessary to postpone much building, which now began to boom. Also, there was now a necessity for a great deal of road improvement, especially with the ever-growing popularity of automobiles, which were beginning to change the lives of everyone. Automobiles could not travel well on the old wagon roads that were

The Ruby Shaft surface plant near Silver City. (Tintic Historical Society)

adequate for a team of horses and a wagon. Automobiles often became stuck in mudholes and had to be pulled out by a horse, creating an increasing demand for better roads.

An ordinance in Nephi prohibited the storage of more than 500 gallons of gasoline within the city limits, prompting the *Juab County Times* to publish an article complaining that many cars and motorcycles passed through Nephi without stopping to get gas. "The writer feels that it is because of the ordinance. . . . Gasoline is only shipped in once a week and there are sixteen cars in Nephi, many of whom gas up twice a week. So no great allowance is made for the many cars which pass through Nephi. Now is the opportune time to make a bid for patronage of a class who have money, and are willing to spend it for their immediate needs," the writer concluded, recognizing that the changing times called for new responses as they brought new opportunities.[25]

A petition in 1917 to install a gasoline tank in front of the Pexton

A Nephi home illustrating the diversity of architectural designs, 1998.
(Wayne Christiansen)

Building on Main Street in Nephi was referred to the county streets
and highways department, as was another petition signed by persons
with businesses in close proximity to the proposed tank complaining

Mining even found its way into the West Tintic area. (Tintic Historical Society)

that there was danger in having such a tank installed.[26] Tanks were installed, because later it was brought to the attention of the mayor and city council that "there was a possibility that the safety of some citizens was being menaced by the presence of tanks within the city limits containing large quantities of gasoline." The city council agreed to investigate.[27]

Newspapers, which often sought to boost their communities, were constantly noting that roads were in need of repair or a new road was necessary. The city and county minutes contain an increasing number of entries concerning new roads and appropriations for road improvements. A special election was held in May 1921 for the purpose of "incurring a bonded indebtedness for building public roads and highways within the county, but outside of the cities." The bond was for $225,200, and it passed by a majority of 390 votes.[28] No mention was made as to what these funds were specifically spent for, but the road work for the next few years was extensive. Between 1922 and 1924 Nephi's Main Street was paved and a number of streets within the city were improved. The road from Chicken Creek to the Millard County line was resurfaced, as was the road from Levan to Chicken Creek. Some work was also done on the Salt Creek Canyon

A spectacular train crash west at Tintic Junction, 1910. (Tintic Historical Society)

Road. In 1929 the road between Nephi and Levan was given an oil and gravel surface and the road between Silver City and Eureka was oiled.[29]

Utah County agreed to build a road between Eureka and the new East Tintic camp of Dividend, and its officials also agreed to do work on the road in Pinion Canyon as soon as the road to Dividend was finished. The Pinion Canyon road had been a subject of discussion in the *Reporter* for some time because it was the only road from Utah County to Tintic and was in pretty rough condition.[30] In 1927 a group of Tintic businessmen met and made plans to finance and improve the road from Eureka to Dividend. C.E. Huish presided at the meeting, and some of those present were W.F. Shriver, Walter Jensen, A.C. Burton, A.E. Booher, J. George Jones, P.J. Fennel, Jos. Fullenbach, Frank Townley, George Forsey, Herman Sylvester, Asa Graham, George H. Ryan, and Henry Davis.[31] Road improvement and construction became a neverending concern for Juab County as it was throughout the whole country.

In 1922 power was brought to Levan from the Big Springs Electric Company in Fountain Green. Men from Levan contracted to

Nephi also fielded a baseball team in the early 1900s. (Pearl Wilson)

put in the poles, and the line was brought down Salt Creek Canyon to Nephi and along the east bench to Levan. On Friday evening, 13 October, electric lights illuminated the town.[32] Electricity arrived in Mona in August of 1929.

In February 1924 a group of Tintic businessmen took control of the Eureka Banking Company. They reorganized the company and elected the following officers: George H. Dern, president; J. George Jones, vice-president; and W.F. Shriver, Dr. Steele Bailey, Jr., and George N. Fitch, directors.[33] In 1925 Harold and Edwin Shriver joined their father as partners in W.F. Shriver and Sons, and in 1928 they opened a store in Provo. Norman and Jensen, which had succeeded the Heffernan and Thompson clothing store, constructed a store-room across from Eureka City Hall in 1926. Business in the Tintic metropolis was booming.

The activity spilled over to drinking establishments. Due to prohibition, saloons were referred to as "soft drink" parlors; but a good drink of liquor was available at many places in Eureka. In Mammoth W.H. Elmer ran a parlor, and B.M. Cornich, Rollo E. Peery, Edwin Simpson, and James H. Whitlock operated billiard halls. Eureka boasted about six "soft drink" and billiards clubs. Among them were

Nephi residents waiting for the southbound train from Salt Lake City. (Fred Chapman)

establishments owned by James and John Gatley and James Crooks, as well as the Snug Pool Hall and Tony Cavilette's "Coal Chutes."[34]

Established firms continued to advertise in newspapers. The City Grocery in Eureka, owned by A.D. Manson, boasted, "Much for the Money," while Cromar & Nelson touted,

> Count on Quick Deliveries when you order from us and you will not be disappointed. Neither will the quality of the goods be other than what you order. We carry a widely assorted line of high grade Groceries, for your selection and guarantee every article we sell. And you will find our charges positively reasonable. Deal here and you may be sure of getting the best groceries at the fairest price.[35]

Tintic had always supported a variety of social and fraternal clubs, and during the 1920s several new ones were added. Among them were the Mah Jongg Club, Five Hundred Club, Trap Shooting Club, Fideles Club, Priscilla Club, Bon Ton Club, Red Wing Club, Elite Club, and Moose Lodge No. 1470. Many of these were com-

Businesses on west Main Street, between Center and First South, Nephi. (Fred Chapman)

posed of people of similar socioeconomic status and were closed to others. Associations thus proliferated.[36]

Organizations also were formed in other areas of Juab County. The Nephi Kiwanis Club was organized in April 1922; it was preceded by the Business and Professional Women's Club in 1920. The Daughters of Utah Pioneers organized locally on 11 June 1930, and, during 1931, five camps were organized in East Juab: Salt Creek Camp, Fort Wall Camp, and Birch Creek Camp in Nephi; Chicken Creek Camp in Levan; and Mt. Nebo Camp in Mona.[37] Mona was incorporated as a town in 1924.

Local newspapers carried novellas and other serialized stories that captured the imaginations of readers. Articles of general interest and humor proliferated during the 1920s. One story from the *Reporter*, entitled "On a Pension," offers an example of newspaper fare:

> When the cage of the Chief Consolidated mine was hoisted from
> the bowels of the earth one day last week it brought to the surface
> "Shorty," who felt the sensation of being in the sunshine for the

Horse and buggy days on Nephi Main Street, looking north from First South. (Fred Chapman)

first time in eight years. "Shorty" is a mule. He was one of twenty three used in the lower levels of the mine to draw long strings of cars loaded with ore to the main shaft. He was beginning to show signs of old age and was not making the necessary time with his long string of mine cars, and so, after eight years under ground, he is hoisted to the top, this time on a pension for life. When "Shorty" was brought to the surface he did not see light, which had been denied him for eight years. A blindfold was around his eyes, for had he been brought into the bright light after so many years in total darkness he would have been blinded. The blind will be left on for a week or more. . . . He will spend the rest of his days in green pastures, which is his reward for faithful service. Less humane concerns might fire a bullet into his brain when his days of industrial usefulness were ended.[38]

Another deposit of gypsum was found in 1925, approximately 1.5 miles north of the Nephi mill, and the mineral was transported to the mill by cars on an aerial tramway. In 1939 the mill was sold to

Westside of Main Street, Nephi, near turn of the century. The Courthouse is visible on the right. (Fred Chapman)

United States Gypsum Company, which manufactured a variety of plaster products sold throughout the United States. By 1947 the local operation employed about thirty men, provided a payroll of about $50,000 yearly, and produced about 30,000 tons of gypsum annually.[39]

From 1925 to 1929 Edward and Fred Kendall were the last ones to work the Nebo Salt Company's salt mill at Red Creek Canyon. The salt was made for table and dairy use only and was sold locally and trucked to parts of southern Utah. By the 1930s it had become impossible for the small business to compete with larger ones on the shores of the Great Salt Lake and elsewhere and it was closed permanently.[40]

Various civic structures were constructed during this period. In December 1917 the federal government purchased property on upper Main Street in Eureka from P.J. Fennell for the construction of a new post office. Soon after, because of the war, all building activity at the site was put on hold, and it was not until fall 1922 that work on it was resumed. The building was finished in the fall of 1924. At a meeting

Outings and picnics were popular diversions in the early 1900s. Here, Nephi residents enjoy a day outdoors. (Fred Chapman)

of the Tintic School District trustees on 17 June 1920, a contract was awarded for the reconstruction of a school building at Mammoth at a cost of $33,230. Tintic High School added a new gymnasium in January 1927.[41]

On 19 April 1918 an election was held in Nephi for the establishment and maintenance of a public library, with the levy of a tax not to exceed one mill on the dollar of all taxable property within the city.[42] The library was approved by voters, and it was installed in two rooms of the county courthouse until such time as the city could build a city hall, where it would be housed. Nephi officials had been planning since 1917 to build a new high school on the east side of Main Street, but because of the war they were unable to begin construction until 1921. According to a district publication of the time celebrating the building,

> The Nephi High School was constructed at a cost of $153,333.00. It is built of red pressed brick and is two stories high. It contains besides the 22 large well lighted class rooms and laboratories, a gymnasium, an auditorium, swimming pool, suitable office rooms, student body office, rooms, showers, and store room. The gymna-

A snow-bound train makes its way along the narrow gauge route near Silver City, ca. 1916. (Utah State Historical Society)

sium is 75 feet long and 55 feet wide. It has a seating capacity of 700. The stage in the auditorium is 55 feet wide and 32 feet deep. Back of the stage is music room 16 feet wide and 53 feet long. . . . The swimming pool is 20 feet wide and 40 feet long. It is four feet deep at one end and slopes to a depth of seven feet at the other end. . . . Taken as a whole the building is a credit to a city the size of Nephi. We have waited a long time for it. But in waiting we now have the best.[43]

In the late 1930s a gymnasium and a mechanical arts building were built near the high school at a cost of $80,000, and in the 1940s a balcony was added to the gymnasium.[44]

Nephi's first LDS Seminary building was dedicated by Dr. George H. Brimhall on 4 March 1923. Prior to this time, seminary classes had been held in the vestry of the Juab LDS Stake Tabernacle. The new building was located on Main Street directly west of the high school and cost approximately $7,000.[45]

Dr. Steele Bailey brought welcomed medical care and facilities to Tintic. The Tintic Hospital, 1912. (Tintic Historical Society)

In October 1924 a special meeting of the Nephi City Council was called for the purpose of considering and authorizing the issuance of bonds for the construction of a city hall. The measure passed by a majority of 95 votes.[46] Work commenced on the building in the latter part of June and was completed in October 1926. The building contained rooms for a library, the American Legion, utility department, fire department, jail, courtroom, and offices for the mayor and city recorder, treasurer, attorney, and marshal.

Juab County held its first county fair on 24 and 25 September 1925. In March 1926, county officials purchased twenty acres of ground (located between Center Street and 200 South and west of 300 West) from J.S. Ostler for the sum of $5,000 to be used for fairgrounds in the future.[47] At about the same time, the Forrest Hotel, owned by the Forrest family, was erected at the northwest corner of Main Street. An open-air dance hall was also built on Main Street in Nephi. The first dance was held on 23 July 1926.

The Service Star Legion constructed a memorial at the intersec-

Mammoth First Graders pose for a class photograph, ca. 1906. (Utah State Historical Society)

tion of Main and Center Streets in Nephi in 1925 to honor the servicemen of World War I. Harriet Brough, Julia Paxman, and Lucille Brough met with the city council and were told that the city would install the electric light pole and lights, a sprinkling device, and place curbing at the intersection. The city would also furnish the electricity and water for the memorial.[48] A star sat on an iron arch which was supported by four iron posts, with a light on each corner. The star had sixty-two colored lights of red, white, and blue. A sign was suspended from the arch giving the information and the purpose of the memorial. Lights were placed in the lawn beneath, with a fountain spray attached to water the grass and flowers.[49] The monument was eventually removed because it was considered to be a traffic hazard.

In 1917 a group of Levan men built a flour mill at the west end of town. The flour of the Levan Milling Company was of high quality and the mill did well at first, but it later went bankrupt because of poor management.[50] In 1923 a group of Nephi and Fountain Green

The Mammoth Brass Band, 1906, added to the "boosterism" of the town. (Utah State Historical Society)

men organized the Juab Mill and Elevator Company and bought the Hague Mill. In 1927 they also purchased the Nephi Mill and Elevator Company.[51]

Agricultural production continued as an important enterprise in west Juab. E.W. Trip reported on 29 October 1926 that 2,400 bushels of alfalfa seed were grown on his farm at Callao the past summer, the most ever produced.[52] Other families engaged in diversified farming, many raising fruit and vegetables for their own use along with alfalfa and grains for market.

In January 1928 a resolution was adopted by the Tintic School Board to discontinue hiring married women to teach school. It was noted that, although there were few married teachers in the district, there had been pressure brought about by some taxpayers who wanted the jobs to go to men or to single women with no married support. "The sentiment against married women being employed as teachers while unmarried and dependent material is abundant has been increasing during the past few years," the board claimed.[53] The move coincided with similar efforts in a number of other Utah school districts.

A new school was completed in Callao in August 1929. John Morley of Eureka and Andrew Steedman of Mammoth, members of the Tintic School District board, were present with school custodian John G. Bunnel to accept the school for the district. A banquet was held, followed by a dance in the new building. Between 350 and 400 people attended. The building was a one-room frame structure, located on a four-acre tract of land and was erected by R.H. Towers at a cost of $2,116.[54]

Tintic celebrated its "Silver Jubilee" on 28 August 1929, the sixtieth anniversary of the discovery of the first claim. For weeks many people worked to make the occasion a big success. Every week the *Reporter* listed activities that would add to the festivities. There would be a baseball game, races, rodeo, and many other events, including the possibility of some spectacular airplane stunts. There also would be a parade in which numerous area old-timers would be honored. Children would be admitted to the games free of charge, and there would be a free barbecue.[55] Approximately 5,000 people attended the event. However, a devastating accident marred the affair. The plane that was taking passengers for rides crashed, striking the bell tower of the Eureka City Hall and then tearing a huge hole in the wall of the Taylor Brothers store next door. The pilot was killed and a sixteen-year-old girl from Silver City was injured.[56]

Economic disasters soon followed, as Juab County residents along with those of the rest of the state and the nation began to suffer from the effects of the Great Depression, which began with the stock market crash of October 1929. Juab County's population decreased by 1,266 people between 1920 and 1930—dropping from 9,871 to 8,605. Most of the population loss was in the Tintic District. The voting precincts had changes as follows: Eureka from 3,908 to 3,114; Nephi from 2,699 to 2,793; Mammoth from 1,125 to 750; Levan from 708 to 644; Mona from 408 to 470; Silver City from 689 to 278; Callao from 256 to 262; Mills from 78 to 122; Trout Creek had no census figures for 1920, the population for 1930 was 63.[57] Mammoth disincorporated as a city in 1929 due to a dwindling tax base and population. The total valuation of Juab County property assessed in 1930 was $11.24 million—down from $11.81 million in 1920.[58]

A shortage of lumber had existed in Juab County since the war; however, now a shortage of money also loomed. As a consequence, many of the homes in the Tintic area were either being torn down and the lumber used for other buildings or they were moved to Juab Valley locations. Many of them ended up in eastern Juab County. Juab County officials and residents were soon caught up in the economic turmoil and emotional despair of the 1930s.

ENDNOTES

1. Richard D. Poll, et al., *Utah's History*, 430.

2. Juab County Commission Minutes, Book 3, 322.

3. *Eureka Reporter*, 26 May 1911.

4. *Eureka Reporter*, 11 June 1911.

5. Poll, et al., *Utah's History*, 424.

6. Richard Campbell Roberts, "History of the Utah National Guard," (Ph.D. dissertation, University of Utah, 1973), 171.

7. *Eureka Reporter*, 8 June 1917.

8. *Times News*, 6 October 1917.

9. See Miriam B. Murphy, "'If only I shall have the right stuff': Utah Women in World War I," *Utah Historical Quarterly* 58 (Fall 1998): 334–50. Also see *"A Driver, Intrepid and Brave" Maud Fitch's Letters from the Front 1918–1919* (n.p.: Jeezel Beezel Partners through Rhino Press, 1995), copy in Utah State Historical Society Library.

10. *Eureka Reporter*, 19 July 1918.

11. Murphy, "Utah Women," 338.

12. Ibid., 339.

13. McCune, *Juab County*, 277.

14. Keith Worthington, et al., *They Left a Record*, 69.

15. Nephi City Council Minutes, 19 April 1918, Book 4, 180–81.

16. See Roberts, "Utah National Guard"; and *Times News*, 25 June 1925.

17. *Deseret News*, 28–29 March 1995.

18. Philip Notarianni, *Faith, Hope, & Prosperity*, 111.

19. Juab Commission Minutes, 12, 13 December 1919, Book 3, 415.

20. Poll, et al., *Utah's History*, 465.

21. Ibid.

22. Notarianni, *Faith, Hope, & Prosperity,* 140.

23. Ibid.

24. Poll, et al., *Utah's History,* 466.

25. *Juab County Times,* 29 August 1913.

26. Nephi City Council Minutes, 7 March 1917, Book 3, 13.

27. Nephi City Council Minutes, 21 September 1917.

28. Juab County Commission Minutes, 30 April 1921, Book 3, 460.

29. *Eureka Reporter,* 26 January 1923, 18 July 1929.

30. *Eureka Reporter,* 9 September 1921.

31. *Eureka Reporter,* 4 November 1927.

32. Maurine Stephensen, *Levan,* 84.

33. *Eureka Reporter,* 15 February 1924.

34. Notarianni, *Faith, Hope, & Prosperity,* 124.

35. Ibid., 126.

36. Ibid., 124, 130.

37. Worthington, et al. *They Left a Record,* 91–92.

38. *Eureka Reporter,* 6 April 1923. This was a reprint of an article in the *Salt Lake Telegram.*

39. McCune, *Juab County,* 98.

40. Worthington, et al., *They Left a Record,* 41.

41. *Eureka Reporter,* 28 December 1917, 23 June, 13 October 1922, 24 August 1923, 14 January 1927.

42. Nephi City Council Minutes, 9 July 1918, Book 4, 180.

43. "Catalogue of the Nephi High School, 1921–22," 3, 4. This was a catalogue issued to each student at the beginning of the year. It included instructions for graduation, a list of classes, fees, and a list of instructors, among other information. The publication was discontinued in the 1930s.

44. Worthington, et al., *They Left a Record,* 73.

45. Ibid., 80.

46. Nephi City Council Minutes, 1 October, 6 November, 1924, Book 4, 330, 331.

47. *Times News,* 26 September 1925.

48. Nephi City Council Minutes, 6 March 1925, Book 4, 334.

49. Worthington, et al., *They Left a Record,* 69.

50. Stephensen, *Levan,* 82.

51. George A. Sperry, et al., *Nephi's Centennial Jubilee,* 36–37.

52. *Times News,* 29 October 1926.

53. *Eureka Reporter,* 20 January 1928.

54. *Eureka Reporter,* 29 August 1928.

55. *Eureka Reporter,* 15 August, 22 August 1929.

56. *Eureka Reporter,* 29 August 1929.

57. *Times News,* 17 July 1930; Notarianni, *Faith, Hope, & Prosperity,* 124.

58. *Times News,* 24 July 1930.

CHAPTER 8

THE GREAT DEPRESSION

Although the Great Depression of the 1930s was to wreak havoc in the economy and social structure and cause great despair in most Juab County residents as it did with most Utahns and Americans, the Depression developed gradually, and initially was seen by many as only a periodic economic downturn of the type the nation had weathered many times before. National and Utah political leaders were generally Republicans, and most believed that the market economy would readjust by itself with little or no help from the government. Many Utahns did not even think of troubled times in the early period of the Depression. However, by mid-1930 effects were beginning to be felt in many parts of the economy, society, and the nation. Unemployment began to rise, and, with less money to spend by consumers, businesses began an ever-increasing tailspin.

In spite of the fact that demand for minerals after World War I had decreased and the price of much agricultural produce had dropped, Juab County residents generally had weathered the farming recession of the 1920s. They repaired and built new roads to accommodate the automobiles which were rapidly replacing the horse-

The poultry train from Utah Agricultural College (Utah State University) makes a stop in Nephi, 1924. (Tintic Historical Society)

drawn vehicles of the past. Even with the decrease in demands, throughout the 1920s Tintic's mines generally were prosperous. Some new mills were erected and mines reopened, until 1929. During the Depression years, the Chief Consolidated Mining Company of Eureka and the Tintic Standard and North Lily on the Utah County side of Tintic Mining District were the district's only producing mines. The effects of fluctuations in the Tintic Mining District and employment reached far beyond the mining industry, extending to a wide array of service industries. Farming was also affected. A ripple effect occurred throughout the county.

Juab County initially did not feel many direct repercussions with the stock market crash of late 1929. As mentioned, even prior to the Depression, farmers in Juab County had faced difficult times, and many had lost their farms or become overextended financially during the 1920s. At the end of the 1929 crop season, the Juab County Agent collected farm records from thirty typical farms of the county. These records were forwarded to the Extension Service office of the Utah State Agricultural College (Utah State University), where they

Thrashing machine doing its work at Little Salt Creek, ca. 1914. (Fred Chapman)

were used to determine if income from the farms existed in proportion to the effort and capital invested in them. Results found that the average size of a dry farm in Juab Valley was 212 acres, with 103 acres of wheat harvested. If each farm produced twenty bushels per acre, at $1.05 per bushel the gross return would be $2,163. After subtracting average expenses (indebtedness, insurance, cost of seed, cleaning and treating, repairs, bags and twine, hauling, labor, and miscellaneous) the average net income would be $874.47. About $1,500 was considered necessary as a family income at the time, therefore the farmer would require a supplementary income of $625.53. To earn $1,500 a farmer would have to dry farm at least 230 acres.[1] The study also determined that farmers were investing too much in machinery, stating,

> In this day of cooperation in most all phases of production it is considered advisable for the wheat farmers in Juab County either to enter into a cooperative agreement each with his neighbor and

Bert Sparks decorated his Ice Cream Wagon for the big parade, probably 4 July 1920. (Dale Worwood)

purchase equipment together so as to cut down and more equally distribute the burden of costs or to hire the machine work [done] on small farms.[2]

Events of the 1930s would reveal the accuracy of this assessment, as they forced many of those farmers who were able to survive to take such economic measures. During the Depression years of the 1930s some of the local ranchers at Mills and other locations who had borrowed on their land were forced into bankruptcy, and most of these men left to find employment elsewhere. Other farmers moved to Nephi and Levan but worked their spreads on a part-time basis.

In November 1930 the poultry and egg farmers of Nephi organized a cooperative association for the purpose of financing and constructing an egg-grading plant in Nephi. Until this time they were trucking their eggs to Payson. The following men were elected as officers: Charles H. Grace, president and director; Earl A. Green, vice-president and director; Alton S. Gadd, secretary and director; Paul E. Booth, treasurer and director; John Richardson, Clarence Warner, J. Walter Paxman, and Clark S. Wood, directors. The association decided to erect a building on the southwest corner of First North

Nephi City outing in Salt Creek Canyon, ca. early 1900s. (Dale Worwood)

and First West. The Union Pacific Railroad built a spur from its tracks to accommodate the plant. Money was borrowed from Nephi banks and Walker Brothers Bank in Salt Lake City. Plans for financing the endeavor stated that: "each one of the poultry men and business men in Nephi will be asked to sign a note to be placed as security for the loan of $5,000, and these notes to be paid off from the profits of the egg grading plant."[3] On 16 February 1931, Nephi Poultrymen, Inc. celebrated the opening of its new grading plant with what the *Times News* called, "one of the outstanding events in the life of Nephi."[4]

Life and activity were quite normal in the area during the first months of the new decade. During 1930, roads were built in Juab County at a cost of over $138,000. State, county, and federal funds were used to build seven miles of road in Salt Creek Canyon; oil ten miles of highway south of Levan; rebuild several bridges on the Silver City-Champlain road; and take out several curves on the Levan-Gunnison road south of Levan. A road also was constructed from the state highway to Burreston Pond through the efforts of the East Juab Fish and Game Association.[5]

Both wagons and early automobiles were used at the warehouse and seeding plant in Nephi, 1924. (Utah State University)

Also in 1930, the Juab County Commissioners and the U.S. Forest Service raised $10,000 to widen the narrow roadbed and construct a graveled road at the back of Mount Nebo, using the remains of a branch of the Sanpete Railroad built in 1890 up Salt Creek Canyon to haul marble which was being quarried from the back of Mount Nebo. After a short time, the quarry had closed and the tracks were removed.[6]

In 1922, after having been closed for several years, the Levan plaster mill was purchased by a Nevada company. The following article appeared in the *Eureka Reporter* of 13 February 1930:

> Sheriff M.M. Kaighn was in the eastern end of the county on Monday of this week to sell the Levan Plaster Mill at public sale. G.R. Ringholtz as plaintiff brought suit against Moses Paggi, J.C. Jensen et al, defendants. The former winning and selling the plant to satisfy judgement. The highest bidder was Dorothy Ringholtz and the price paid was $5,303.12. According to Sheriff Kaighn the Plaster Mill was one of the most modern plants of its kind in this country and was sold for only a fraction of its worth.

Salt Creek crib dams, 1925. (Utah State University)

In 1935 the mill again changed hands. It was purchased by A.V. Smith, who modernized the plant, using diesel power to operate the machinery and trucks to haul the gypsum. The mill operated until 1942, when Smith closed it and moved away.[7]

Lawmakers were beginning to be concerned over possible revenue shortfalls. In 1930 the Utah Legislature passed a graduated personal and corporate income tax. Before this the government had depended on property tax to provide about 81 percent of needed state and local government revenue.[8] The *Times News* published an article urging support of this tax, maintaining,

> decide whether you are going to continue to pay all the taxes for the support of government, or whether the legislature shall be given the power to compel those whose income is from salaries and securities to bear some of the tax burden. Three fourths of the income of the people of Utah is from other sources than property. Why then should property pay all the taxes?[9]

When the Juab School Board met in June 1930, it decided to transport Levan High School students to Nephi. Since this meant that Nephi would be the only high school in the district, they also initiated a name change from Nephi High School to Juab High School.[10] It took the Nephi students a few years to fully accept the change.

By 1931 Juab County officials were finding it necessary to provide some aid for the unemployed. The Nephi City Council Minutes include numerous instances where people were permitted to do work to pay their electric and water bills. Widows and the indigent were allowed to pay the minimum amount of one dollar per month. In October 1931 the *Times News* announced that the Juab County Commission would permit taxes to be paid in three installments: "This does not postpone the final date of settlement, but it does give the tax payer, who cannot pay all his taxes at one time, a decided advantage over the present practice, in that it relieves him of the three per cent penalty and the twelve per cent annual interest charges on the amount of taxes he is able to pay."[11] Later county commission minutes during the 1930s contained references to people who were permitted to pay a portion of their property taxes each month. The documents also recorded property which had been sold at tax sale, or, because it was not purchased by anyone, had become county property.

The published financial statements for 1931 showed the Juab School District to be in adequate condition, but, due to lack of funds, in 1932 the school year ended early—on 22 April.[12] This was the earliest date that would give students who planned to go on to college enough credits to be accepted. Costs were also cut the next year by combining Domestic Science and Domestic Arts classes and curtailing expenses for the Music Department. Superintendent Owen L. Barnett voluntarily accepted a 10 percent reduction in his salary. All teachers, janitors, and others who received less than $100 per month were given a 10 percent reduction in salary, with a 15 percent cut for those receiving over $100 per month.[13] In 1934 the district applied for a $7,000 government loan, but due to the fact that only $4,620 was received, school closed on 25 May that year.[14]

By 1932 Utah's economic situation had been seriously affected by the developing economic depression. Gross farm income had declined from $69 million to $29 million, and the value of mineral production had declined from $115 million to $23 million.[15] Needless to say, Juab County suffered a direct hit. In addition, 1931 proved the

Entertainment proved important to community life. Nephi's Venice Theatre. (Fred Chapman)

driest year on record in Juab County—only 7.42 inches of rain had fallen in the twelve-month period. Following that, rainfall at the Nephi weather station measured 84 percent of normal for 1932, 73 percent for 1933, and only 65 percent in 1934.[16] The drought began to seriously affect farm production and the very livelihood of area farmers.

Some building did occur in the early 1930s. A new power plant was built for Nephi east of the existing one. Later the two plants, supplemented by Telluride Power Company, supplied power for Nephi. The Juab LDS Stake Tabernacle received a facelift in the summer of 1931. A new facade was constructed and several new classrooms added to the building.[17] A law was passed in 1930 authorizing new federal buildings in towns where post offices showed receipts of over $7,500 and under $10,000. Buildings were to be constructed in towns where the government owned the sites on which they would be located. Nephi fit these requirements: receipts for 1929–30 had been just over $7,000 and the government had owned property at the northeast corner of Main and Center Streets for the past twelve years.

Nephi High School was dedicated on 3 January 1923, by James W. Paxman. (Fred Chapman)

Nephi's civic clubs and other organizations sent requests to Washington D.C., asking that Nephi be considered for such a building. As a result, the federal building which would house the post office and local offices of the United States Forest Service was constructed. The cornerstone for the $55,000 building was laid on 25 July 1932; occupancy commenced in late January 1933. John E. Lunt was the postmaster at that time, with W.C. Cole, assistant, and A.D. Kendall, as custodian. Homer K. Lunt and C.R. Lomax were city postal carriers.[18]

In 1932 the Levan Town Board, with the help of a group of men and boys from the town, volunteered to improve a U.S. Forest Service-designated park and recreation area known as "Saw Mill Flat," located in Chicken Creek Canyon east of Levan The Utah Fish and Game Department also planted trout in the creek.[19]

Until the election of Franklin D. Roosevelt in 1932, most aid was provided by private charitable organizations and individuals, although on both the state and national levels Republican politicians were beginning to advocate and promote some governmental assistance plans. The churches and Red Cross were the most significant

Levan LDS Church with later addition. (Golden Mangelson)

charitable organizations in the county at this time. Juab County's Red Cross central committee included Raphael Garfield, Mona, chair; Mrs. H.E. Hall, Eureka, secretary; Mrs. Edna Cazier, Nephi; J.R. Hansen, Levan; J. Osrol Webb, Eureka; Bigelow Bradley, Mammoth; and E.R. Higginson, Silver City.[20] The purpose of the committee was to pass upon the applications for assistance submitted by LDS ward committees and others. Each of the county's LDS wards had a committee that received applications and distributed food, clothing, and other supplies to the needy.

In the fall of 1931 the Juab County Red Cross began distributing surplus food that had been purchased by the federal government to bolster food prices. During 1933 they dispensed 800,000 pounds of wheat and 3,420 sacks of flour. They also distributed through the LDS Relief Society organizations the following material, valued at $2,908.40: hosiery, underwear, overalls and trousers, shirts, blankets, comforters, sweaters, and cloth material. The group also provided a Red Cross Nursing Service. For example, according to a report submitted by Mrs. Joey Olpin, local Red Cross nursing representative, which itemized the work of Nina Little, this consisted of the following: visiting five schools; 1,152 pupils were given dental inspections;

Christensen Shoe Shop, located at about 41 East Center, Nephi, n.d. (Fred Chapman)

820 pupils received dental care; 1,090 vision tests were given; eighty-seven pupils were found to have defective vision; fifty-three conferences were held with parents; two pre-school clinics were set up in Nephi; twenty children were examined by a physician; five home hygiene classes were held; thirty home hygiene certificates were issued; 860 typhoid inoculations were given; 281 diphtheria inoculations were given; and sixty-two visits and conferences were held on behalf of the Red Cross Nursing service.[21]

In April 1932 Governor George H. Dern proclaimed 8 May as a fast day for Utah. Everyone was asked to fast for three meals and contribute the money not spent for the skipped meals to relief agencies. By June 1932 the Red Cross had received from various sources 800,000 pounds of crushed wheat feed that was allocated to stockmen, with 200,000 pounds going to poultrymen. They had dispensed 1,420 fifty-pound bags of flour and had turned over 1,020 bags of flour to the LDS Relief Society to be distributed to the needy.[22] East Juab also, at this time, donated what Mrs. J.E. O'Connor, secretary of

Students from the Silver City Public School, 1928. (Pearl Wilson)

the Tintic unit of the Red Cross, estimated at "well over $1,000.00 worth of food" to the people of Tintic. The food was distributed to 135 families. Mrs. O'Connor expressed the sincere appreciation of recipients to donors in a letter to the *Times News*.[23]

Franklin D. Roosevelt was elected president by a great majority in 1932, with a majority of Utahns also voting for the Democratic candidate. Fellow Democrat Henry H. Blood became governor of Utah. Both supported more aggressive government involvement in combatting the Depression.

In March 1933, in the face of the economic crisis, Governor Blood declared a bank holiday for the state of Utah. Only banks which could show fundamental soundness would be permitted to reopen for business. The Nephi National Bank had closed on 1 December 1931 and began liquidation in 1932.[24] A receiver was appointed on 26 January 1932, and the estate closed on 8 August 1936. The First National Bank of Nephi absorbed the Bank of Fountain Green in 1932 but was not licensed after the banking holiday. It was placed in the hands of a conservator in 1933, remaining

Sisters of the Holy Cross ran St. Joseph's school in Eureka for many years. Class photo, ca. 1920s. (Tintic Historical Society)

under that control until a receiver was appointed on 5 February 1935. The estate closed on 22 December 1939.[25]

The Eureka Banking Company moved to Nephi on 5 October 1933, changing its name to the Central Utah Bank in 1934. It was absorbed by the Commercial Bank of Nephi on 27 May 1935.[26] In late October 1934, Juab School District sued and was awarded a judgement by a federal court jury of $4,368.19 from the defunct First National Bank of Nephi. The district, through its treasurer James H. Ockey, sued for school funds deposited in the bank, protected by a depository bond, which the bank had refused to turn over to the district after it suspended business.[27]

Roosevelt began his famous New Deal—a barrage of public programs and agencies to help citizens gain employment to get back on their feet economically. The federal government soon initiated programs to provide work for the unemployed, and by late 1933 these were augmenting the earlier few direct relief programs. In 1933 Congress established the Federal Emergency Relief Administration (FERA) and the governor appointed a Utah State Advisory

Manson Brothers Grocery Store became a fixture on Eureka's Main Street for many years. Photo from ca. 1918–22. (Tintic Historical Society)

Committee on Public Welfare. A special session of the Utah Legislature on 10 July passed the Utah Industrial Recovery Act (UIRA) and a 2 percent sales tax, which would be used to match funds from FERA for an expanded public welfare program.[28]

The Civil Works Administration (CWA) and the Civilian Conservation Corps (CCC) were early agencies that provided work opportunities for some Americans. In 1935 the Works Progress Administration (WPA) was established to provide work for the unemployed. The Social Security program was created to provide for the partial financial support of dependent children, the blind, and the aged. Utah subsequently established a Department of Public Welfare.

In October 1933, 395 men from Nephi, 76 from Mona, 129 from Levan, and 11 from Mills signed up for work on resurfacing the road from Nephi to Leamington. The federal government had planned to employ a number of men for the project, but because the number of unemployed was so large, it was decided that between twenty-five

Minnie Bates, postmistress at Silver City, picking up mail delivered by train, ca. 1930s. (Tintic Historical Society)

The automobile hit it big in the Tintic Mining District. An early truck delivery in Silver City, n.d. (Tintic Historical Society)

and thirty men, practically all of them with teams, would be hired at a time. Each man would be given forty-eight hours work—six days at eight hours per day. Resident Engineer M.C. Moffat headed the surveying, while Evan Harris, county road supervisor, guided construction.[29] Fifty-five men from Nephi also were employed graveling and grading that city's streets. Twenty-five men were hired to clean up the cemetery and grade streets in Levan. In Mona, twenty men worked at cleaning the cemetery and improving the city streets.[30]

The CWA was organized locally in Juab County in December 1933, with the following committee members: I.M. Petty, chairman; J. Earl Reid, Nephi; C.E. Rife and Frank Townley, Eureka; and Carl Eager of Mammoth.[31] The CWA began registering women for employment if there were no other members of the family working. Women's projects included quilting, rug making, cording wool, and nursing. Centers were established in various towns in the county to accommodate sewing projects.[32]

By April 1934 Juab County had received $68,452.08 from the CWA: Tintic District received $33,390.31, Nephi $19,905.49, Levan $5,117.00, Mona $4,578,88, Mills $495.38, women's projects

Leather helmets and sparse padding provided little protection for the Silver City football team in 1925. (Tintic Historical Society)

$2,194.70, predatory animal control $713.94, and administrative needs $1,038.38.[33] A majority of the work projects were for road work and improving municipal water supplies. The Mechanical Arts Building at the Eureka School was rebuilt and an addition was made to the Mammoth School. An outdoor swimming pool was constructed at Nephi and two concrete tennis courts were built.[34]

Other needs also received funding. At Nephi, the springs which supply culinary water to the city were developed and 21,300 feet of water pipe was laid. In Eureka 11,350 feet of water pipe was installed. Levan's city springs were developed; and, at Mona, 4,000 feet of water pipe was installed. Buildings were painted and repaired and school playgrounds were improved. A monument was constructed in Nephi City Park to cover a part of the adobe wall built by the early settlers. A 160-foot water tunnel was built near Levan that increased the town's supply of water by 144,000 gallons per day. Concrete sidewalks were installed in Mona. Because Eureka is located in a canyon and had been subjected to destructive floods, a stone-lined sewer was built through the center of town to alleviate this problem. A road was built to the Eureka cemetery from the highway, and the streets in the

The pump house at Cherry Creek provided the much needed water for the mine and town at Mammoth. (E. Steele McIntyre)

cemetery were improved. A tennis court was also built at Tintic High School.[35]

The enacting bill for the Civilian Conservation Corps (CCC) was introduced by President Roosevelt on 21 March 1933, and, by 31 March, the measure passed both houses of Congress.[36] Identified as "An act for the relief of employment through the performance of useful public work, and for other purposes," the bill gave the president authority to hire unemployed men for works of a public nature on state and federal lands for prevention of forest fires, contol of floods and soil erosion; plant, pest and disease control; and construction, maintenance, or repair of paths, trails, and fire lanes. Provision also was made for the extension of work into private and municipal lands when it was felt to be in the public interest.[37]

The CCC camps, or "Cs," as they were sometimes called, were organized to provide employment for young unmarried men. Recruits were to be trained under U.S. Army supervision. Headquarters for Utah CCC Camps was to be located at Fort Douglas in Salt Lake City. Utah initially was allotted 1,000 unmarried

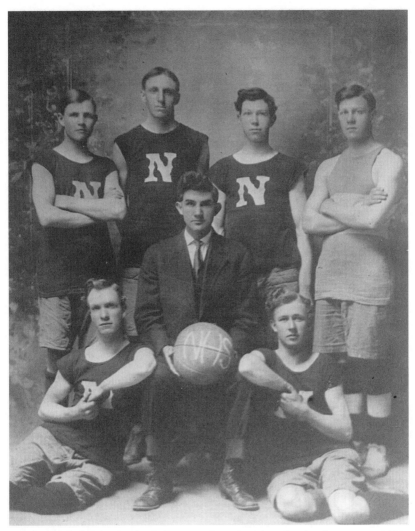

Nephi High School basketball team played with only six players, ca. 1910. (George E. Wilson)

men between the ages of eighteen and twenty-five, and to this number, 1,300 local enlisted men (LEMs) were hired from the unemployed carpenters, lumbermen, miners, and others who could serve as project leaders.[38]

The young enlistees were given food, clothing, shelter, and thirty dollars per month, twenty-five dollars of which was to be sent home

The Nephi Post Office, as in many communities, proved to be a center of activity. (Wayne Christiansen)

to their families, leaving them with five dollars to spend as they wished. Enrollment was to be completely voluntary. Applicants had to be U.S. residents who were at that time listed on relief rolls.[39] Camps usually operated in six-month enrollment periods; this later changed to two years, and changed again in 1937 so that any unemployed young man was eligible for service.[40]

Four of the original camps in Utah were built of lumber; the others consisted of six-man tents with lumber frames and floors. Juab County was allotted one of the lumber camps, which was to be located at the base of Mount Nebo on the banks of Salt Creek and would be identified as Camp Nebo. Lieutenant W.R. Irish, a West Point graduate, was captain; later in the summer, G.L. Barron of Springville, a former captain in World War I, became the civilian superintendent.[41]

The young men were issued army clothing to wear. Bert Powell recalled, "I believe I was the first man to join the CCC Camp in Nephi," and he also served as camp reporter for the *Times News*. Construction of the camp began in May 1933. The men slept in

Eureka's Main Street bustled with activity in the 1920s. (Utah State Historical Society)

eight-man squad tents for the six weeks required to build the four barracks, which would each hold fifty men. They also built a mess hall and recreation center.[42] They worked on cattle trails, flood- and erosion-control projects, cleaning recreational areas, and building benches, tables, and restrooms. They also built the ranger station. In June 1933, twelve young men from Eureka and four from Mammoth were sent to the Nebo Camp.[43] On 6 November the camp was moved to Washington, near St. George. The following April it was reopened by another group.[44]

During the summers of 1933 and 1934 the men worked on the Mount Nebo Scenic Loop Road, This twenty-mile road begins about twelve miles from Nephi and runs northeasterly, and then north, behind Mt. Nebo. It reaches an altitude of 10,000 feet, and continues until it connects with Payson Canyon. It is advertised as one of Utah's most beautiful scenic drives. In 1936 the CCC workers repaired damage which had occurred during floods due to heavy rainfall the pre-

Holiday lights adorn Nephi Main Street, 1930s. (Fred Chapman)

vious spring.[45] The 145 young men who came in 1936 from the vicinity of Bismark, North Dakota, and 165 from Missouri replaced the previous group of veterans, who were transferred to a camp in California. The newcomers worked on flood control in Marsh Canyon, which was the site of the springs that supplied Nephi's culinary water and had been badly damaged by floods during the previous few years.[46]

In September 1933 the Utah Board of County Commissioners and other public officials appealed to Governor Blood and members of Utah's Congressional District to lobby to have CCC camps established in western Juab, Millard, Beaver, and Iron Counties. At this time they were unsuccessful, and they were told by Colonel Robert Fechner, head of the Conservation Corps, that the "President will not consent to working any of the men of the conservation corp on the public domain until congress passes a bill placing the public domain under federal administration."[47]

Sheep men gather at Jericho for a wool sale. (Utah State University)

The Juab County Commission again contacted the Utah congressional delegation and the area's district supervisor of national forests in 1935, requesting their help in obtaining a camp in western Juab County. A camp then was established at Jericho, and the first group of men arrived in the latter part of November 1935. Within a few days they were working on the old pioneer road from Silver City to Utah County.[48]

By the end of November 1937 they had completed a variety of projects, including the reconstruction of the six-mile pioneer road at Silver Divide and the development and cribbing of an old well at an unnamed spring. The crib stored 5,000 gallons of water and the well delivered a flow of thirty gallons per minute. Metal troughs were installed and a pumphouse built to house a small pumping unit that would deliver forty gallons per minute. A spring at Mud Springs was dug out, cribbed, and covered. The water was piped underground and flowed into a twenty-foot trough. A small reservoir was constructed to store the overflow. The first section of the ninety-mile Cherry Creek Road was built to extend from Highway 26 near Jericho to the Nevada line. A stock-watering project called Desert Mountain Reservoir consisted of an earth dam with the face and spillway rip-rapped. Coyote Knoll Reservoir and Hole-in-Rock Reservoir (located in Little Sage Valley) were also built, as were four earthen dams to

Service Star Legion planting trees in the new park at Nephi, 1931. (Utah State University)

check erosion and spread out the water at Hop Creek Wash. A Goshen cattle corral was constructed of quaking aspen poles, with graveled sorting pens, a squeeze chute, and watering troughs. The River Bed Excavation Reservoir was dug and the dirt used for a long fill on a road across a low portion of the old riverbed. Feeder ditches were made to increase water storage. Emergency snow removal projects provided a means for feeding approximately 20,000 snowbound sheep. Roads leading to homes in Cow Hollow were also cleared. A project called the No-Name Corral was made with cedar posts and old railroad ties. During the summer of 1936, crickets infested the area near Hassell ranch. The camp secured the loan of 5,000 turkeys, provided transportation for them, herded them during the battle, and returned a much-fattened flock at the end of a three-month campaign. The method proved to be very successful and national publicity resulted from this novel means of eradication.[49] This is just some of what the CCC camp accomplished while it was in west Juab County.

The *Eureka Reporter* included "Jericho CCC Camp News" as a column in its regular weekly paper from 1935 to 1941. It covered the

Workers preparing the grounds for landscaping at the poultry plant in Nephi, 1934. (Utah State University)

work the corpsmen accomplished as well as their sports activities, educational projects, increases and decreases in enrollment, and other things. The Jericho camp also published its own monthly paper. It was originally planned to be called the *Deseret Breeze,* but the name was changed to the *Walls of Jericho.* Further changes followed, however, and it was finely first published as the *Jericho Journal* in June 1938.[50]

The young CCC corpsmen were generally accepted by those in the surrounding communities; in fact, some of them married girls from Utah and took them back to their homes, while others stayed in Utah. Joseph Bernini, who was born on New York City's east side, came to the Jericho camp in 1939 and worked cutting cedar posts for fence lines, seeding desert tracts, and building storage dams for watering livestock. Bernini later served in the United States Navy during World War II and then returned to Tintic, where he married Grace Green from Silver City, raising a family in Eureka. He served as Eureka City Marshal for thirty-eight years, and in 1978 he was appointed Juab County Commissioner to finish the term of Fred Johnson. Except for two years from 1984 to 1986, Bernini has been reelected to that position. He won reelection in November 1998 to serve another four years.[51]

CCC workers labor at project number 1, loading gravel at Silver Divide, 1935. (Utah State University)

In the fall of 1938 four new CCC camps were added to the Division of Grazing program, including the Callao CCC Camp, which was located 121 miles northwest of Delta. At first, Kenneth Wolf, CCC liaison officer of the Ninth Corps, was reluctant to situate a camp so far away from a hospital and where there was no recreation for the young men. Finally, however, Governor Blood wrote to the CCC director and reminded him that Utah had spent money for the camp and for fuel, the county had helped build a road to the camp, and livestock interests were anxiously awaiting improvements to the area's facilities. The CCC finally decided that Callao was a suitable place for a summer camp and agreed to let the corpsmen stay provided the Division of Grazing would stand the expense of moving the company to Kanosh on 1 January 1939. Corpsmen did go back to Callao on 1 April 1940 and stayed until 30 September 1941.[52]

To adequately cover all the projects completed in the county by the CCC camps during the time would be a difficult task. Needless to say, in Juab County as elsewhere, the CCC was greatly appreciated and did much to improve the land and its utilization. The agency constructed roads and stock trails in western Juab which continue in use as winter grazing routes for numerous sheep herds during the winter months. The men also worked to prevent soil erosion and

Mess hall at the CCC camp in Callao, 1939. (Dick Seal)

control flooding, and the public continues to enjoy the scenic roads built during the time.

In April 1936, at a meeting held in the Juab LDS Stake Tabernacle, Soren M. Nielsen of Mt. Pleasant, president of the North Sanpete Stake, was selected chairman, and A.H. Belliston, president of Juab Stake, was chosen to be vice-chairman of the LDS church relief program for the Millard, Deseret, Tintic, Juab, Moroni, North Sanpete, South Sanpete, and Gunnison Stakes. Under the new program, agricultural property would be rented and unemployed men and women would be put to work on church projects. They would be fed, clothed, and given some money to pay such things as utility bills. Members of the LDS church would be asked to pay an honest tithing, either in money or produce. Every member also would be asked to fast for two meals on the first Sunday of every month and contribute the amount saved, either in money or produce, to their bishops. The money and produce collected and the crops raised would be placed in bishops' storehouses. Each region was to have a regional storehouse where the surplus from the bishops' storehouses could be stored and distributed to the needy members of the region. President Frank Birch of Tintic Stake described a mining project

Callao CCC camp number 116, 1939, attracted many men from the Midwest. (Dick Seal)

being worked in the stake in which the church provided capital for unemployed members to lease claims and earn a livelihood from working them.[53]

The Nephi South Ward added a $35,000 amusement hall and classrooms to its building during the Depression years, and the addition also included a new Relief Society room and storage space.[54] Work began on an addition to the west end of the Juab County Courthouse in the spring of 1936. With a WPA grant of $12,000 to cover the cost of the labor, workers removed thirty feet of the building and replaced it with a fifty-four-foot extension. A basement was built for vaults, storage, and a garage. The first floor housed the offices of the county recorder and the county sheriff, and two restrooms. The second floor had eight office rooms to be used by other government agencies.[55]

In February 1935, Dr. P.L. Jones, who was president of the Sons and Daughters of the Pioneers and Indian War Veterans, met with the Nephi City Council and told them that a meeting would be held soon to determine where the next Black Hawk War celebration would be held. He believed that Nephi had a good chance of hosting it if the community was interested.[56] The Black Hawk War celebration subsequently was held in Nephi that summer. It ended with a rodeo. Center Street was closed to traffic between Main and First East to accommodate the event. The local tennis courts were used for dancing, and the city leased the county fairgrounds. A professional rodeo company presented three performances. An arena and a racetrack were constructed at the Juab County Fairgrounds and over 100 head of stock were shipped in for the races and rodeo. Other festival programs were presented by Utah County, Tintic, and southern Utah organizations. Governor Henry H. Blood attended on the second

The military nature of the CCC is evident as workers "stand retreat" at the Callao camp, 1939. (Dick Seal)

day.[57] The next year, the event became known as the Ute Stampede and was held from 10–13 July. It later was changed to a three-day event and continues to be held annually, attracting thousands of visitors and county residents to the festivities.

In 1938 the people living on Center Street in Nephi presented a petition to the City Council requesting that the street not be used for the Ute Stampede. It was held there that year, but the following year a vote was taken to determine if the citizens of Nephi were willing to support the continuation of the celebration. The council minutes merely stated, "It will be held."[58] The Ute Stampede has been held at the county fairgrounds since then and has developed into an important event for almost everyone who has lived in Nephi and much of Juab County. School and family reunions are planned to coincide with the event, and other former residents plan vacations so they can attend.

A Ute Stampede Queen and a Miss Nephi, each with two attendants, are chosen each year and a float is made for each group to ride on as they attend other celebrations in the state. A parade is held each day of the event: a Western Parade on Thursday, a Mammoth Parade on Friday, and a Bathing Beauty Parade on Saturday, although recently there have been some complaints about holding the last. The three rodeo performances are the main attraction and are presented annually by the same group.

Eugene Lunt, Commander of Battery E, 145th Field Artillery, met

A lonely sheep camp adorns the wide open spaces at Callao, 1939. (Dick Seal)

with the Nephi City Council on 20 August 1936 and informed them that it was possible Nephi could qualify for an armory building. The federal gvernment would provide 90 percent of the cost if Nephi could raise the remaining 10 percent, which would amount to approximately $3,000. Also, the city would have to purchase property for the building, which was to be constructed through the Public Works Administration. The plan was accepted, and by October the site on First East, between First North and Center Streets, had been purchased. Construction was begun and the new armory was dedicated on 24 September 1938. It was constructed of brick, with the west portion two stories high and the large assembly hall one story.[59]

In 1938 the Juab School Board decided to construct a new building for high school physical education and mechanical arts classes. They felt that it was important to "construct a building to take care of the modern trend in education, that of vocational work instead of solid academic teaching . . . so the student who shows a trend toward mechanics will have a chance to prepare himself for a trade which, in later years, will prove valuable."[60] The new gym was located on the school campus, south and slightly east of the high school building.[61]

The upper floor would be used for basketball and other indoor sports activities. It would include a large gymnasium floor with plenty of seating for spectators. The lower floor would be used for mechanical arts classes, including woodworking, metal work, and mechanical construction. Voters approved the issuing and sale of bonds amounting to $50,000 for the school district's share of the construction of the $90,000 building. They also applied for and obtained a grant from the government for the remaining $40,000.[62]

The Great Depression was hard on a rural county like Juab, and Depression-era government programs proved extremely beneficial for much of the county. The WPA and CCC were especially significant. People endured the hardships, awaiting relief from the economic and social disaster. The New Deal programs helped, but another type of disaster—the Second World War—brought an end to the Depression by mobilizing the country's resources to fight a political enemy.

ENDNOTES

1. *Times News*, 3 April 1930 Although not mentioned in the article, this survey was probably done through the experimental station south of Nephi.

2. Ibid.

3. *Times News*, 2, 10 November 1930.

4. *Times News*, 19 February 1931.

5. *Times News*, 9 January, 22 May 1930.

6. *Times News*, 20 March 1930.

7. Maurine Stephensen, *Levan*, 72.

8. Richard D. Poll, et al., *Utah's History*, 484.

9. *Times News*, 23 October 1930.

10. *Times News*, 19 June 1930.

11. *Times News*, 8 October 1931.

12. *Times News*, 3 August 1931.

13. *Times News*, 31 March 1932.

14. *Times News*, 22 March, 5 April 1934.

15. Poll, et al., *Utah's History*, 482.

16. Kenneth W. Baldridge, "Nine Years of Achievement: The Civilian

Conservation Corps in Utah" (Ph.D. dissertation, Brigham Young University, 1971), 174.

17. *Times News,* 19 March 1931.

18. *Times News,* 7 August 1930, 28 July 1932, 12 January 1933.

19. *Times News,* 17 November 1932.

20. Ibid.

21. *Times News,* 26 October 1933.

22. *Times News,* 28 April, 9 June 1932.

23. *Times News,* 14 April 1932.

24. *Times News,* 3 December 1931.

25. Roland Stucki, *Commercial Banking in Utah, 1847–1966* (Salt Lake City: Bureau of Economic and Business Research, 1967), 174, 176.

26. Ibid., 165. The Nephi City Council Minutes for 7 December 1933 stated that the Eureka Banking Company at Nephi was "holding Tax Amount," with the notation that the Nephi National Bank was now closed.

27. *Eureka Reporter,* 1 November 1934.

28. Poll, et al., *Utah's History,* 486.

29. *Times News,* 9 November 1933.

30. *Times News,* 30 November 1933.

31. *Eureka Reporter,* 7 December 1933.

32. *Times News,* 21 December 1933.

33. *Times News,* 5 April 1934.

34. "A Report of the Works Division, April 15, 1934–October 31, 1935" (Utah Emergency Relief Administration), 178.

35. Ibid.

36. Baldridge, "Civilian Conservation Corps," 2.

37. Ibid., 10.

38. Ibid., 19.

39. Ibid., 24, 73.

40. *Times News,* 23 September 1937.

41. Bert Powell, interview with Pearl Wilson, 8 January 1999.

42. Ibid.

43. *Eureka Reporter,* 15 June 1933.

44. Baldridge, "Civilian Conservation Corps," 46, 364.

45. *Times News,* 18 July, 20 August 1936.

46. *Times News,* 30 July, 13 August 1936.

47. *Times News,* 21 September 1933.

48. Juab County Commission Minutes, 4 May 1935, Book 4, 58; *Eureka Reporter,* 28 November, 5 December 1935.

49. This information appeared in the *Times News* and the *Eureka Reporter* on 11 November 1937.

50. Baldridge, "Civilian Conservation Corps," 287.

51. *Deseret News,* 21 January 1996; Powell, interview.

52. Baldridge, "Civilian Conservtion Corps," 121, 372–73, 375–76.

53. *Times News,* 30 April 1936.

54. *Times News,* 25 March 1937.

55. *Times News,* 12 March 1936.

56. Nephi City Council Minutes, 21 February 1935, Book 6, 246.

57. *Times News,* 1, 8 August 1935.

58. Nephi City Council Minutes, 2 June 1938, Book 7, 145, 2 March 1939, 179.

59. *Times News,* 15 September 1938.

60. *Times News,* 23 June 1938.

61. The building is now referred to as the "Old Gym" and is used for community sports such as Junior Jazz basketball and roller skating.

62. *Times News,* 23 June 1938.

CHAPTER 9

JUAB COUNTY IN THE WORLD WAR II ERA

Juab, like many other rural Utah counties, experienced an over-all decrease in population as a result of the Depression years. People were put into motion as the ravages of the Depression caused stress and strain on both the economic and social fronts. Like the migrants fleeing the midwestern dust bowl, many families left Utah for the west coast, while others moved to the urban counties of the state. World War II subsequently changed the economic picture of the nation and had a great impact on Juab County and the rest of the Beehive State.

The 1940 census showed the population of Juab County to be 7,393, a decrease of 1,211 people from the count ten years earlier. Nephi had gained 263 residents, making its population 2,836, and Mona had grown from 328 to 357. However, Eureka showed a decrease of 751 people, Mammoth 288, Callao 38, Mills 57, Silver City 167, and Trout Creek 40.[1] The Juab County Commissioners decided that the population in Silver City, Trout Creek, and Mills were not large enough to justify the expense of maintaining a voting precinct; therefore, it was decided that Silver City would be part of

Men who constructed the CCC camp at Salt Creek Canyon in 1933. (Dale Worwood)

the Mammoth precinct, Trout Creek and Callao would become the Trout Creek-Callao precinct, and Mills would be added to the Levan precinct.[2] The 1940 Census of Agriculture showed Juab County had 391 farms, as compared with 524 in 1935 and 496 in 1930.[3]

Overall events signaled some reasons for optimism as the new decade commenced, yet some economic ups and downs continued as effects of the Depression were still felt. Ore shipments from the Tintic District showed a considerable decrease in 1939 because a large amount of dump material had been shipped and only a small amount taken from the underground workings. The dumps were being shipped as a final gleaning process to procure everything that was possible. The Mammoth Mining Company shipped some dump material, but most of what it shipped came from underground operations. The Chief Consolidated Mining Company showed a large increase of 391 carloads shipped over the preceding year, and in March it reported that new ore bodies had been developed and the outlook was much better for the future.[4] Yet, the mining was diminishing; when the local Safeway grocery store closed, the *Eureka*

Reporter stated, "This indicates a trend which has been apparent for years, and it also indicates the fact that . . . this town is going down by degrees."[5]

Nephi established a nursery and planted 2,700 seedling trees to beautify the city. Mayor P.L. Jones said that officials expected to have enough to plant trees on both sides of each street within the city limits. In order to resurface its off-highway streets, Nephi bought a new gravel crusher and located it northeast of the city near an abundant gravel supply. The city's officials also modernized the road-sprinkling truck. At a cost of $22,500, the Juab Mill and Elevator Company built a new mill in 1940 in Nephi. It included additional storage elevators and new machinery, making it adequate to handle the large amount of wheat grown in Juab Valley.[6]

In July 1940, Eureka purchased from the Chief Consolidated Mining Company half-interest in six wells located in Homansville in Utah County along with the equipment and lines necessary to bring the water to the reservoir which supplied water for the city. The cost was $18,524. Prior to this time, Eureka officials had been purchasing water from month to month for the city.[7]

Also in July, the International Union of Mine, Mill and Smelter Workers in the state voted to strike if they were not granted a new wage scale. They voted for the strike but were persuaded by a wire from union official J.R. Steelman to wait while the matter was negotiated further. After five weeks of negotiation, an agreement was reached that affected thirteen operating companies and approximately 8,000 men in Utah. Major points agreed upon included: recognition of the union as exclusive bargaining agent for a period of two years; a wage increase, to be retroactive to 1 June, although the amount was not divulged; provisions for vacations with pay; and grievance procedures designed to prevent strikes and lockouts.

The feature which attracted the most attention was the union demand for vacations with pay. Union officials claimed that if this was granted it would be the first contract in the country in the metal mining industry to carry such a provision. The contract that was agreed upon provided for one week's vacation with full pay for everyone who had been employed for one year or more. In October, due

Eureka residents helped to build the Salt Creek camp in 1933. (Dean Manson)

to the increase in the price of copper, miners in Utah were given a twenty-five cent per day raise.[8]

Despite such gains for miners, school registration in the Tintic School District showed a 5 percent decrease for the 1940–41 year, further evidence of the declining population. The high school had nineteen fewer pupils, Eureka public schools had twelve fewer, Mammoth one less, while Callao and the west end of the county stayed the same.[9]

Four more miles of the highway over Dog Valley from Nephi to Millard County were constructed in 1940–41. This road improvement had been a state and county project that had been underway for approximately seven years. The intention was to build an oiled road from Nephi to Lynndyl and Leamington in Millard County.[10]

During the 1930s, while the United States and much of the world was working its way through the Depression, war had erupted in Europe and the Far East. On 1 September 1939, after other strife in previous years, World War II began when Adolf Hitler's Nazi troops invaded Poland. War was declared on Germany by France and Great Britain. The United States initially tried to stay out of the conflict, although the government's sympathies and covert support were with Great Britain and its few remaining allies.

During the first half of 1940, President Roosevelt asked Congress for additional funds for defense. He called for the United States to produce 50,000 planes a year, and the War Department authorized aid for Great Britain in the form of out-of-date arms, munitions, ships, and planes.

On 16 September 1940, Congress passed the Selective Training and Service Act, making it mandatory for all men between the ages of twenty-one and thirty-five to register for one year of military training. Approximately 16.4 million men registered. Wednesday, 16 October, was designated as the first registration day. On that day, 290 men registered from Nephi, 287 from Eureka, 83 from Levan, 34 from Mona, 74 from Mammoth, and 29 from Callao—making a total of 797 Juab County men. The first young man from Juab County to volunteer for the army was Robert Gwen Hutchinson of Eureka. He and five others from Eureka—Ivan J. Warr, Clarence William Bant, Howard Rudolph Towers, Melvin Thomas Burke, and Benjamin F. Allinson—volunteered to serve for one year.[11]

Congress had authorized the mobilization of the National Guard in August 1940, and, on 7 February 1941, Governor Herbert Maw received a radiogram from Secretary of War Henry L. Stimson calling for the "induction into service of the United States, effective March 3, 1941, all federally recognized elements of the Fortieth Division of the National Guard of the United States, of the State of Utah and all personnel of both active and inactive National Guard assigned thereto."[12] Most of the affected companies were quartered in their own armories for training until they began to leave for San Luis Obispo, California. Battery E of the 145th Field Artillery was mobilized to leave on 26 March.

Mayor P.L. Jones of Nephi issued a proclamation to the effect

Jericho CCC camp, 1935. (Tintic Historical Society)

that 10 March be set aside to honor all the young men who had or would be drafted or would volunteer to leave for a year's training.

> NOW THEREFORE, it has been deemed advisable that insomuch as these boys have displayed a willingness to serve us in the protection of our inalienable rights that we do honor them in various ways.
>
> SO THEREFORE, be it proclaimed that Monday, March 10, be set aside in Nephi City for the purpose of paying tribute to the youth who will participate in the defense program, and we urge all the people of Nephi and East Juab county to participate in the events of the day."[13]

The "events of the day" began with a parade that included Battery E and its equipment, followed by the Juab High School band and other groups. Also represented were the American Legion, Veterans of Foreign Wars, Selective Service, and civic authorities from Nephi, Levan, and Mona, along with other patriotic citizens and organizations.

On 26 March the members of the 145th were escorted to the train by the high school band and a large group of Juab County citizens, many of them family members of the departing soldiers.[14] On 25 November 1941 the 2nd Battalion of the 145th received orders to embark for the Philippine Islands, the first of the Utah units to be assigned overseas duty. On 6 December 1941 they boarded the transport ship *U.S.S. Tasker H. Bliss,* but when the ship was approximately 400 miles out to sea they received word that war with Japan had been declared after the surprise Japanese attack on Pearl Harbor. They were ordered back to San Francisco. After the bombing of Pearl Harbor changes were made in assignments. It became necessary to implement the "Rainbow Plan," which would provide for the defense of the west coast of the United States.[15]

The 145th were soon sent to Honolulu, Hawaii. On 22 January 1944 they left Hawaii for the Marshal Islands. On 15 June 1944 they were among the forces that invaded the island of Saipan in the Marianas. After twenty-four days of fighting, Siapan was taken, as were the other islands of the chain.[16]

On 30 November, the unit left for the Philippine Islands, landing on 6 December 1944. It had been just three years since they left the United States for what they thought would be the Philippine Islands. On 1 April 1945, they were with the troops that invaded Okinawa and were there when the war with Japan ended on 14 August 1945. Throughout the conflict, these and other servicemen from the county performed heroic and valiant service, at least twenty-four making the ultimate sacrifice of giving their lives for their country and its ideals.[17]

The Home Front

Meanwhile, the people of Juab County kept occupied with the business of trying to keep conditions stable at home. The *Eureka Reporter* mentioned almost every week that the area was deteriorating economically, with such headlines as, " Eureka Main Street Buildings Prominent By Vacancy," and "Condition of Mining Industry Not Very Encouraging."[18] The amount of mineral shipped from the Tintic District declined in 1941 for the fifth consecutive year. The Mammoth Mine, which had been producing since 1871, closed in February, and the Blue Rock Mine shut down in April. The Tintic Standard Mine, along with some of its other holdings in East Tintic in Utah County, was doing well, however. In June it "opened a new ore body running high in lead and silver, being one of the most important discoveries in the property in recent years," it was claimed.[19]

Officers of the Jericho CCC camp, 1935.

The Jericho CCC Camp left the county in May and the Callao Camp in August 1941. The army draft and enlistments, along with other young men going into defense-related jobs, had greatly reduced the CCC enrollment, and the entire program soon was terminated nationally.[20]

Life continued on in Juab County. Nephi City decided to hold a Ninetieth Homecoming Anniversary with the Ute Stampede in 1941. One day of the Stampede was dedicated to the early settlers of Nephi and honored W.A.C. Bryan, the only surviving original settler. Bryan came to Nephi in 1851 and had recently celebrated his ninety-second birthday. Special invitations were printed and sold at both of the town's drug stores. They were in post card form, with a picture of Mount Nebo and a small message on the front. The reverse side carried an invitation, with enough room for a personal message. A new 1,000-seat grandstand was constructed at the fair grounds.[21]

All National Youth Administration projects in Juab County were closed in June 1941. Some of the projects completed in the previous years included construction of ski hills and skating rinks in Nephi, Levan, and Mona. In Levan, the youths had cut timber and made swings, teeter-totters, and sandboxes for the local park. In Mona, twenty-five bridges were made and placed over irrigation ditches along Main Street. The exhibit buildings and bleachers at the fair-grounds were repaired and painted. Also, numerous trees were planted.

On 14 November 1941, Levan town board members met with the Nephi City Council to discuss a problem that had developed. At that time and for some years previous, Nephi had been using Levan's line from Fountain Green to transmit energy, while Levan had been using Nephi's transformers at Fountain Green to get its electricity. Since Nephi had recently signed a contract with Telluride Power Company and would no longer be getting power from Fountain Green, it was necessary that some changes be made. After much discussion, they decided to hook Levan to the transformers at the new substation. Levan officials would then build two miles of new line to connect with the old line and abandon about sixteen miles of their old line to Fountain Green.[22]

In late 1941, Juab residents began to notice a change in the econ-omy as a result of the war. So many of the young men were serving in the armed forces that unemployment was no longer a problem; in fact, it was now somewhat difficult to find men to work. Nephi had planned to build a new bridge across an area of Main Street with help from WPA workers but had to postpone it because there was a short-age of labor and money.[23] With the declaration of war, tires and sugar soon were rationed and people were being urged to produce more food by planting gardens and raising more animals. The price of food crops was rising and the government was asking that growers pro-duce as much as possible to be canned for both domestic use and to aid allies.[24]

The Protective Division of the East Juab County Unit, Council of Defense, was taken over and supervised by the members of local Post No. 1 of the American Legion. The duties of the division included training men for police duty. This included about twenty men who would be available to assist the regular police in case of an emergency. There were also Departments of Fire, Debris Clearance and Demolition; Rescue, First Aid, and Evacuation; and Air Raid Precautions and Aircraft Observers—all to be trained and supervised by members of the American Legion.[25]

A later issue of the *Times News* called for more volunteers to be

One building housed the theater, recreation hall, and store at Mammoth. The complex was located next to the Mammoth LDS Church, 1935. (Utah State University)

trained as auxiliary firemen, rescue squads, auxiliary police, air raid wardens, fire watchers, for emergency food and housing assistance, public works repair, emergency medical service, nurse's aids, demolition and clearance crews, road-repair crews, gas decontamination squads, and Boy Scout messengers. "Let's get on the bandwagon, people of Nephi. Nephi is like the United States. . . . If it's worth living in, it's worth protecting and fighting for. We may have to fight for it, so lets learn how to protect it. . . . Now," proclaimed the paper.[26] Juab County's first war casualty, Clarence V. Brough, was killed on 28 January 1942, at Corpus Christi, Texas, when a plane he was piloting went into a spin and crashed.[27]

In 1942 Cecil Fitch, president and general manager of the Chief Consolidated Mining Company, announced plans to hire a large crew of men for work in installing pumps to drain and develop ore deep in the company's workings. He had received a telegram from a government committee in Washington, D.C., offering him premium price on all lead and zinc produced. The company had more than 100 mines with underground workings. Fitch exclaimed, "Eureka will boom again."[28]

The Defense Department had authorized $190 million for the creation of the Geneva Steel plant in Utah County in 1941. Approximately 10,000 men were employed in the construction, which was completed in February 1944.[29] Some 1,500 steel workers were then hired. A number of the men hired were from surrounding areas, including Juab County. Men from Juab County also worked during the construction of the plant, which provided a boost to the county's economy.

In September 1942 a committee representing several service clubs met with the Nephi City Council to discuss the possibility of the council underwriting the cost of a bus to transport workers from eastern Juab County to the Geneva Steel plant. There would be some thirty-five men riding the bus every day. The council voted to appropriate $400.00 to underwrite the bus operation, which would be operated by Rio Grande Motorway and would begin service on 1 October. By 1 November the service had not cost the city anything—it was paying for itself.[30]

Despite rationing, labor shortages, and other inconveniences caused by the war, morale in Juab County was high, as patriotism was extolled constantly and citizens united to defeat a common enemy and great threat. Everyone was trying to work together to accomplish what was expected of them, whether in military or other government service or to provide food and other needs of the country. They were also trying to build a base for the future, when those who were away working or serving in the military would return. A Million Dollar Club was organized locally with the goal to increase the net income of Juab County by $1 million a year within the next five years.[31]

Religious and social organization's participated vigorously in the war effort. Members of the local LDS Stake presidency—Will L. Hoyt, James H. Ockey, and Herman W. McCune—urged people not to just grow Victory Gardens for their own use, but to grow enough so they could contribute to the nation's food supply.[32] Members of the Kiwanis Club bought $6,068.75 worth of war bonds. The Nephi City Council purchased $1,000 in bonds, and the Juab County Commission agreed to urge their employees to purchase war savings bonds on a payroll deduction basis. The ladies clubs of the county helped to sell $4,311 worth of war bonds and savings stamps.[33]

Nephi's National Guard unit in 1929. (Pearl Wilson)

Extensive drives were conducted to collect used fat, rubber, and "junk" metal. The city provided trucks, and men and boys volunteered to collect these items. They were very successful.

In October 1943 Myrtle Davidson, assistant director for home economics at Utah State Agricultural College, sent the *Times News* a report on her recent visit to Callao, then a community of about fifty-four families.

> Much of the land in the Callao area is homestead property paid for with sweat, toil and effort in the early days of 1858 and '59. An old blacksmith shop still marks that spot where mail carriers used to stop for a change of horses in the days of the Pony Express. Such names as Carrigan, Thomas, Neff, Bennion, Tripp, Bagley and others belong to its early history.
>
> Most of the Callao families own their own farmsteads and all of them are out of debt. Their livestock consists of sheep and cattle, and of course, as a western frontier, they too had their quarrels to determine whether wool or hair should run the ranges, but all that has been quieted for many years. The most serious livestock hazard is the hungry coyote who sneaks into nearby fields to take his toll of young animals or poultry. . . .
>
> Some of the areas have too little water for very good gardens

while others grow fruit and most vegetables. All homes are surrounded with shade trees. Through exchanges with neighbors and
some importation every cellar is filled with home cured and
canned meat, home stored dried and canned vegetables and fruit,
home-made butter and cheese, and plenty of milk. Most of the
families make their own bread, a goodly portion being whole
wheat. Eggs and poultry meat are available the year around. No
need for ration stamps in Callao.[34]

The report seemed to confirm that rural Utahns actually enjoyed
some benefits denied their more urban counterparts during the
Depression and war years—that is, those with gardens and farm animals might have butter, milk, or more abundant food to eat.

Davidson's observations after her visit to Callao are worth further quotation, providing insight into the western part of the county
during the war period.

Do they know there is a war? Yes, indeed they do, the lack of
manpower is quite acute. The young girls occupy themselves by
participating in school operettas, inter-school debates, dramas, and
various church or civic activities during the winter. During the
summer they respond to the need for help by donning levis of
slacks to drive the mower and hay rake or haul the hay. Each has a
favorite riding horse and beautiful ones they are. The cattle must
be driven to the mountains or fields, and an occasional trip must
be made to check on the animals.

It is not too strenuous on those farms for one father told us
that he always took time out during the heat of the day for his
daughters to rest. "You see, we work for ourselves and can decide
together what days or hours we work, when we need a fishing trip,
or some of mother's ice cream under the trees," he said.[35]

In the early morning of 8 September 1943 the Juab High School
building was almost totally destroyed by fire. The fire apparently
began in the kitchen of the home economics department and spread
to the ceiling and attic. Payson, Spanish Fork, and Mt. Pleasant fire
crews were contacted for help and responded with remarkable speed.
The building, constructed in 1922, had been occupied by Nephi
Junior High School and Juab High School, which served Nephi,
Mona, Levan, and Mills. After the fire, the high school students occu-

The Nephi Processing Plant provided returning soldiers with work, 1940s.
(Fred Chapman)

pied the city equipment building, which had been purchased from
the Utah National Guard after the new armory building was constructed. Junior high students were placed in the Central School and
the "old shop building." In the new Mechanical Arts building, both
junior and senior high school pupils were given instruction in physical education, mechanical arts, farm mechanics, agriculture, and
music.[36]

Local events and business took place despite wartime concerns.
In January 1944, 5,500 "Food For Freedom" broiler chickens were
shipped from Nephi to San Francisco. The chickens were grown by
George Ostler, Edward and Clarence Wilkey, and the Check-R-Feed
Farms and brought 90 cents each to the growers.[37] George Bigler was
honored by the United States Gypsum Mill for his long service. Bigler
went to work in September 1894, when the company was known as
the Nephi Plaster Company. He supervised the rebuilding of the mill
in 1909.[38] William A.C. Bryan, at that time in his ninety-sixth year,
was honored in Salt Lake City on the eighty-third anniversary of the
linking of the transcontinental telegraph lines. On that day Bryan
tapped out a message originally sent from Brigham Young to
Abraham Lincoln at the time of the Civil War: "Utah has not seceded
but is firm for the Constitution and the laws of our once happy coun-

try, and is warmly interested in such successful enterprises as the one so far completed."[39]

Juab County reached its War Bonds Fund goal, due in part to the fact that Nephi Central School students purchased $2,307 worth of war bonds and stamps during a period of eight weeks. They had set a goal of $1,950, which was the purchase price of a field ambulance. They were then able to have a decal placed in an ambulance with the following inscription: "This marker is placed here in recognition of the purchase of War Bonds in the amount equal to the price of the equipment of this type by Nephi Central School, Nephi, Utah, U.S.A.—Type of Equipment—Field Ambulance."[40]

The War Labor Board unit of the county asked the Juab County Commission to cooperate with the War Food Administration of the United States to find agricultural workers to help relieve the present shortage. The commission agreed to act as employers for Mexican workers supplied by the agency under provisions of a treaty between the United States and Mexico. They contracted for ten workers on 1 April 1945 and ten workers on 1 June 1945.[41]

In June, as the war was winding down, the county treasurer was authorized to purchase $10,000 worth of war bonds from the road fund.[42] On 12, 13, and 14 July, Nephi held the Ute Stampede. It was advertised as "the best show in Utah this year," and "the west's wildest and roughest show." Some of the country's most famous rodeo performers had signed to participate. This was the first big event to be held in Nephi since 1941.[43]

In July, Mona Irrigation Company completed 1,415 feet of reinforced concrete canal to carry water from Bear Canyon across the gravel bench on the mountainside above Mona. It was figured that this would save enough water to irrigate twenty-four acres of land every day. The U.S. Soil Conservation District supplied technical assistance and equipment.[44]

On 14 August, President Harry S. Truman announced that the Japanese surrender had been accepted, ending the war. V-J Day was celebrated everywhere, including Juab County. The *Times News* stated that the people of Nephi began to gather to celebrate almost before the siren blew when the news was broadcast over the radio. The high

Parade in Eureka passes by the Miner's Union Hall, 1947. (Tintic Historical Society)

school band marched up Main Street and the cars lining the street blew their horns. Following a few numbers by the band, the Nebo Knights began to play for a street dance which lasted several hours. The *Times News* recounted that, "A bonfire was built in the street where a headless 'Tojo' was burned in effigy."[45] More than 900 young men and women from Juab County served their country in World War II, and twenty-four gave their lives.[46]

The war changed lives and economies in Juab. Earlier, in 1943, after a meeting of the newly organized Million Dollar Club, 7,000 baby turkeys were ordered by area farmers, and turkey raising became a growing industry in Nephi. In 1945 a group of men formed a corporation, the Nephi Processing Plant, to process turkeys for sale. The officers were Milton L. Harmon, president and general manager; Ned T. Ostler, vice-president; Earl H Steele, secretary-treasurer; and George Ostler and James P. McCune, directors.[47] The plant advertised for seventy-five workers on 11 October, and on 25 October they advertised for fifty more. During its first year the Nephi Processing Plant produced 1,500,000 pounds of turkey meat. This operation helped to add some economic stability to Juab both immediately after the war and in subsequent decades.

The Post-war Years

C.E. Rife died in 1942, and his wife subsequently was unable to manage the *Eureka Reporter* newspaper, which was eventually moved to Springville. Following Rife's death, Japanese-Americans who had been interned at Topaz in Millard County wanted to lease or buy the paper, but although the Japanese would have continued to print the *Reporter,* many people in Eureka opposed them. Therefore, in 1947 the townspeople talked to a printer named Conover in Springville about printing the paper, and he agreed to do so if they would sell enough subscriptions to make the print run feasible. Conover bought the rights to the paper from Mrs. Rife, and Rusty Rife went to work for him (continuing until 1972). Belle Coffee was the reporter for a time. Grace Bernini was longtime editor.

Nephi City had been considering the installation of a sewer system to cover the business district, school buildings, and a portion of the residential district since April 1941.[48] Finally, in 1947, it became a reality. When Thermoid Western Company came to Nephi it became necessary that some improvements be made in the water supply as well as the method of sewage disposal. As one historian of the town expressed it:

> The question of paying for the sewer system presented a problem to the City Council. As not everyone was attached to the sewer system, it would not have been fair to meet the debt through a general obligation bond, Mayor Jones said the Council met many hours each night for weeks and fincly worked out an ordinance in which all those who had sewer connections would pay for [them] with their sewer bill. If they did not pay for the sewer bill their water would be disconnected.[49]

A water and sewer bond election was held on 17 October and was approved by a large majority.[50]

Dedication of the Nephi Municipal Rose Garden occurred on 13 April 1947. It served as a memorial in honor of veterans and was placed just north of the armory building. The marker, sponsored by

1948 proved to be a monumental one for snow. This house on Railroad Street in Eureka proves the point. (Tintic Historical Society)

the ladies clubs and Nephi City, was established through contributions from the clubs, the city, and various individuals.[51]

With this symbolic end of wartime Juab, the county's cities and towns began to build for the future. Roads, hospitals, and improvements in other infrastructure would be an important part of post-World War II county life. The dream of a two-lane oiled highway between Leamington and Nephi finally became a reality. The contract was given to J.M. Sumsion of Springville, who bid $142,887. The grade of the road on Dog Valley Hill was also lowered by about thirty feet and the road was moved to the north in some areas. Both Juab and Millard Counties participated in the financing of the road.[52]

In 1944 Juab County commissioners began investigating the possibility of constructing a hospital in Nephi. Tentative plans included the LDS church contributing 20 percent of the cost, Nephi City 20 percent, Juab County 20 percent, and the Citizens Hospital Fund 10 percent by subscription. The commissioners favored the plan and agreed to pledge 20 percent of the total cost, up to $75,000, providing the others participated accordingly.[53] The *Times News* of 18 January 1945 stated, "Indications are reported to be favorable for the construction of a 20-bed hospital to cost between $50,000.00 and

$75,000.00. It is probable that construction will not begin until there is a relaxation of war-time building restrictions." The project was put on hold for a number of years.

In August 1949 an election was held to determine if Juab County would issue general obligation bonds in the amount of $60,000 towards the cost of acquiring, constructing, and equipping a county hospital. Election results were favarable for the construction of the facility: 288 against and 1,087 for.[54] Bids were accepted for the hospital construction on 25 August 1950. They included: general construction bt Talboe and Wooton for $118,780; Millard Electric and Appliance for $17,726; Brown Plumbing and Heating for $89,000. Members of the first hospital Board were George D. Haymond, Nephi, John H. Harmon, Nephi, Ida P. Belliston, Nephi, Alberta B. Jones, Nephi, J.H. Andrews, Nephi, W. Arnon Garfield, Mona, and H.R. Francom, Levan.[55] The Juab County Hospital soon was built and began operations.

In 1947, on the occasion of the centennial celebration of the arrival of Mormon pioneers to Utah, the Daughters of Utah Pioneers (DUP) published Alice Paxman McCune's *History of Juab County*. This history, part of a statewide effort by the DUP, stood for many years as the only extended treatment of Juab County's past. Such works attest to the observation that to better understand the present, one must have a sense of the past—something the present work also hopes to provide.

Nephi City officials wanted to better coordinate community development. On 14 January 1948 the mayor and city council presented an ordinance that would provide for a city manager, who would be responsible for utilities in the city and would recommend and advise the city council on matters of civic improvement. The manager could attend council meetings and voice his opinion, but did not have a vote, and could also discharge city employees if they were considered to be incompetent. The city council was authorized to discharge the city manager if the mayor and council considered it advisable. Daniel Davis served in an unofficial capacity as city manager for a short time. In 1948 George Matkin, a native of Idaho and graduate from Utah State University, became the Nephi City Manager.[56]

The Pioneer Centennial in 1947 provided an occasion for many celebrations. Here Irene Mangelson reigns as queen in the Nephi Centennial Ball.

Fifteen students began the 1949 school year; before it ended there were twenty-nine. Both the Partoun church building and the new schoolhouse had to be used for classes during the 1950–51 school year.[77] At the school board meeting on 26 October 1949, a letter was read from Mrs. Olive Kunz, the secretary of the newly organized parent-teachers association in Partoun. A report stated that,

> Mrs. Kunz requested a high school for the nine students . . . , hot lunches for the elementary school, better seating facilities in the Partoun school. . . . Superintendent Blight read his answer, in which he stated that new seats had been ordered for both schools, but that a high school in that region at the present time was an utter impossibility, and that he was working on a plan to serve hot lunches. The people in Partoun sent a petition to the Tintic School Board in 1950 requesting a high school in Partoun. It took thirty years for it to finally happen, but in 1980 it became a reality.[78]

There were nine families living in Partoun in 1998.

Mining and Other Developments. The year's output from the mines of Tintic District for 1949 amounted to 6,797 carloads of ore.

Alexander Blight, of Eureka, taught school and became the superintendent of the Tintic District schools. Photograph taken in 1947. (Tintic Historical Society)

Chief Consolidated properties shipped 2,096 loads, which was over 30 percent of the total output. The Tintic Standard company, which included the Eureka Standard and Iron Blossom Mines in Utah County but still in the Tintic District, shipped 1,887 loads. The next largest shipper was the North Lily Mine, with 1,075 carloads.[79]

A reserve of some 500,000 tons of halloysite, a hydrous aluminum silicate clay used as a catalytic agent in oil refining, was discovered in Dragon Consolidated Mining Company property south of Eureka. An estimated 200,000 tons were blocked out in 1949. An average of 450 tons of clay were being shipped weekly to Filtrol Corporation in Los Angeles. The Illinois Clay Company milled and sold halloysite to the Ford Motor Company of Canada for use in cast-

Dr. Steele Bailey operated a medical practice in the Tintic District for many years. (Tintic Historical Society)

ing molds. The Dragon Consolidated Company, which had been incorporated by a Provo group including members of the Knight family, was now controlled by the North Lily Mining Company, a part of the International Smelting and Refining Company, a subsidiary of Anaconda Copper Company.[80]

In 1936 brothers Chad and Ray Spor had discovered fluorspar on the west flank of Topaz Mountain. They had heard rumors that there was tungston in the area and were looking for it but instead found fluorspar and travertine. Between 1936 and 1944 the brothers staked claims in the area and worked them periodically. In 1944 their father, George C. Spor, their mother, and their brothers and sisters raised a few hundred dollars and moved to the claim, living in tents and a trailer before building a comfortable cabin. The area has since been known as Spor Mountain. The men in the family took turns operating their garage in Delta and working the claims. By March 1949 the mine had become inactive, but the family was actively developing the ground adjacent to the mine.[81]

In May 1947 Earl Willden, Tass Claridge, and another man, while looking for a quartz outcrop Willden and his older brother had found fifteen years earlier, stumbled onto a promising fissure on the east side of Spor Mountain. They staked a claim that day and later staked ten more. This claim later was sold to Ward Leasing Company of Salt Lake City. The Willdens continued their prospecting and in May 1948 found a rich fluorspar deposit they called the Lost Sheep Mine.[82]

In the spring of 1948 Dock Black and Scott Chesley began searching the area between the Spors' mine and the Ward Leasing Company operation. They uncovered four substantial ore bodies and put them into production. They bulldozed a road more than a mile up the steep mountainside to get to their claims. By 1949 they had shipped forty-five railroad cars of ore. Geneva Steel was an important consumer of fluorspar.[83]

In 1949 the Hermansen family of Spanish Fork bought all of the stock of the Juab Mill and Elevator Company. It was later purchased by a California company and called the Nephi Milling Company; however, in June 1991 it was destroyed by fire.

At mid-century, with 5,981 inhabitants counted by the 1950 census, a substantial drop from the 7,392 counted in 1940, Juab County was in a mild state of decline, but residents shared the post-war optimism of most Americans that the brighter economic times they had begun to enjoy were going to continue. In the case of Juab County, however, such hopes seemed still tied to the mining industry, which would continue to suffer locally in the coming years.

ENDNOTES

1. *Times News,* 13 June 1940.

2. Juab County Commission Minutes, 31 May 1940, Book 7, 223.

3. *Times News,* 13 June 1940.

4. *Eureka Reporter,* 11 January, 28 March 1940.

5. *Eureka Reporter,* 22 February 1940.

6. *Times News,* 18 April, 27 June 1940.

7. *Eureka Reporter,* 18, 24 July 1940.

8. *Eureka Reporter,* 4, 11 July, 10 October 1940.

9. *Eureka Reporter,* 5 September 1940.

10. *Times News,* 19 December 1940.

11. *Times News,* 10, 17 October, 14 November 1940.

12. Richard C. Roberts, "History of the Utah National Guard," 302.

13. *Times News,* 6 March 1941.

14. According to the *Times News,* 6 March 1941, there was one young man from Mona, one from Eureka, one from Manti, one from Fairview, and one from Idaho in the group. The remaining thirty-eight were from Nephi.

15. Roberts, "Utah National Guard," 314.

16. Ibid., 392, 394.

17. Ibid., 394. See Alice P. McCune, *History of Juab County,* 278, for a list of those killed in the war.

18. *Eureka Reporter,* 24 April, 7 August 1941.

19. *Eureka Reporter,* 2 January, 20 February, 24 April, 6 June 1941.

20. *Eureka Reporter,* 8 May, 14 August 1941.

21. *Times News,* 12, 19 June 1941.

22. Nephi City Council Minutes, 4 November 1941.

23. Nephi City Council Minutes, 17 July 1941, Book 6, 18.

24. *Times News,* 26 February 1942.

25. *Times News,* 22 January 1942.

26. *Times News,* 23 April 1942.

27. *Times News,* 5 February 1942.

28. *Times News,* 11 June 1942.

29. Richard D. Poll et al., *Utah's History,* 501–2.

30. Nephi City Council Minutes, 24 September 1942, Book 8, 62; 5 November 1942, Book 8, 65. See also *Times News,* 24 September 1942.

31. *Times News,* 4 March 1943.

32. *Times News,* 18 March 1943.

33. Juab County Commission Minutes, 3 May 1943, Book 7, 336; Nephi City Council Minutes, 6 August 1943, Book 8, 81; *Times News,* 22 April, 29 July 1943.

34. *Times News,* 7 October 1943.

35. Ibid.

36. *Times News,* 9 September 1943.

37. *Times News,* 6 January 1944.

38. *Times News,* 28 September 1944.

39. *Times News,* 26 October 1944.

40. *Times News,* 14 December 1944.

41. Juab County Commission Minutes, 6 March 1945, Book 7, 383.

42. Ibid., 387.

43. *Times News,* 12 July 1945.

44. *Times News,* 2 August 1945.

45. *Times News,* 16 August 1945.

46. McCune, *Juab County,* 279–91.

47. Keith Worthington, et al., *They Left a Record,* 96; *Times News,* 4 March 1945.

48. Nephi City Council Minutes, 17 April 1941, Book 6, 9.

49. Worthington, et al., *They Left a Record,* 100–1.

50. *Times News,* 23 October 1947.

51. *Times News,* 10 April 1947.

52. *Times News,* 5 June, 31 July, 14 August 1947.

53. Juab County Commission Minutes, 9 October 1944, Book 7, 371.

54. Ibid., 8 August 1949, Book 7, 455.

55. Ibid., 25 August 1950, 475, 23 March 1951, 520.

56. Worthington, et al., *They Left a Record,* 101.

57. Nephi City Council Minutes, 11 January 1934, Book 5, 198, 202.

58. Ibid., 1 December 1938, 166; Worthington, et al., *They Left a Record,* 99.

59. Nephi City County Minutes, 23 December 1943, 94; 14 February 1944, 103.

60. Worthington, et al., *They Left a Record,* 100.

61. Ibid.

62. *Times News,* 15 April 1948.

63. Ibid.

64. *Eureka Reporter,* 30 January 1948.

65. *Eureka Reporter,* 28 May 1948.

66. *Eureka Reporter,* 18 June 1948.

67. *Eureka Reporter,* 25 June, 4 August 1948, 25 February 1949.

68. *Eureka Reporter,* 5 November 1948.

69. *Eureka Reporter,* 3 December 1948.

70. *Eureka Reporter,* 28 January 1949.

71. *Eureka Reporter,* 4, 14 February 1949.

72. *Eureka Reporter,* 19 August 1949.

73. Marlene Bates, "North Snake Valley," 86.

74. *Salt Lake Tribune,* 8 May 1949.

75. *Eureka Reporter,* 9 September 1949.

76. Ibid.

77. Bates, *North Snake Valley,* 232.

78. Ibid., 233.

79. *Eureka Reporter,* 30 December 1949.

80. Ibid.

81. Cecil A. Fitch, Jr., James Quigley, and Clarence Barker, "Utah's New Mining District," *Engineering and Mining Journal* (March 1949): 64–65.

82. Ibid., 64–66.

83. Ibid.

CHAPTER 10

CONTEMPORARY
JUAB COUNTY

After World War II Juab County faced the continued ups and downs of previous decades, although there were changes in economic conditions that agriculture and mining had to respond to. The towns of Juab sought new industries and ways in which families could make a living. In many ways, county social life mirrored that of the rest of the country, as technological innovations such as television and increased automobile use changed American society. The last half of the twentieth century witnessed changes in practically all sectors of life. Highway construction, with increased traffic of tourists, although interstate freeways now carry traffic around Nephi, has changed county business activities, prompting some to look back to gentler, less hectic times in the county's history. In the 1980s and 1990s, mining resources in the county generally became uneconomical to pursue. Agriculture remains an important component of the economy; but, as is the case in many other Utah counties, tourism is viewed as an industry of the present and a hope for the future.

Billboard making a pitch for East Juab County; located just outside of Levan, 1997. (Wayne Christiansen)

Juab County Industry

Discharged soldiers returning to Juab County following World War II found their job options limited, although some had places waiting on the family farm. Employment in the Tintic mines was on the decline. The once-prosperous local gypsum industry was on its last legs. In January 1946, Juab County recorded only 280 jobs in mining and fifty-six in manufacturing.[1]

In the fall of 1945, local prospects had got a little brighter with the opening of the Nephi Processing Plant, a logical extension of the developing local turkey industry. Shortly after the opening of the plant, the *Times News* stated, "The Processing plant is an industry which has been needed for some time past, not exactly as a part of the turkey industry, but as an industry that will give a payroll for Nephi's women and children who in the past have had practically nothing from such a source." The article continued in a hopeful tone, "The industry, from the time the turkey is hatched, until the final processing can be one of the biggest businesses the East Juab valley has ever known."[2]

In 1946 the plant processed about 2.5 million pounds of turkey and employed an average of 116 people. After an expansion in 1953, annual production reached about 6 million pounds of turkey and the

New industries brought some life to Nephi, including this rubber plant located just north in the city, 1997. (Wayne Christiansen)

payroll reached a peak of about 135 people. However, as the earlier *Times News* article suggested, jobs at the processing plant generally were not by themselves enough to sustain a family. In 1946, for example, the plant was in operation only sixty-six days.[3]

The 1947 announcement that the Juab Valley Feed Company would build a mill to process feed for livestock also brought the promise of a few jobs for Juab County residents. In 1956 the Utah Poultry & Farmers Cooperative bought the mill and built an addition.[4] However, both of these industries were linked to the ups and downs of the agricultural economy. The county needed something that would provide some balance to the economy and offer steady year-round employment.

News that a manufacturer of rubber products, the Thermoid Western Company of Trenton, New Jersey, had chosen Nephi as the site of its new plant was greeted—by some residents, at least—as the answer to the area's economic doldrums. In March 1947 the *Times News* published this open letter to Fred E. Schluter, president of Thermoid Company, from "the people of Nephi."

Nephi's new Juab County Jail illustrates the growth in the county, 1997. (Wayne Christiansen)

Greetings, and hearty welcome, Mr. Schluter, on your first visit to Nephi since beginning of construction of Thermoid Western Company's plant here. May your visit to Nephi be such that you will have a sincere desire to return on many, many occasions.

We may be, as a body, delinquent in expressing our appreciation for your company's decision to locate here. We feel that this is one of the most fortunate things that could happen to our community—to give it a balanced economy, to give much needed employment to our youth in order that they may remain here to seek their livlihood, [sic] and rear their families.

In forecasting the future, it is obvious that our community will be changed from an overbalanced agricultural area, to one of a balanced economy, with a prosperous growth. Prosperous growth means better living conditions which reflects into all walks of life.

That's only a little of what your company is going to do for Nephi, Mr. Schluter, and here's our pledge: We shall do all within our power to make your business operations here materialize beyond your greatest expectations. We pledge our cooperation to the fullest degree your business here will be sound and profitable, and to vindicate great wisdom in your decision to locate "in the valley of the mountains."[5]

By some measures, Thermoid's choice of Nephi for its new plant made little sense. There was no nearby source of raw materials and no large nearby market for the company's products, so freight rates would be higher. Nevertheless, Thermoid officials said they were drawn to the area by the "quantity and quality of Utah workers." Schluter later told a group of business leaders that he had been persuaded to locate in Utah by David O. McKay, president of the Church of Jesus Christ of Latter-day Saints, and Gus P. Backman, executive secretary of the Salt Lake City Chamber of Commerce. "They convinced us that we should invest in the fine character of Utah citizens," Schluter said.[6]

Construction of the Thermoid Western plant began late in 1946, and, by the end of 1947, the plant had produced its first shipment of transmission and conveyor belting. In the following months, the plant also began producing automobile fan belts, various types of industrial hose, and other molded rubber products. About 3,000 people attended the dedication of the plant in June 1948.[7]

By 1953 the Thermoid plant was employing about 300 people— about one-third of the total labor force of eastern Juab County—with an annual payroll of more than $1 million. In April 1953 the *Utah Economic and Business Review* published a study of the plant and its impact on the community that said in part:

> To the people of Nephi and the surrounding area, Thermoid Western Company means employment opportunity, the maintenance of purchasing power, and a progressive equilibrium in a predominantly agricultural community. To Thermoid Western Company, Nephi and its people mean a pleasant, cooperative community, and a reliable, stable, enthusiastic labor force.
>
> The new industries have contributed directly and indirectly to numerous civic improvements. The Nephi city fathers, service clubs and groups have developed civic improvements far beyond that found in most communities of similar size. A new culinary water supply has been established, involving 22,000 feet of main pipeline and 32,000 feet of distribution lines. There are a new 12-mile sewer system and a complete sewage treatment plant (one of

The architectural heritage in Nephi became the subject of a 1970s historic preservation study. (Wayne Christiansen)

the few in the state) and a new Main Street lighting system. More than seven miles of streets have been hard surfaced. The City's electric utility has been expanded and a new county hospital has been constructed.

Thermoid's specific affects [*sic*] on other business in Nephi have not been measured. Certainly, however, service and trade industries have benefitted substantially. Based on employment ratios in Utah, the 300 workers in the Nephi Thermoid plant may directly and indirectly create employment for 450 additional workers in complementary services and trades in Nephi and surrounding communities in the state.[8]

"In the five years since Thermoid located its rubber products plant in Nephi it has established itself firmly as a good citizen of Nephi and Utah," the *Salt Lake Tribune* wrote in a 1953 editorial. "It has brought increased population and prosperity to Nephi, which is today one of the most progressive small cities in the state."[9]

Thermoid's importance in the local economy became evident during a strike at the plant in the early 1950s. Harlow Pexton, who

The City of Mona welcomed visitors in 1997. (Wayne Christiansen)

operated a wholesale grocery business, reported that his sales in Nephi dropped 50 percent during the strike.[10] Despite the enthusiasm expressed both by Thermoid officials and area publications, the relationship between the plant and its employees was not always cozy.

On 16 January 1951, 240 members of Local 1663 of the International Association of Machinists walked off the job after the union and the company could not reach an agreement on a new contract. Three days later, a lump of coal crashed through the front window of the home of William Peterson, superintendent of the strike-bound plant, hitting his nine-year-old daughter playing on the living room floor. In February, the general manager of a trucking company that had been crossing picket lines to make deliveries at the plant charged that one of his drivers had been threatened by certain Juab County residents. "The driver was forcibly taken from the truck," the general manager said in a complaint to Utah Attorney General Clinton D. Vernon. "However, he was allowed to return to the truck and continue on, being followed by these residents. Later the pursuers fired several shots at or into the truck in almost a direct line with the driver."[11]

In March Utah Governor J. Bracken Lee called for a state investi-

Monument identifies this structure as a "historic pioneer cabin" in Mona, 1997. (Wayne Christiansen)

gation of alleged criminal incidents related to the strike. The strike lasted until a wage settlement was reached in late March. The union threatened a work stoppage in December 1955, charging that workers at the Nephi plant were paid 30 percent less than other employees in the industry. There was a brief wildcat walkout in March 1957. A strike in 1959 lasted about four months.[12]

Despite these problems, the plant, under a series of owners, remained a critical part of the local economy. In December 1958 it was acquired by the H.K. Porter Company of Delaware. In 1964 Porter built a new wing on the plant, bringing the potential of up to sixty more jobs to Nephi. Two years later, Porter announced a second expansion.[13] In March 1970 Gates Rubber Company of Denver bought the Nephi plant. However, in 1971 the Federal Trade Commission ordered Gates to sell the Nephi plant, charging that the Denver company's ownership of the plant was stifling competition in the markets for automotive belts and hoses. In 1973 Gates sold the plant to a private corporation known as NRP Incorporated. In 1974 NRP Incorporated was acquired by Omnitec Corporation of Phoenix, Arizona. The new owners phased out fan-belt production at the plant and focused on the manufacture of industrial hose for specialized markets such as oil exploration and drilling.[14]

In the late 1970s, labor troubles returned to the plant, whose workers by then were being represented by the United Rubber Workers union. In August 1975 the union local called a strike following a failure to reach a new contract agreement with plant management. According to a *Times News* article,

It doesn't take much of a mathematician to divide the annual payroll paid by NRP, Inc.'s Nephi plant into 52 pieces and to see that the strike, now some five weeks old, is costing the Nephi, Levan, Mona and Fountain Green area thousands upon thousands of dollars each week in lost payroll. NRP's annual payroll is said to be about $2.7 million, and this hurridly breaks down to $51,230 weekly. . . . But the loss to the individuals and to their families is not all. The dollar the worker earns goes to help support the families of grocery store employees, of service station operators, and employees of the hardware and clothing store, as well as countless other stores and enterprises in town—all of whom provide needed services.[15]

The dispute was settled after six weeks; however, there was a short wildcat strike in June 1977 and another six-week strike in 1978.[16] Such labor disputes could cause divisive feelings in the communities, the agrarian residents not being traditionally too sympathetic to the workers, especially when the economic ripple effects of the strikes began to be felt in other areas of the economy and society. Supporters of the laborers countered that their well-being was essential to the county's economy in the long run.

NRP continued to be a vibrant part of the local economy through the 1970s. However, by 1982 there were signs of trouble. The national economy was floundering, with high unemployment and soaring interest rates. At the same time, oil prices were starting to drop, prompting oil companies to trim their exploration and drilling budgets. Less drilling meant fewer orders for the company's hose products. By June 1982, through a series of layoffs, NRP had cut its work force from 250 to 140 people. The United Rubber Workers union agreed to postpone scheduled raises in 1982 and 1983, but this wasn't enough to prevent the company from closing its doors for four months in 1982. That November,

New Mona LDS Church, 1997. (Wayne Christiansen)

Juab County had the highest unemployment rate in Utah—21.2 percent.[17]

By April 1983, when NRP was sold to Bastian Industries of Grand Haven, Michigan, the plant's work force was down to eighty people, who worked only when there was demand for their product. In August 1984 the plant closed its doors amid rumors of serious financial problems. "Several workers at the plant say there are no raw materials at the plant from which to make products, and that the company cannot secure credit to get the raw materials," the *Times News* reported on 30 August.

The closing of the plant came about a month after traffic moved onto a newly completed stretch of Interstate 15, routing travelers around Nephi's business district. In July 1985 a story in the *Salt Lake Tribune* described the bleak picture in Nephi:

> The double blow to commerce and employment has plunged the Juab County seat's economy into a depression that some citizens say only revival of the plant could lift. Downtown stores, their shelves no longer replenished by new deliveries, now go for hours without shoppers. Window after window stares darkly at cars, which hurry along Main Street, rarely stopping. It can be dif-

Interstate 15 runs just east of Mona, 1997. (Wayne Christiansen)

ficult to distinguish businesses still open from those that have given up.

"When NRP started going under, you could see its effects here in the store that some minute," said JoAnn Tolley, cashier in Tolley's variety store. "People don't buy many things when they don't know where their next dime is coming from." . . .

Despite the loss of jobs, few people have left Nephi in search of work, according to realtor David Blood. In fact, he said more people want to move into the city than move out. Blood said he has not heard of even one former NRP employee leaving town.

"The former employees are convinced the plant can be operated more efficiently than before and at a profit," said [city administrator Randy] McKnight.

The city and county are concentrating on getting the plant reopened. Two rubber hose manufacturers are considering a joint purchase of the plant, and McKnight said a group of former NRP employees also is looking into financing for a buyout.[18]

In October 1985 a bankruptcy court approved the sale to a partnership of Jones Enterprises of LaPorte, Indiana, and the Cypher Company of Pittsburgh, Pennsylvania. They formed a new company, Nephi Rubber Products, Incorporated. The sale came over the objec-

Levan's welcome sign indicates community values, 1997. (Wayne Christiansen)

tions of the group of former NRP employees who were also interested in buying the plant; however, because they failed to file written objections before a specific deadline, the court accepted the Jones and Cypher bid.

An issue in the negotiations was a $700,000 federal grant awarded to the city of Nephi by the U.S. Department of Health and Human Services to help restore operations at the plant. Since federal rules would not allow the city to give the money directly to the new owners, the city used the money to buy stock in Nephi Rubber Products. The plant reopened in December 1985 with fifty-three employees. By May 1986 the payroll was up to seventy-eight people.[19]

Nephi Rubber Products was a notable success story in providing non-agricultural jobs to the residents of east Juab County. However, it only took a prolonged strike or layoff to remind people of the risks of relying too heavily on one employer. In an attempt to lure other industries to the area, in 1956 the Nephi Chamber of Commerce had published a brochure entitled "Industrial Opportunities" that highlighted some of the area's attractions to businesses. An article in the *Times News* said in part,

Consisting of text, maps, photographs, and charts, the brochure tells the story of "good reasons for expanding in Nephi" pointing out that for coastal and intermountain markets, Nephi has a central location.

The 25-page brochure lists the facts that the Nephi area has a location near the center of Utah, with good economic opportunity for an industry desiring to serve the western eleven states. Always important to industry, the transportation facilities serving this area include good rail, highway and airport facilities. The brochure also points out that the area is served with low cost electrical and coal facilities, and the necessary water resources are available. Almost unlimited industrial sites are available in the Nephi area, the brochure states, adjacent to transportation and utilities.[20]

In 1961, when Rancho Trailer Manufacturing Company, a manufacturer of mobile homes and camping trailers, started looking at Nephi as a possible site for a new plant, the Nephi Chamber of Commerce launched a campaign to buy the land for the facility. "Response from the residents of Nephi, Mona and Levan 'has been very gratifying,' according to Chamber of Commerce officials, and solicitors were starting Wednesday to make personal contacts to raise the balance of the money needed," the *Times News* reported. The company was induced to come to the area, and the first locally produced trailer was completed in January 1962. By the early 1970s Rancho was employing between 30 and 180 people, depending on the season, and adding about $750,000 a year in its payroll wages to the local economy.[21]

In 1964 a manufacturer of men's and boys' sportswear, Pacific Trail Sportswear Company, announced plans to establish a sewing plant in Nephi. The plant, later acquired by Catalina Sportswear, provided jobs for as many as 180 people, making it one of the county's largest employers at the time.[22]

In spite of a few success stories, however, the economy of Juab County struggled in the late 1950s and early 1960s. The county's unemployment rate was consistently higher than that of the state as a whole. In 1959, for example, 12.4 percent of Juab County's work force was unemployed, compared to 4.3 percent for the state. In 1962, even

Brick home illustrating the early architecture of Levan, 1997. (Wayne Christiansen)

with the help of the Rancho payroll, 11.9 percent of county workers did not have jobs, compared to 4.6 percent of those statewide.[23]

Distressing as those numbers were, they did have a silver lining: they helped the county qualify for funding under a new federal program created by the Area Redevelopment Act (ARA) of 1961. Signed into law by President John F. Kennedy, the program offered low-interest loans to businesses in depressed areas. "Because of the continued high rate of unemployment in some areas of Juab County, together with a low farm income rate, Juab County has been designated as a 'redevelopment area' eligible to participate in the program," the *Times News* told its readers on 22 February 1962.

A newly created group, the Juab County Economic Development Corporation, applied for ARA funds to rehabilitate the twenty-seven-year-old Nephi Processing Plant. The group proposed that more than $402,000 be spent on the project, of which $251,000 would come in the form of an ARA loan, another $89,000 in loans from First Security Bank, and the remainder from local individuals. In the fall of 1962 the group received word that its ARA application had been approved. According to Utah Senator Frank E. Moss, ARA loans ulti-

Old barn remains one of few buildings in Mills, 1997. (Wayne Christiansen)

mately helped create about 537 new jobs in Utah, including 113 at the Nephi turkey-processing plant. "Crews have been kept busy since last season in order to get renovation work completed before starting another year's run of birds at the plant," Moss said in August 1964. "Turkey processing started at the end of June and all indications point to the longest season of operations ever experienced at the Nephi plant."[24]

In 1968, Juab and five other counties in central Utah—Millard, Sanpete, Sevier, Piute, and Wayne—joined forces to form the Six County Economic Development Committee. By pooling their resources, the counties hoped they could be more successful in attracting new development to the area. The main office of the new organization was to be in Nephi.[25]

One of the means used to attract new industries that was particularly popular in the 1970s was the creation of industrial parks. This typically involved the purchase of a large tract of land, often with the participation of local government, in an area with convenient access to utilities and transportation routes. This land would then be divided into smaller parcels and offered at favorable rates to companies interested in building facilities there. In 1975, Juab County, the

Hay derrick and corral in Mills, 1997. (Wayne Christiansen)

city of Nephi, and a private business-promotion group, Nephi Enterprises, Inc., agreed to buy acreage north of the Vine Bluff Cemetery from Alice F. Bailey. When this area later proved unsuitable for large industrial buildings, it was subdivided into residential lots and the proceeds from the sale of the lots were used to buy a new industrial park site north of Nephi Rubber Products. In August 1977, five acres in the new Nephi Industrial Park were deeded to the first tenant, Utah Candy Makers, Incorporated. In November, Utah Senator E.J. "Jake" Garn and Utah Governor Scott Matheson were on hand for the official groundbreaking at the new industrial park. Although Congressman Dan Marriott could not attend, a representative read from a prepared statement: "In the finest traditions of pioneering, we're here to break ground. This park has the potential of a thousand jobs in the next few years."[26] In spite of the early optimism, however, few businesses followed the lead of Utah Candy Makers. Eight years later, the park was still largely unoccupied.

"Industries not interested in coming to Nephi, council told," said a front-page headline in the the *Times News* on 27 June 1985. The speaker was Mark Fuhriman, director of the Juab Community Development Office, another agency created to bring new businesses

to the area. According to the the *Times News,* Fuhriman said he had
tried to induce many firms to locate to Nephi, but without success,
"because the community does not have sufficient labor reserves. . . .
The area also lacks the 'amenities' companies are looking for, such as
universities, job training, and cultural activities, Fuhriman said. . . .
For many companies, Fuhriman says, it does not makes sense to
locate in Nephi because raw materials must come from the larger
areas of the state, principally Salt Lake City, and finished materials
have to be shipped back to the larger areas." What the area needed,
Fuhriman claimed, was an industrial park in the northern part of the
county where it could attract workers from Utah County.

Members of the Nephi City Council were understandably cool to
the idea. However, in September the Juab County Commission
approved a zoning change that would allow an industrial park to be
built in the northern part of the county. As Fuhriman had noted,
businesses remained reluctant to relocate in Juab County. To make
matters worse, the construction of Interstate 15 bypassing Nephi had
siphoned away much of the tourism revenue that had supported
motels, gas stations, and restaurants. "Today, several gas stations
along Nephi's main thoroughfare are boarded up and surrounded by
weeds," the *Salt Lake Tribune* reported on 27 July 1985. "Nearly
vacant parking lots surround the motels and restaurants. 'Business is
slow; it's always slow,' said one restaurant cashier."

In the mid-1980s, Juab County still consistently had one of the
highest unemployment rates among all Utah counties. In the first
quarter of 1985, it reached a staggering 24.7 percent. In October 1985
the county received some more bad news: Catalina Sportswear
planned to close its Nephi sewing plant, which at that time had sixty
workers on its payroll. The company blamed foreign competition for
the shutdown.[27]

In 1986 the county unveiled a new economic program with a
new name and a new director. Glenn W. Greenhalgh was chosen as
director of the new Community Economic Development Agency.
Greenhalgh said he had no plans to pursue the plans of his prede-
cessor, Mark Fuhriman, to build an industrial park in the north end
of the county. "He said that as far as Nephi City is concerned, the
development agency needs to concentrate its efforts on filling the

Farm house in Mills, 1997. (Wayne Christiansen)

existing industrial park," the *Times News* reported on 16 January 1986.

Greenhalgh had his work cut out for him. Almost a decade after the grand opening of the Nephi Industrial Park, only two buildings had been constructed, including one that housed a workshop for the disabled. Local officials were understandably delighted in November 1989 when Greenhalgh landed his first catch: Mid-State Consultants Incorporated, a firm with sixty employees specializing in communications engineering.

"When I first heard Mid-State was considering building in Nephi, I felt we had to go after them with all we had to get them here," former mayor Boyd Park said at the groundbreaking for company facilities in February 1990. "All we've had in our industrial park is a weed patch and it's hard to sell weeds. This is a beginning." The company's 12,000-square-foot building was dedicated in September 1990. By 1995 Mid-States Consultants had an annual payroll of about

Rocky Ridge community lies in Juab County, just south of the Utah County line, 1999. (Tintic Historical Society)

$3.5 million and was planning a 6,600-square-foot addition to its building.[28]

By the mid-1990s, Nephi's "weed patch" was attracting attention from several other companies. In 1995 Sunset Rail, a steel fabrication company, announced plans to spend $1.2 million to move its plant from Lehi to Nephi. In 1996 Horizon Metals, a company manufacturing ferrous and non-ferrous castings, said it was moving its foundry, machine shop, and other operations from Salt Lake City to the Nephi Industrial Park. The economic development agency produced a ten-minute video, "America's Best Kept Secret," extolling the area's virtues, which was shown at trade shows around the country. It contained testimonials from several of the state's best-known citizens, including Governor Michael Leavitt and Senator Orrin Hatch.[29]

Echoing the prosperity of the state as a whole, the economy of Juab County made a dramatic recovery in the 1990s. By 1997 Juab's unemployment rate had dropped to 4.1 percent, and state economists were predicting that the number of jobs in the county would increase by 65 percent in the following twenty years.[30] Among other industries that are helping to support the county economy is the Ash Grove cement plant. Built in the early 1980s near the Millard County line,

The Callao welcome sign stands in direct contrast to those in East Juab County,1997. (Wayne Christiansen)

the plant employs about 100 people, about half of whom come from the Nephi area.

As Juab County prepares to enter the twenty-first century, its economy looks very different from that of fifty years ago, when virtually all jobs came from three industries—farming, mining, and the manufacture of rubber products. Although the economy will undoubtedly continue to go through periods of prosperity and poverty, the county at present seems much better equipped to handle those swings than it once did.

Public Health and Safety

As mentioned briefly in the preceding chapter, a fund-raising campaign by the Nephi Hospital Association fell short after World War II, and the Juab County Commission called for a bond election. The measure passed in September 1949 by a margin of 799 to 254. In August 1950 the Juab County Commission awarded contracts to three area companies for the construction of a modern fourteen-bed hospital on Fourth East Street in Nephi. "The building of a hospital here will be the realization of a dream of many years standing, and will be the climax of a campaign started several years ago by civic groups," the *Times News* reported. Additional funding for the project came from the state and federal governments.[31]

Excavation for the new building began in September 1950 and the $298,000 hospital accepted its first patients in March 1952. In 1953, its first full year of operation, the hospital treated more than 800 patients. A total of 154 babies were born there during the year. In addition to residents of Juab County, patients also came from surrounding counties.[32] During its first four years, the hospital's average occupancy was 9.7 patients per day. However, by 1959 this figure had increased to 15.4 per day. "Many times during the past years 25 patients have been in the hospital, and on October 30 of this year there were 28 patients and a waiting list for admittance," the *Times News* reported on 3 November 1960.

This heavy use led to a move to expand the hospital facility. In April 1959 the Juab County Commission passed a resolution calling for an expansion of the hospital to twenty-five or thirty beds. After several revisions, plans were approved by the commission, the hospital board, and the U.S. Department of Health. In June 1960 the county commission authorized an architect to proceed with working drawings, and in February 1961 the commission awarded a contract for a fourteen-bed addition, essentially doubling the hospital's in-patient capacity. The $110,000 expansion was completed in November 1961.[33]

In January 1972 the Juab County Hospital Board of Directors announced that a medical-dental clinic would be built on a site adjacent to the hospital. In the early 1970s the building held offices and examination rooms for two doctors; it later served as headquarters for the the Central Utah Health District. Built with federal aid, the building reverted to the Federal Housing Administration (FHA) not long after it was built. Juab County bought the building from the FHA in 1975.[34]

By the mid-1970s, Juab County Hospital was in trouble. Nonpayment of bills was increasing, malpractice insurance costs were soaring, and the patient load was dropping. "During the last three years the hospital has experienced a financial problem of great magnitude," the *Times News* reported on 5 February 1976. "In 1973 the

Old school at Callao later became a county road building, 1997. (Wayne Christiansen)

hospital operated with a year-end deficit of $78,052.77. In 1974 the deficit was $95,898.82, and the 1975 deficit was $55,381.00." The patient load had dropped from a daily average of fourteen in 1973 to twelve in 1975—lower than it was when the hospital was expanded in 1961. The county commission and the hospital board sent a questionnaire to county residents asking for direction. Two-thirds of those who responded to the questionnaire said they wanted the hospital to stay open. Three-quarters rated the hospital's services either good or very good. People were about evenly divided as to whether to create a special taxing district to underwrite hospital costs.[35]

Compounding the hospital's problems was the county's inability to keep doctors in the area. Early in 1979, hospital administrator David Peterson told the county commission that one area doctor had recently moved his practice to Delta and two others had also expressed interest in moving to other areas. "If we are left without doctors in the area, we'd have to close the hospital down," Peterson said. "And if we closed the hospital down, about half of my 65 employees would have to leave the community also."[36] According to an editorial in the *Salt Lake Tribune,* Juab County was facing a prob-

An old homested at Callao, 1997. (Wayne Christiansen)

lem common to rural communities: "Simply stated, the lure of the large city is just too great for a doctor to resist. It offers a chance to practice where facilities, staff and advice are readily at hand, where the phone can be taken off the hook now and then and where the money is more certain."[37] However, in August 1979, county residents were relieved to hear that two Texas doctors, Dr. Fred Catrett and Dr. Wayne Viehweg, were planning to set up practice in Nephi.

In March 1979 the county signed a contract with a private company, Advanced Health Systems, Incorporated, to manage the hospital. However, that arrangement lasted less than two years. In January 1981 the commission voted to terminate the contract, apparently unhappy with the rates Advanced Health Systems charged its patients. Soon afterwards, the county discovered that it still owed Advanced Health Systems about $650,000 for management fees, remodeling costs, and inventory needed to run the hospital. To repay the debt and finance other improvements to the hospital, the commission asked county voters to approve an $800,000 bond issue. In a vote of confidence in April 1981, county voters approved the bond by a margin of 566 to 116.[38]

In November 1984 the Juab County Commission heard a pro-

Log home with addition, Callao, 1997. (Wayne Christiansen)

posal from Rural Medical Services Foundation, a local nonprofit corporation formed specifically to lease the hospital from the county. "Everybody will be benefited by removing the hospital from the political arena," said Gaylord K. Swim of Levan, a director of the new foundation. The commissioners apparently agreed. On 31 December 1984 they agreed to lease the hospital to the new group. In its first two years running the hospital—renamed Central Valley Medical Center—the foundation managed to do what the county had rarely managed to do: make money. In May 1987, hospital administrator Mark Stoddard told the commission that the hospital had shown a profit of $44,160 in 1985 and $18,431 in 1986. The foundation also had made a number of improvements to the building, including the installation of a new heating system and insulating windows.[39]

However, by the fall of 1995, the building was showing its age. State inspectors found a number of deficiencies that, Stoddard estimated, would cost more than $500,000 to correct. Many of the deficiencies related to standards established after the hospital was built. Was the hospital worth that kind of investment? officials asked. At meetings in 1995 and 1996, the commission and the foundation debated the fate of the aging building. Finally, in the fall of 1996, offi-

cials of Central Valley Medical Center told Juab commissioners that
they would begin raising money for a new facility. The price tag was
$6–7 million.

"Although the center's medical staff and services are up to date,
its facility is not," fund-raiser David Wanamaker told the commission. "Due to its age, the building requires such major renovation that
engineering and architectural consultants recommend that a new
facility be constructed." Although county funds would not be
involved, hospital officials asked the county to sponsor them in getting loans for the project.[40]

At the time of this writing, hospital officials are working to raise
money for the project. They can take comfort in the knowledge that
they currently are running a successful program even without the
advantages that an up-to-date facility would bring. In 1997 a leading
health-care management consulting firm listed the Central Valley
Medical Center among the most successful small rural not-for-profit
hospitals in the United States.[41]

Highways

Nephi's position at the intersection of major highways—U.S.
Highway 91 and Utah Highways 321 and 28—played a critical role in
the growth of the town's economy. Gas stations, restaurants, and
motels grew up in response to the demands of travelers, most of
them driving north or south on U.S. Highway 91.

In September 1956, the highway committee of the Nephi
Chamber of Commerce announced an advertising program to keep
and increase traffic on Highway 91. Signs would be posted along the
route to advertise private industry and promote local scenic attractions. "Because of the increase of tourist travel in the State of Utah
along Highway 91 each year, the economy of the communities as well
as the entire state of Utah can be strengthened by a coordinated program," the *Times News* reported on 6 September 1956. "Benefits of
the tourist travel to the communities is, and can be, of tremendous
importance in the economy."

However, by February 1959, local businesses were facing a more
difficult challenge. Instead of just trying to lure travelers off two-lane
U.S. Highway 91, they would soon have to contend with a high-speed

Tintic School District's new Callao school, 1997. (Wayne Christiansen)

limited-access divided highway, part of the new national interstate freeway system being constructed. That month, the Utah State Road Commission held a meeting in Nephi to discuss alternative routes for proposed Interstate 15, which would run north-south through Utah. The new road threatened to bypass the Nephi business district and slice through prime irrigated farmland west of the city.[42]

As it turned out, it took another fourteen years before a route finally was chosen through the Nephi area. The highway was a subject of debate throughout the 1960s and well into the 1970s. In February 1964, the Utah State Road Commission presented its plans in a public meeting in Nephi. Its preferred route would enter the county from the south at the location of Highway 91, pass to the west of Levan and Nephi, continue northeasterly, and pass to the east of Mona before continuing on to Santaquin Hill.

A number of Nephi-area farmers didn't like the plan, and said so. Nine days after the meeting, they circulated to the area newspaper a petition with about 300 signatures in which they spelled out their objections:

> The proposed routing of this highway immediately west of Nephi
> City will cut through the heart of the finest irrigated section of

Old boarding house at Utah Mines, Fish Springs Mining District, 1997.
(Wayne Christiansen)

> Juab Valley and will necessitate construction of two railroad over-
> passes and four or more underpasses which we believe can be
> avoided by routing the highway east of the main part of Nephi
> City. Such routing would permit the taking of bench lands of
> small value and not irrigated, instead of the irrigated fields adjoin-
> ing the city on the west. It would place the highway where it
> would command a scenic view of Juab Valley instead of destroy-
> ing its best agricultural area.[43]

In spite of these objections, however, there were indications that the
state was still favoring the western route when another hearing was
held in July 1967. By 1971 the climate had changed, however; new
environmental restrictions were prompting the state to take another
look at a route east of the city.[44]

Another round of hearings was held in early 1973; and in May
1973 the Utah State Road Commission made its decision: the highway would pass east of Nephi, connecting with a section already
under construction from Santaquin.[45] The actual construction of
Interstate 15 through Juab County took place in several stages. Work
on the first stage, a 10.5-mile stretch from Santaquin Hill past Mona

Juab County volunteer fire station at Mammoth, 1997. Note the Utah Historic Site marker indicating that the building is a part of the Mammoth Historic District, Tintic Mining District. (Wayne Christiansen)

to the northern edge of Nephi, began in the fall of 1973; it was opened to traffic in July 1975.

In the meantime, discussion continued on the proposed location of interchanges on the remainder of the route through the county, stretching about 35.5 miles from north Nephi to the Millard County line. In a May 1975 public hearing, a delegation from Levan, led by Mayor Farrell Wankier, asked for an interchange to serve their community. Other leaders asked for an interchange at the intersection with Utah Highway 132 east of Nephi. The manager of Sierra Motel in Nephi said he liked things just the way they were, with all traffic going down the city's Main Street.[46]

In July 1977 the Utah Department of Transportation submitted its proposal to the Federal Highway Administration. It called for four interchanges: one north of Nephi, one south of Nephi, another at Mills Junction, and a fourth near the entrance to Yuba State Boating Park. "An interchange is not scheduled at the present time on U-132 east of Nephi but property will be acquired in the area so that the interchange can be constructed at a later date," the Times News told its readers on 28 July 1977.

By the spring of 1983, construction was either completed or in full swing on the remaining 35.5 miles of freeway, which had been divided into five separate projects. A six-mile stretch between Mills Junction and the Sevier River was already open to traffic. Interchanges were under construction north and south of Nephi, with surfacing of the highway in that 6.3-mile section scheduled to begin in the fall of 1983 or the spring of 1984. Grading and installation of drainage systems was underway on several other sections.[47]

By this time, although Nephi-area merchants were still dreading the loss of business expected when the completed freeway would bypass the city, there was a growing sense of urgency tied to the completion of the freeway. One reason was that U.S. Highway 91 from Nephi to Scipio in Millard County had become one of the deadliest stretches of road in the country. The road acted as a funnel for completed sections of Interstate 15 to the north and south. Large volumes of traffic traveling at high speeds were detoured onto the two-lane road, and the results were disastrous. "Some years ago, Elden C. Sherwood, then of the Highway Patrol, said that before the freeway

The Gemini headframe stands as a testament to the importance of mining in Eureka, 1997. (Wayne Christiansen)

by-passed our area, we would be screaming for it. That prophecy has come to pass," *Times News* editor Roy E. Gibson wrote in his column on 16 January 1975. "We feel that drivers, coming off the freeway to the north and to the south momentarily forget that they are now driving on a 'two-way' highway, with resultant head-on crashes. The Nephi to Santaquin Hill stretch of Highway 91 has been the scene of four recent fatalities."

The worst year for traffic fatalities in Juab County was 1977, when twenty-three people died on the county's highways. Seventeen deaths came in July and August alone. An entire family of eight died when their van collided with a truck on U.S. Highway 91 about a mile north of the Millard County line. That accident triggered an investigation by the National Transportation Safety Board. The state's newspapers began referring to U.S. Highway 91 between Nephi and Scipio as the "Nephi Death Strip." In February 1983, *People* magazine included the Nephi Death Strip in a story on the ten most dangerous roads in the United States.[48]

In the summer of 1984, the section of Interstate 15 bypassing

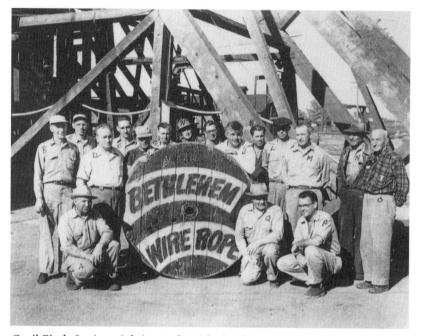

Cecil Fitch Sr. (on right) stands with the department heads of the Chief Consolidated Mining Company, 1951. (Brooks Baker)

Nephi was opened to traffic. In December 1985, traffic was routed onto a thirteen-mile section between Mills Junction and Scipio. The last remaining section, from south Nephi to Mills Junction, opened in April 1986. That gave motorists an uninterrupted stretch of freeway from Tremonton in extreme northern Utah to the Arizona state line. Utah Governor Norman Bangerter attended a dedication ceremony celebrating the death of the Nephi Death Strip.[49]

As expected, Juab County's highway death toll dropped dramatically following the completion of Interstate 15. So too did the number of customers in Nephi's tourist-oriented businesses, however. An Associated Press story in the *Salt Lake Tribune* in July 1985 painted a dismal picture of the downtown Nephi business district with its boarded-up gas stations and nearly vacant parking lots:

> Everitt Thomson has held on desperately to his fading business. Thomson bought his Conoco gasoline station in 1968 and

Loren Rawlings, a pioneer of Partoun, 1997. (Wayne Christiansen)

used to pump 1,500 to 2,000 gallons of gas on a normal summer day. On Wednesday, he sold less than 200 gallons.

"They said these places can come back, but I don't see it happening here," Thomson said. Given the right price, he said, he probably would sell out—something he never imagined in the old days.

"I love this business. I love the city. But it's just not worth it anymore," he said.[50]

Despite the economic ups and downs, Nephi and Juab County remain on the main north-south route through Utah and will continue to see heavy amounts of traffic through the area. As other Utah communities attempt to cope with changing times and needs, Nephi and Juab will join other locales looking for additional and novel ways of luring tourists and travelers off the major highways to spend some of their time (and money) in the county.

Juab County at Play

Juab County has a long tradition of being a playground for locals as well as visitors with diverse interests. As mentioned, the Ute Stampede has become an event of regional prominence. Recreational possibilities, including the Mount Nebo Loop, Yuba Reservoir, Little Sahara Recreational Area, Fish Springs National Wildlife Refuge, and the Tintic Mining District on the National Register of Historic Places site all are found in Juab.

Yuba State Boating Park. Built in 1913 on the Sevier River at the southern tip of Juab County to control flooding and store water for irrigation, the Yuba Dam reservoir became a haven for fish and a favorite of local boaters and fishermen. It also featured some of the finest sand beaches in the state. In 1964, lobbying by the Nephi Chamber of Commerce and the Nebo Boat Club, and the donation of about forty acres by the Sevier River Water Users Association, paved the way for the Utah Parks and Recreation Commission to approve the construction of a state park at the dam. The plans included the construction of a boat ramp, improvement of the access road, and, over the long term, development of overnight camping, drinking water, and restroom facilities.

"Boating has become a major recreation in East Juab County in recent years, and with both the Mona Reservoir and the Yuba State Boating Park available during the 'season' the area will become the center of boating for the entire central Utah area," the *Times News*

Old school at Partoun, ca. 1970s. (Tintic Historical Society)

reported on 9 April 1964. In June 1964 the Nebo Boat Club used proceeds from powerboat races at Mona Reservoir to help develop the facilities at Yuba State Boating Park. By spring 1965, a bulldozer was hard at work, beginning construction of a twelve-foot-wide, eighty-foot-long concrete boat ramp.

The new boating park was to be connected to U.S. 91 by a new hard-surfaced road between Scipio and Levan. In June 1966, state and county officials, along with representatives of the Sevier River Water Users Association, gathered to dedicate the new park. "Combined with the dedication of the State Boating Park on Sunday will be the annual Nebo Boating Club's speed races," the *Times News* reported on 23 June 1966. "The races previously have been held at Mona Reservoir, but because of greater water surface area and the new and improved boat launching facilities at Yuba, the races will hereafter be run here, according to Jack Cotton, Commodore of the club."

By the early 1970s, Yuba State Boating Park had become one of the most popular boating destinations in northern Utah. During the Fourth of July weekend in 1971, state park officials counted more than 5,700 people entering the park, with 200 boats on the water at

West Desert Elementary, Partoun, 1997. (Wayne Christiansen)

one time. In 1972–73, a major renovation was launched at the park. Crews, aided by several hundred men from the Utah National Guard, developed a new campground and built a new road into the park.[51] By 1976, public use of the park had increased to the point that local officials, along with a delegation from nearby Sanpete and Sevier Counties, were pressing the state to build additional boat ramps. They told the Utah Parks and Recreation Commission that on weekends people were waiting as long as two hours to launch their boats. "The problem, made acute by the terrific use of the facility in southern Juab County, is expected to become more acute in the near future because power boats have recently [been] prohibited in Palisades Park near Manti," said the *Times News* on 20 May 1976. According to a report from the Bureau of Land Management, the number of people using the area for recreation increased from 34,000 in 1972 to about 86,500 in 1976.[52] The state responded quickly. By June 1976 planning was underway for a new boat ramp in the Painted Rocks area on the east shore of the reservoir.

In 1980s and 1990s use of the facility has increased greatly, including use on the lake of new craft such as sailboards and jet skis. Some improvements have been made to the facility, and more are

Granite Ranch, located between Callao and Trout Creek, 1997. (Wayne Christiansen)

talked about, as it continues to be a popular playground for locals and visitors alike.

Little Sahara Sand Dunes. By the mid-1960s, a new rite of spring was becoming established in Juab County—spending Easter on the sand dunes about twenty-five miles west of Nephi. In 1967 an estimated 8,000 people—more than the entire population of the county—"Eastered" at the dunes on Sunday alone. "Groups began camping on the desert as early as Thursday, and a great number used the Sand dunes area Friday and Saturday," the *Times News* reported on 30 March 1967. "Sheriff [A. Duane] Sperry stated that the suggestion is being made by several that efforts proceed toward the establishment of a State Park at the Sand Dunes area. Popularity of the spot is growing 'by leaps and bounds,' especially for week ends such as Easter," the paper continued.

Driving the interest in the sand dunes was the growing popularity of off-road vehicles (ORVs), including dune buggies, dirt bikes, and four-wheel-drive vehicles. By 1972 an estimated 100,000 people a year were visiting the area. In August of that year, the federal Bureau of Land Management (BLM) announced a management plan for the nighty-eight-square-mile Little Sahara Recreation Area, as the dunes were being called by then. Little Sahara contains sagebrush flats, juniper-covered hills, and free-moving sand dunes believed to have been deposited by ancient Lake Bonneville. About sixty-two square miles of the recreation area would be designated for off-road vehicle use, including the Sand Mountains in the southern part of the area, which were becoming famous as a site for competitive hill climbs. However, vehicles would be excluded from the ecologically unique northwestern section, which would be designated as the Rockwell Natural Area. The plan called for several picnic and camping areas. The BLM also announced plans to build new access roads into the area from U.S. Highway 50/6. A few years later, the facilities at Little Sahara were expanded to include a solar-heated visitors center and a developed 114-unit campground, featuring picnic tables, grills, firepits, paved roads, flush toilets, and drinking water.

During Easter weekend in 1974, about 25,000 people flocked to Little Sahara, stretching to the limit the resources of Sheriff Sperry and his deputies. That weekend, nine people were arrested on drug charges. According to a newspaper account, some people tried the current fad of public nudity: "'We even had streakers,' Sheriff Sperry said. He pointed out that several were noted riding cycles and dune buggies—but none were arrested. 'We picked them up and told them to get dressed and all complied,' the Sheriff said."[53]

As it turned out, streaking was a passing fad. However, the county's law-enforcement headaches at Little Sahara were just beginning. On Easter weekend in 1977, for example, a child was killed after being thrown from an off-road vehicle in one of forty-two accidents reported to the sheriff's patrol. According to Sheriff Robert L. Painter, ambulances made sixteen runs from the dunes to area hospitals. In 1978 Sheriff Painter began what would become an annual tradition—issuing a public warning before Easter weekend that no "malarky" would be tolerated. "Last year there were 15 arrests for intoxication, seven fights (two of them with guns), and one fatality," Painter told the newspaper. "We had 45 people admitted to the Juab County Hospital in Nephi and 43 admitted to the Payson Hospital from accidents at the dunes during Easter. We want to change this picture—we're going on the offensive rather than the defensive."[54] As

Newly-constructed LDS Church, Trout Creek, 1997, shows a renewed vitality in the West Desert community. (Wayne Christiansen)

part of that strategy, Painter enlisted the help of thirteen officers from the Utah Highway Patrol in 1978 and also borrowed a "jail bus" so that several people could be taken to the county jail at one time. The strategy also involved setting up roadblocks at entrances to the dunes and checking vehicles for illegal alcohol and drugs.

Although officers continued to have their hands full with visitors at Easter and certain other holidays, by 1987 Painter's successor, Sheriff Dave Carter, was claiming that law-enforcement efforts had made a difference in the climate at Little Sahara. "We will continue to enforce the law at the dunes so it will be a place where families like to visit and can have a good time," he told *the Times News.* "Those who like to cause trouble no longer are coming to the dunes. I think we finally have discouraged them and they are going elsewhere."[55] However, in a meeting with county and BLM officials held in June 1987, Carter also noted that pressure on Little Sahara was no longer confined to Easter weekend. Crowds also were flocking to the dunes at other times, particularly popular holidays such as Memorial Day weekend. "Every week there is something, where we used to have troubles just on Easter weekend," Carter said. At that meeting, County

Eureka's new Tintic High School was constructed in 1982. (Wayne Christiansen)

Commissioner Richard M. Brough appealed to the BLM to pay a larger share of the county's law-enforcement costs, since providing those services for outside visitors was taking scarce county funds, with little appreciable return—a problem also faced in other counties with popular recreation spots, such as Moab in Grand County.[56]

More than 30 years since the tradition began, Utahns continue flocking to Little Sahara for Easter weekend. For Easter 1998 there were some 17,000 visitors, 200 arrests, and one fatality counted. It wasn't anything like the late 1970s, Sheriff Carter told the *Deseret News.* "But overall, it was quite a hectic weekend."[57]

Fish Springs. In 1954 Joseph Schribner of Ogden utilized 100 acres of marsh land at Fish Springs for the commercial harvesting of bullfrogs. Landing barges were hauled to the area for use as rearing pools. The large spring, known as the Frog Pond, was encircled by dikes to form a water reservoir for the hatchery.[58] In 1959 the United States Fish and Wildlife Service purchased all privately owned land and some public land owned by the State of Utah—a total of about 3,775 acres. An additional 14,097 acres was withdrawn from the pub-

Josie Mae Bailey, wife of Dr. Steele Bailey, dedicates the monument erected at the site of the Mammoth Hospital in Robinson, 1976. (Tintic Historical Society)

lic domain by the Department of the Interior. This was used to establish the Fish Springs Federal Wildlife Refuge, which has become a popular spot for nature lovers willing to travel to its rather remote location in the northwestern corner of the county.

The Times News

The Times News traces its roots back to October 1909, when Jacob Coleman started the *Juab County Times*. Among his first employees was fifteen-year-old A.B. "Abe" Gibson. In 1912 J.M. Christensen bought a half-interest in the newspaper from Coleman and assumed the role of editor. A year later, Gibson bought Coleman's remaining interest and became the paper's manager. Christensen apparently alienated some of the Nephi's leading citizens, who responded in 1916 by starting a competing weekly, the *Nephi City News*, published by Dennis Wood and Ralph J. Henroid. However, advertisers balked at placing ads in two local newspapers and pushed for a consolidation. In 1917 Abe Gibson and Dennis Wood bought out their respective partners and combined the two publications as the *Times News*, with Wood as editor and Gibson as manager.[59]

Until the *Times News* purchased its first typesetting machine in 1918, all type had to be set by hand. One of the two women who held that job was Camilla Miller (later Mrs. Camilla Duckworth). She relived her typesetting days in a 1971 interview with Roy E. Gibson, Abe's younger brother. "She couldn't recall just how much type she could set in a day, but we in the industry know that these young ladies were fast at typesetting," Gibson wrote. "And when one considers that each individual letter and space had to be picked from the case, placed in the 'stick' and then the line tightly spaced so it would 'lift,' not too much could be set in a shift."[60]

In January 1926 Dennis Wood resigned to accept a job as clerk of the Juab School District Board of Education, selling his share of the *Times News* to Abe Gibson. Gibson was active in the Utah Press Association, served as its president in 1930, and in 1960 was the first person to receive the association's Master Editor and Publisher award. In 1930, Roy Gibson joined his older brother on the staff of the newspaper. When Abe took a road-construction job shortly afterwards, Roy ran the paper. The two brothers later formed a partnership that lasted until 1942, when Abe acquired the *Pleasant Grove Review* and moved to Pleasant Grove. He later sold his interest in the *Times News* to his younger brother.[61]

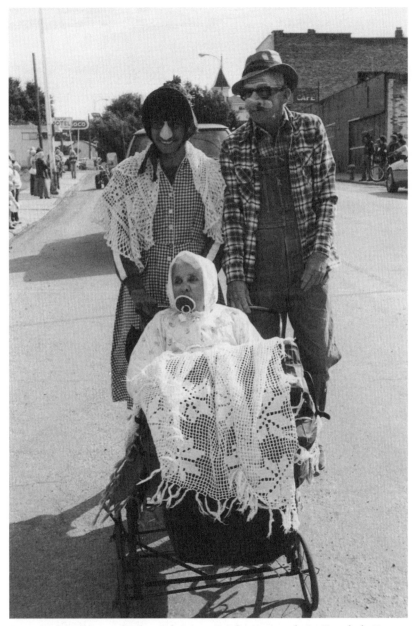

Larcel McNulty, and Lily and Oscar Erickson parade in Eureka's Depot Days festivities, 1982. (Gary B. Peterson)

"Depot Days" parade, Eureka, 1982. (Gary B. Peterson)

Roy Gibson served as editor and publisher of the *Times News* until 31 December 1976, when he turned the business over to his sons, Vance P. and Allan R. Gibson. During Roy Gibson's tenure, the newspaper won many state and national awards, including the coveted Utah Press Association General Excellence award, emblematic of the best overall weekly newspaper in the state in its circulation category. In 1972, toward the end of his tenure, the paper took the next step in the evolution of newspaper technology by abandoning the old mechanical hot-lead typesetting machine in favor of an electronic device that set type on long strips of photosensitive paper. Those strips, in turn, were pasted onto a grid to form the newspaper page.[62]

In 1976 Roy Gibson followed in his brother's footsteps by being named Master Editor and Publisher by the Utah Press Association.[63] "Being the editor of the paper meant many long, hard hours of work, and many sleepless Wednesday nights," Vance Gibson wrote in a tribute to his father that ran in the *Times News* on 15 June 1978.

> Many times he got the forms "locked up" and on the press and received a call that someone had died or that there had been an accident. That meant many more hours of setting type, moving

Tintic Historical Society's book committee watch *Faith, Hope, & Prosperity: The Tintic Mining District* come off the presses at Community Press in Orem, 1982. (Gary B. Peterson)

articles around, and getting the paper back to the press so that the news would reach the public Thursday morning.

As a boy I remember coming to work on Thursday morning. It was my job to take the papers to the post office as soon as they were printed, folded and addressed. I was often greeted by a father who had spent the entire night setting type and was usually covered from head to toe with printer's ink, but a better father a boy couldn't ask for.

Roy Gibson died on 17 June 1978, two days after his son's tribute appeared in print.

In January 1977 Vance and Allan Gibson became the second generation of Gibson brothers to run the *Times News*. Vance was the editor and was responsible for production and job printing; Allan was responsible for advertising, photography, and layout. In their first year at the helm of the paper they won a number of awards from the Utah Press Association including General Excellence, best spot news photograph, and best front page among Utah weekly newspapers in their circulation category.[64]

Schools

In January 1923, the new Juab High School opened on Main Street in Nephi. Students who had moved from the cramped old school into the spacious new facility were in awe. "In contrast to what we had, it was heaven," recalled Fred L. Gadd, who was a sophomore when the building was completed. The school had a spacious library, a gymnasium in the basement that doubled as a lunchroom, and even a swimming pool. "And, of course, there was the big auditorium that we never had before," Gadd reported.[65] Prior to the opening of the new building, school plays had to be held in various church halls. In the late 1930s, a new gymnasium and a mechanical arts building were added at a cost of about $80,000.

The building served its students well until 5 September 1943, a week before the 1943–44 school year was due to start, when fire broke out in the school's home economics department. Before Nephi's volunteer firefighters and crews from surrounding towns could bring the flames under control, they had destroyed almost everything except the east wing, which housed the auditorium, gymnasium and swimming pool. According to the local paper:

> In probably the worst disaster which has ever occurred in Nephi, the Juab high school building was almost completely gutted by fire of unknown origin. The building's walls, one or two second story floors, some of the desks, and other equipment on the ground floor and the gymnasium-auditorium wing remain of one of the most beautiful rural high schools in the state of Utah.
>
> The fire was discovered shortly after 1:15 A.M. Sunday morning in the kitchen of home economics department, and quickly spread throughout the ceiling attic space, bursting through the built-up, tarred roof in spots several feet square at a time. Because the fire burned between the roof and the ceilings of the upper rooms, water would not reach it.
>
> Soon after the Nephi fire department arrived on the scene, and laid two hose lines, it was apparent that more assistance would be needed to save any portion of the structure, because of the fast spreading of the fire, and calls were placed for the Payson and Spanish Fork departments of Utah county, and the Mount Pleasant company of Sanpete county. . . .

June McNulty, Tintic Historical Society, presents a copy of the Tintic book to American Association for State and Local History Director, Gerald George, 1984. The Tintic group was given the prestigious Corey Award from AASLH. (Gary B. Peterson)

Mayor P.L. Jones and Fire Chief E.R. Shaw of Nephi were high in their praise of the work of the two neighboring city departments, and stated that without their help, the entire building would probably have been destroyed.[66]

It took about three years to rebuild the school. In the meantime, classes were moved into the old armory building and the shop building next to the Central School.

In the spring of 1953, construction began on a new elementary school on Fourth East Street in Nephi. The school was dedicated in January 1954. In the fall of 1954, work began on a new athletic field at the high school with facilities for football, tennis, track, softball, and baseball. The new field allowed Juab High School to begin playing competitive football in the fall of 1955.[67]

In 1954, the state school superintendent had recommended the consolidation of school districts within three of Utah's less-populated counties, including Juab. In January 1957 a bill in the Utah legislature called for the consolidation of all school districts within any county having fewer than 4,000 students. At that time, Juab and Tintic districts had a combined total enrollment of about 1,500 students—and enrollment was dropping.[68]

The boards of both the Juab and Tintic school districts opposed the plan. "Neither the geography, nor the general economy of the two districts lend themselves to any further collaboration," the Juab Board of Education said in a prepared statement. "Tintic District is strictly a mining area and Juab District is predominantly an agricultural area. We are over forty miles apart with a mountain range between us. After careful study, we cannot visualize further economies by consolidating the two districts. We have a firm mandate from the people whom we represent to do everything possible to defeat the consolidation of the Tintic and Juab School Districts."[69]

The boards were successful in appealing the proposed consolidation, which was never enacted. Juab County remained with two school districts.

A survey of the Juab School District conducted during the 1957–58 school year found 402 students at Juab High School, 310 at the Central School, 247 at Nephi Elementary School, 150 at the Levan school and sixty-five at the Mona school. Besides their accomplishments in the classroom, the students at Juab High School gave the community something to cheer about in 1959 and 1960 by winning back-to-back Class-B state basketball championships.[70]

In the spring of 1960, taxpayers in the Juab School District were asked to approve a $360,000 bond issue that would have added another ten classrooms, a kindergarten, and a library to Nephi Elementary School. According to the plan, the high school would then expand into the old Central School building. The bond issue also would have helped fund the construction of a new multipurpose room at Mona School. However, voters wouldn't buy it—in a March election, they turned down the plan by almost a two-to-one ratio.[71] Even without a bond issue, school district officials managed to find the funds to build a vocational arts building next to Juab High School. The $143,000 building, with facilities for business, secretarial, home-economics, drafting, and industrial-arts classes, was dedicated in November 1964.[72]

In April 1966 the Juab school board voted to start busing seventh- and eighth-grade students from Mona and Levan to Juab High School rather than have them continue to attend the elementary schools in their own communities. The board argued that the high school could offer these students a much broader curriculum than they would receive in their local schools.[73]

In April 1970, still without increasing its bonded indebtedness, the school board asked for bids for an addition to Nephi Elementary School. When completed, the enlarged school would replace three of the district's aging elementary schools. "The Nephi Central School, the Levan Elementary School and the Mona Elementary School have served the residents of this area well," the *Times News* reported on 30 April 1970. "Their design and present physical condition make them inadequate educationally for a modern elementary education program, structurally unsound and unacceptable to the standards of the State Fire Marshal."

According to Superintendent Ralph W. Menlove, the district could finance the project by using special funds that had been set aside during the previous five years and by dividing the expansion project into two phases. Construction of the first phase began in the summer of 1970 and was completed in time for the start of the 1971–72 school year. The second phase was completed by the summer of 1974. "This will complete the elementary school and make it one of the finest anywhere," one official told the *Times News*.[74]

The same could not be said for the high school, however. By 1975 the east wing of the school was more than fifty years old, and the portion rebuilt after the fire in the mid-1940s was approaching thirty years old. In May 1975 a citizens' committee recommended that the district build a new high school/middle school complex rather than invest any more money in the old buildings. A year later, district voters were asked to approve the sale of $3.8 million in bonds for a four-year high school and a separate three-year middle school in a new location.[75] The vote was closer than in the previous bond election, but the outcome was the same: voters refused to approve the bonds, this time by a margin of 625 to 546.[76]

A report from the school planning section of the Utah State Board of Education described Juab High School's building as "educationally intolerable," according to a story in the *Times News* on 16 December 1976. In May 1977, voters were once again asked to approve a bond issue for a new high school/middle school campus. However, by this time the availability of matching state and federal aid had reduced the burden on local taxpayers to about $2 million; and this time the bond issue passed, 740 to 502.[77]

In January 1978, plans for the new secondary-school complex were shown at a public hearing in the old high school. The plans showed a high school, middle school, and vocational center on a thirty-six-acre lot on the corner of Fourth East and Seventh North Streets in Nephi. The complex included a gymnasium with seating for 500 and an auditorium capable of seating 700 people. Construction began in the spring of 1978, and, in November 1979, students moved into the new middle school. The high school building was finished in time for the opening of the 1980–81 school year. The $4.9-million complex was dedicated on 10 September 1980. In a four-way transaction, the ownership of the old high school facilities was transferred to Juab County, Nephi City, and the Nephi Stake of the Church of Jesus Christ of Latter-day Saints.[78]

During the 1960s and 1970s, enrollment in the Juab School

District averaged about 1,100 students. Had this number remained constant in the 1980s, the school construction program might have slowed down following the completion of the new high school and middle school. However, by 1980 there were signs that the county's school buildings wouldn't be able to contain the student population for long. In November 1980 the board was told that enrollment had increased 3.8 percent—from 1,104 to 1,146—in the previous year. In 1981, enrollment increased by another 113 students, or 9.9 percent. The growth continued in subsequent years, reaching 1,481 students by the fall of 1984. These numbers reflected an increase in county population. After reaching a twentieth-century low in the 1970 census count, with 4,574 residents, the county population jumped to 5,530 by 1980 and continued an upward trend through the 1980s and 1990s.[79]

In April 1982, the Juab Board of Education had tried to address both the immediate and the long-term needs, ordering three mobile classrooms to relieve overcrowding at Nephi Elementary School and scheduling another bond election to fund another building program. That $4.5 million in bonds would be used to build, in order of priority, an elementary school in Mona, an addition to Juab Middle School, an elementary school in Levan, and a second elementary school in Levan. "The action follows a decision by the board that when school buildings are needed, they should be placed near where the students live—when it is economically feasible to build them," the *Times News* reported on 15 April 1982. Although it was the second bond issue in five years, district voters didn't flinch. They authorized the $4.5 million bond sale by a three-to-one margin. Construction of a 24,800-square-foot school in Mona began in September 1982; the school officially opened in November 1983. Built at a cost of $1,165,000, it had an initial enrollment of 150 students.[80]

The Tintic School District also underwent growing pains and changes in facility needs. By the late 1970s, age and weather had exacted a toll on district buildings in Eureka and new building plans were made. A new Tintic High School opened for the 1982–83 school year. Located east of the older structure, the modern high school building allows students access to services and equipment that enhance their education.

In the mid-1990s new challenges faced most rural school districts, including Tintic. Growing pains were projected in 1995. An article in the *Salt Lake Tribune* stated that Tintic School District's student body increased by forty-six, a 17 percent surge for the "tiny west-central Utah district. Increases are expected to continue in Tintic as well as neighboring Nebo and Juab districts."[81] Increases throughout the state generally were viewed as a reflection of in-migration and a healthy economy, although it could put financial pressure on many of the smaller districts, including those in Juab County.

Nutritional needs of students became a growing concern in the 1990s. In this regard, the Tintic School District captured headlines in 1995: "Anti-Hunger Group Praises Tintic But Gives Utah Overall Grade of C," was a *Salt Lake Tribune* headline. The article continued,

> Tintic School District has improved its participation in the school breakfast program by 200% over last year, garnering an A+ for its efforts from Utah anti-hunger advocacy group. . . .
>
> But the real beneficiaries are students in the remote west desert communities of Eureka and Trout Creek who are getting a healthy morning meal that also is a good value for parents, said Tintic Superintendent Patricia Rowse. . . . In fact, the participation has been phenomenal. At Eureka Elementary School, where school meals are served to first through 12th graders, between 40 and 50 students eat school breakfast every day.
>
> At West Desert High School, in Trout Creek, breakfast is served to 40 students from all grades. With a total of 60 students—40 in high school and 20 in grade school—that's two-thirds of the student body, Rowse pointed out.
>
> Part of the reason for the higher participation at West Desert is that many students are bused to school and arrive in time for breakfast, and parents who are commuting to jobs find it a convenient way to ensure their children are getting a nutritious meal. Secondary reasons for initiating the breakfast program were: trying to get students to school on time, and providing a "calming" period between arriving at school and starting class work.[82]

Such programs were welcome in the small county district, which had to struggle in many areas due to its lack of students.

Other County Developments

In 1951 a flood destroyed the upper power plant equipment and the facility was closed. In November 1985 Nephi began purchasing electricity from the Utah Municipal Power Association.

Mona. The church built in Mona in 1884 was used until a new Mormon chapel was erected in 1949. Since then the members at Mona remodeled and improved the church several times. Juab School District gave the ground on which the earlier brick school stood to the town of Mona and officials turned it into a park. According to a local historian,

Volunteers tore the old building down. built the memorial monument, hauled in the dirt, planted grass, furnished the playground equipment, planted the trees, installed the drinking fountain, and fixed up the ball field. The Park was dedicated in July of 1976.

The bell from the brick school built in 1907 is the same bell used in earlier schools as an Indian alarm or emergency signal in the early days, or as a call to school. It is enshrined on the memorial monument. This monument was laid with sandstone and bricks from the old school. It was built by Everd Squire.[83]

In the early 1950s the town of Mona began surfacing its roads with asphalt. The project was continued as finances became available until all of the roads in the town were surfaced.

Agriculture, Ranching, and the Military. Agriculture still thrives in much of eastern Juab County, although with consolidation into larger farming operations some small communities have essentially gone from the map. Dean Howard stayed on in Mills after his children married and moved away and his wife died, living there until he died in December 1990. Beginning in about 1997, three families had purchased property and were living in Mills.

With hard work and sacrifice, John Ingram of Nephi eventually owned 5,000 sheep. As his sons grew, they helped with the sheep, and when Ingram died in 1939 two of his sons—Clarence with his sons Don and Dick, and Angus with his son John—took over the business. Angus Ingram finally sold his herd in 1973 and Clarence and his sons sold theirs in 1974. These were the last sheep herds of any size remaining in the East Juab area.

In western Juab County there is some farming, but ranching is still seen as a better way to utilize the land. Outside of Callao and Partoun, few people live in the wide expanses of western Juab County. With fewer than 200 people scattered over some 2,000 square miles, western Juab County beyond the Tintic Mountain Range has often taken a back seat to the eastern part of the county, where most of the people, industry, and roads are concentrated.

The wide open spaces of the so-called west desert have from time to time attracted the attention of federal officials looking for places to build or test weapons systems or other military programs. In the late 1970s the federal government believed that the area would make an ideal location for its proposed MX missile system.

As proposed by the U.S. Air Force, the MX system would have involved building about 1,000 concrete missile shelters a year for four-and-a-half years in the desert valleys of western Utah and eastern Nevada. The shelters would have been connected by a network of roads, allowing missiles with nuclear warheads to be moved from shelter to shelter, thus effectively shielding them from enemy attack. The Air Force estimated that about 25,000 workers would have been required during the peak years of construction, and a permanent operating force would have involved about 10,000 people. All told, the project could have brought as many as 100,000 people to western Utah and eastern Nevada, according to government estimates.[84]

At a hearing in Nephi in November 1979, area citizens voiced concerns about becoming military targets, and wanted to know whether the federal government would help the county deal with the expected influx of a large number of people. Among the skeptics was Callao resident Cecil Garland, who told government officials that their missile program would destroy his lifestyle as certainly as would a Russian bomb. "I've run and run . . . just to find a little peace and quiet and now you're gonna come and take that away from me," he said.[85]

A poll conducted in the spring of 1980 by Congressman Dan Marriott revealed that most county residents agreed with Garland. By a 56 to 37 percent margin they said they would not support the system even if it were in the national interest. And by a 51 to 40 percent margin they said they would oppose the system even if environmental and economic impacts were resolved.[86] Therefore, most residents breathed a sigh of relief when eventually the military scrapped the plans for the MX system. However, the relief was short-lived. In 1987 the U.S. Army and Air Force announced that they were planning to use the west desert as practice range to develop their electronic warfare capabilities. The vast openness of the area's land continues to provide a temptation that it be used for military purposes—something some favor and others vehemently oppose.

Quality of Life and Historic Preservation

Juab County's history points to the value of understanding the past to help understand and meet the challenges and opportunities of the present and future. Political and social debates in the 1990s settled squarely on issues of the "quality of life" in Utah communities and counties. Most agree that a sense of the past is essential in understanding the present into order to plan for the future. This concern about a "sense of place" loomed as especially significant at the dawn of a new millennium. History and historic preservation remain at the center of this issue.

In the late 1970s the Utah State Historical Society and its Historic Preservation Office sought to expand their work of identifying cultural and historic resources throughout the state. Under funding from the federal government and the National Park Service, the preservation program looked to conform to preservation legislation passed in previous years. A main goal was to increase Utah listings in the National Register of Historic Places.

As part of a U.S. bicentennial project, state officials at the Utah State Historical Society journeyed to Eureka in 1975 and 1976 to assist the then fledgling Tintic Historical Society, founded in 1973. That early group consisted of Paul and Bernie Mogensen, June and Coleen McNulty, Sylvia and John Campbell, Oscar and Lily Erickson, Joe and Grace Bernini, and Mac and Lucille Bigler. The Tintic group expressed a desire to establish a museum and document Tintic's history, and the state historical society responded. Philip F. Notarianni, on contract from the Salt Lake office, began a long-term study of the Tintic Mining District.

In 1979 the Tintic Mining District was listed officially in the

National Register of Historic Places as a Multiple Resource Area. The efforts of the Utah Historic Preservation Office also meant National Register designations for other Juab sites, including the George Carter Whitmore mansion (1978); the Edwin Booth house, at 94 West 300 South, Nephi (1979); the Oscar M. Booth house, at 395 East 100 South, Nephi (1982); the Fish Spring Caves Archaeological District (1981); and the Juab County Jail, at 45 West Center, Nephi (1987). The Nephi Mounds had received a Utah State Historic Site designation in 1975.[87]

Historic preservation activities, establishment of the Tintic Mining Museum, programs of the Tintic Historical Society, and the publication of a history on the Tintic Mining District in 1982 led to national acclaim for the group from Eureka. On 3 October 1983 the Tintic Historical Society won the Albert B. Corey Award, the highest honor bestowed on a local historical society in the United States and Canada by the American Association for State and Local History (AASLH). In February 1984, AASLH Executive Director Gerald George traveled to Eureka to present the award and an accompanying $500 check to the society and its president, Lily Erickson, who stated, "This is the biggest thing that ever happened to us."[88]

Gerald George later wrote about the Tintic group and his visit in *History News*.

> It is evident, however, that the society's success stems from more than a knack for coming up with cash. Also essential is the way the society uses history to generate a spirit of community in its economically struggling locality. Equally important, the society's members have not been afraid to go outside for help from professionals. They have again and again insisted on receiving it. The Tintic Historical Society seems a model for the field of how professional state agencies and volunteer local societies should interact continuously to make history an enriching part of life for everybody.[89]

George echoed the observation of Philip Notarianni that the Tintic Mining District "had a heritage and the buildings to prove it."

The Utah statehood centennial in 1996 generated numerous state and local celebrations and projects. Two projects were particularly important in chronicling the history of Juab County. One focused on the writing of new and updated histories of all twenty-nine of Utah's counties—a genuine contribution to the history of the state. This book is the Juab County part of that project. A second project was the gathering of information related to all historical markers and monuments that exist in Utah. A concerted effort meant a site form completed on hundreds of sites in Utah, including thirty-three in Juab County. Markers and monuments identified in Juab include: Bagley's Ranch, Willow Springs Pony Express Station, Eureka and Mammoth Historic Districts, Fish Springs, Pony Express Monument, Levan Sons of Utah Pioneers and Daughters of Utah Pioneers markers; Mona Bicentennial Park and the Old Pioneer Cemetery, various sites in Nephi, and the Burraston Ponds.[90]

Both the centennial of Utah statehood in 1996 and the Mormon Pioneer Sesquicentennial of 1997 heightened the awareness of many Utahns of their history and heritage. With efforts such as those described above, Juab County residents also became more aware of their past and its effects upon the present. Many smaller rural areas are discovering the economic value of "cultural tourism," as many modern tourists desire historical information about the sites and locales they visit. Juab County has much to offer in this as in many other areas—a variety of historic resources that bode well for future interest in the county.

An example of Juab County's commitment to the preservation of history and historical resources can be seen in the vote by county residents in 1980 to reuse the old Juab High School and Vocational Arts Building as the new Juab County Courthouse and for other county functions. In addition, a portion of the old county courthouse contains a museum operated by the Juab Daughters of Utah Pioneers to preserve the county's historic and cultural artifacts.

Juab County stands at a crossroads, geographically and socially, as a new millennium nears. The traditionally agricultural-based eastern end of the county remains poised to benefit from growth and its geographical position on Utah's main north-south corridor. The western portion of Juab remains a sparsely populated vast area, where ranching and a fluctuating mining industry have dominated existence. Juab County remains a county with a dual identity.

Population projections indicate but a slight growth pattern into the twenty-first century. In 1990, Juab contained some 5,817 residents; with an annual percentage change estimated at 1.16 percent, the population of the county is projected to climb to about 8,219 by the year 2020—much less than many other areas of Utah, particularly those along the Wasatch Front.[91] Historically, the mining industry has been susceptible to the upturns and downswings of the economy, and no mining booms are forecast for the county in the immediate future. More populous eastern Juab faces a dwindling agricultural economy and increasingly has come to rely economically on tourism and travel. Population growth depends on the county's ability to pursue economic development.

Beryllium has become important to the county. According to one writer, in a 1990 journal article,

> Open pit beryllium production commenced at Spor Mountain in 1959 and the mines are now the nation's largest domestic source of beryllium, with an estimated 6 million tons of disseminated bertrandite ore in reserve. When the writer first visited Topaz Mountain in 1946, gem-quality topaz was everywhere. Even the dirt roads sparkled with topaz crystals, but now, the area has been virtually picked clean.[92]

The Topaz area is perhaps the most popular area in Utah for mineral collecting. People come from all over the country in hopes of finding topaz and other minerals. The Bureau of Land Management has set aside an area in Topaz Valley (Topaz Cave) for collectors. In spite of the large number of visitors, topaz and many other minerals are still abundant—among them red beryl, bixbyte, garnet, and amethyst.[93]

Rocky Ridge, located just south of Santaquin across the county line, became Juab's newest community in 1998. Property had been purchased in 1971 by Thomas Bronson, M. L. Allred Sr., and Ronald A. Allred. In 1997 Rocky Ridge incorporated, named Juab County voting district number thirteen. Marvin Allred was elected the first mayor in 1998. other communities may follow.

Challenges face Juab, as they do most other rural Utah counties. The people of Juab have been survivors in fluctuating economies and periods of difficulties. In the long run, the county, marked by lush fields on one end and a harsh desert on the other, contains features and lifestyles that various people find attractive and that foster a desired quality of life. The projected growth may be small, but many Juab County residents actually prefer it that way as they look to life in the coming century.

ENDNOTES

1. "Beaver-Millard-Juab Counties, Industrial Pattern as of September 30, 1947" (Salt Lake City: Utah Department of Employment Security, 1947), 34.

2. *Times News,* 25 October 1945.

3. *Times News,* 13 February 1947, 30 July 1953, 28 October 1954; Worthington, et al. *They Left a Record,* 96.

4. *Times News,* 20 March 1947, 15 November 1956.

5. *Times News,* 6 March 1947.

6. John R. Christiansen, Sheridan Maitland, and John W. Payne, "Industrialization and Rural Life in Two Central Utah Counties," (Logan: Utah Agricultural Experiment Station, 1959), 12; *Salt Lake Tribune,* 4 November 1953.

7. *Times News,* 10 June 1948.

8. "Thermoid Western at Nephi, Utah," *Utah Economic and Business Review* 13 (April 1953): 4–5.

9. *Salt Lake Tribune,* 4 November 1953.

10. Christiansen et al., "Industrialization and Rural Life," 31.

11. *Times News,* 18 January, 22 February, 22 March 1951; *Salt Lake Tribune,* 21 January 1951, 2 April, 6 August 1959.

12. *Times News,* 8, 15 December 1955, 19 January, 23 February 1956, 7 March 1957, 2 April, 6 August 1959.

13. *Times News,* 8 January 1959, 5 March, 24 September 1964, 18 August 1966.

14. *Times News,* 19 March 1970, 24 June 1971, 2 August 1973, 5 December 1974, 13 February 1975.

15. *Times News,* 4 September 1975.

16. *Times News,* 18 September 1975, 16 June 1977, 28 September 1978.

17. *Times News,* 10 June, 30 December 1982.

18. *Salt Lake Tribune,* 27 July 1985.

19. *Times News,* 10 October 1985, 6 February, 8 May 1986.

20. *Times News,* 4 October 1956.

21. *Times News,* 14 September 1961, 25 January 1962, 4 April 1974.

22. *Times News,* 6 November 1964; Utah Bureau of Economic and Business Research, "County and Community Economic Facts," 1980.

23. See "Juab County, an Economic Profile," 1962, Bureau of Economic and Business Research, University of Utah.

24. *Times News,* 15 November 1962, 6 August 1964.

25. *Times News,* 14 November 1968.

26. *Times News,* 6 November 1975, 10 March, 4 August, 17 November 1977; Worthington, et al, *They Left a Record,* 123.

27. *Times News,* 13 June, 17 October 1985.

28. *Deseret News,* 2 February 1990, 24 December 1995.

29. *Deseret News,* 12 July 1995, 14 October 1996.

30. *Deseret News,* 18 September 1997.

31. *Times News,* 20 July, 31 August 1950.

32. *Times News,* 14 January 1954.

33. *Times News,* 3 November 1960, 2 February, 9 November 1961.

34. *Times News,* 13 January, 7 September 1972, 20 November 1975.

35. *Times News,* 26 February 1976.

36. *Times News,* 25 January 1979.

37. *Salt Lake Tribune,* 10 February 1979.

38. *Times News,* 22 January, 26 February, 23 April, 30 April 1981.

39. *Times News,* 29 November 1984, 3 January 1985, 14 May 1987.

40. *Deseret News,* 3 November 1995, 5 March, 4 November 1996.

41. *Times News,* 4 June 1997.

42. *Times News,* 12 February 1959.

43. *Times News,* 27 February 1964.

44. *Times News,* 27 July 1967, 18 March 1971.

45. *Times News,* 1 February, 17 May 1973.

46. *Times News,* 1 May 1975.

47. *Times News,* 12 May 1983.

48. *Times News,* 7 June 1979, 24 February, 1 September 1983.

49. *Times News,* 2 August 1984, 24 December 1985, 24 April 1986.

50. *Salt Lake Tribune,* 27 July 1985.

51. *Times News,* 8 July 1971, 14 September 1972, 14 June 1973.

52. *Times News,* 16 February 1978.

53. *Times News,* 18 April 1974.

54. *Times News,* 14 April 1977, 23 March 1978.

55. *Times News,* 23 April 1987.

56. *Times News,* 11 June 1987.

57. *Deseret News,* 14 April 1998.

58. Marlene Bates, "North Snake Valley," 86

59. *Times News,* 19 February 1970, 2 January 1975.

60. *Times News,* 11 March 1971.

61. *Times News,* 12 February 1976.

62. *Times News,* 20 February 1958, 28 December 1972.

63. *Times News,* 19 February 1976.

64. *Times News,* 6 January 1977, 16 February 1978.

65. *Times News,* 15 December 1922, 2 October 1980.

66. *Times News,* 9 September 1923.

67. *Times News,* 19 March 1953, 7 January, 9 September 1954, 18 August 1955.

68. *Summit County Bee,* 25 November 1954; *Times News,* 31 January 1957; "Juab County, An Economic Profile," 1967, 52.

69. *Times News,* 31 January 1957.

70. *Times News,* 29 January, 19 March 1959, 24 March 1960.

71. *Times News,* 25 February, 31 March 1960.

72. *Times News,* 12 November 1964.

73. *Times News,* 14 April 1966.

74. *Times News,* 7 May 1970, 30 September 1971, 25 July 1974.

75. *Times News,* 29 May 1975, 15 April 1976.

76. *Times News,* 13 May 1976.

77. *Times News,* 28 April, 26 May 1977.

78. *Times News,* 19 January 1978, 8 November, 27 December 1979, 4 September 1980.

79. *Times News,* 26 November 1980, 25 November 1981, 22 December 1983, 27 December 1984; Powell, *Utah History Encyclopedia,* 433.

80. *Times News,* 20 May 1982, 3 November 1983.

81. *Salt Lake Tribune,* 2 November 1995.

82. *Salt Lake Tribune,* 9 November 1995.

83. M. Clark Newell, *Mona and Its Pioneers,* 19.

84. *Salt Lake Tribune,* 8 November 1979.

85. *Salt Lake Tribune,* 21 November 1979.

86. *Salt Lake Tribune,* 17 April 1980.

87. See National Register files, Historic Preservation Office, Utah State Historical Society.

88. *Eureka Reporter,* 21 October 1983, 16 February 1984; *History News* 39 (May 1984): 19.

89. *History News* 39 (May 1984): 19.

90. See "Utah Historical Markers and Monuments Site Forms," Utah State Historical Society.

91. *Statistical Abstract of Utah 1996* (Salt Lake City: Bureau of Economic and Business Research, 1997), 12.

92. Edgar B. Heylmun, "Dry Placers in Utah," *California Mining Journal* 59 (April 1990): 67.

93. See Philip D. Richardson, James R. Wilson, and Paula N. Wilson, "Mineral Collecting in Utah," *Rocks and Minerals* 68 (November-December 1993).

Selected Bibliography

Allen, James B., and Ted J. Warner. "The Gosiute Indians in Pioneer Utah." *Utah Historical Quarterly* 39 (1971): 162–77.

Alter, J. Cecil. *Early Utah Journalism.* Salt Lake City: Utah State Historical Society, 1938.

Baldridge, Kenneth W. "Nine Years of Achievement: The Civilian Conservation Corps in Utah." Ph.D. dissertation, Brigham Young University, 1971.

Bates, Marlene. "North Snake Valley, Part 1." Marlene Bates, Gandy, Utah.

"Beaver-Millard-Juab Counties Industrial Pattern as of September 30, 1947." Salt Lake City: Utah Department of Employment Security, 1947.

Bolton, Herbert E. *Pageant in the Wilderness: The Story of the Escalante Expedition to the Interior Basin, 1776.* Salt Lake City: Utah State Historical Society, 1972.

Boswell, Stephen R. *History of Dry Farming on the Levan Ridge.* Special Collections and Archives, Utah State University, Logan.

Brooks, Juanita, ed. *The Journal of Martha Spence Heywood 1850–56.* Salt Lake City: Utah State Historical Society, 1978.

Cardon, Philip V. "Minor Dry Land Crops at the Nephi Experiment Farm."

Utah Agricultural College Experiment Station Bulletin 132 (March 1914).

———. "Tillage and Rotation Experiments at Nephi, Utah." Bulletin of the U.S. Department of Agriculture 157 (1915).

Carr, Stephen L. *The Historical Guide to Utah Ghost Towns.* Salt Lake City: Western Epics, 1972.

Carr, Stephen L., and Robert W. Edwards. *Utah Ghost Rails.* Salt Lake City: Western Epics, 1989.

Carter, Kate B. *Heart Throbs of the West,* vol 2. Salt Lake City: Daughters of Utah Pioneers, 1940.

———. *Our Pioneer Heritage,* vol. 7. Salt Lake City: Daughters of Utah Pioneers, 1964.

Chittenden, Hiram Martin. *The American Fur Trade of the Far West,* New York: Press of the Pioneers, 1935.

Christiansen, John R., Sheridan Maitland, and John W. Payne. "Industrialization and Rural Life in Two Central Utah Counties." Logan: Utah Agricultural Experiment Station, 1959.

Coleman, Jacob. "Nephi." *The Arrowhead* (October 1912).

Copeland, James M., and Richard E. Fike. "Fluted Projectile Points in Utah." *Utah Archaeology* 1 (1988): 5–28.

Egan, Howard R. *Pioneering the West 1846–1878. Major Howard Egan's Diary.* Richmond, Utah: Howard R. Egan Estate, 1917.

Fike, Richard E., and John W. Hadley. *The Pony Express Stations of Utah in Historical Perspective.* Bureau of Land Management Cultural Resources Series No. 2, 1979.

Fitch, Cecil A., Jr., James Quigley, and Clarence Barker. "Utah's New Mining District."*Engineering and Mining Journal* 150 (March 1949): 63–66.

Fitch, Maud. *"Driver, Intrepid and Brave," Maud Fitch's Letters from the Front 1918–1919.* Jeezel Beezel Partners through Rhino Press, 1995. Copy at Utah State Historical Society.

Frisch, Paul A. "Labor Conflict at Eureka, 1886–97," *Utah Historical Quarterly* 40 (1981): 145–56.

"George Carter Whitmore Mansion." National Register of Historic Places Inventory Nomination Form. Historic Preservation Office, Utah State Historical Society.

Gottfredson, Peter. *Indian Depredations in Utah.* Salt Lake City: Skelton Publishing, 1919.

"Grading Exercises of the Nephi High School," (1900). Pamphlet 13826, Utah History Information Center, Utah State Historical Society.

Heylmun, Edgar B. "Dry Placers in Western Utah." *California Mining Journal* 59 (April 1990): 67–69.

Jacobs, G. Clell. "The Phantom Pathfinder: Juan Maria Antonio de Rivera and His Expedition." *Utah Historical Quarterly* 60 (1992): 200–23.

Jennings, Jesse D. *The Prehistory of North America.* New York: McGraw-Hill, 1974.

———. "Prehistory of Utah and the Eastern Great Basin." University of Utah Anthropological Papers, No. 98, (1978).

"Juab County, An Economic Profile." Salt Lake City: Bureau of Economic and Business Research, 1967.

"Juab County Courthouse File." Historic Preservation Files, Utah State Historical Society.

Juab County Records. Juab County Courthouse, Nephi, Utah.

Lindsay, LaMar W., and Kay Sargeant. "Prehistory of the Deep Creek Mountain Area, Western Utah." Antiquities Section Selected Papers, No. 14 (1979).

Lipe, William D. "The Southwest." In *Ancient North Americans,* ed. by Jesse D. Jennings. New York: W.H. Freeman and Company, 1983.

Madsen, David B. "The Human Prehistory of the Great Salt Lake Region." In *Great Salt Lake: A Scientific, Historical and Economic Overview,* ed. by J. Wallace Gwynn. Utah Department of Natural Resources Bulletin No. 115 (1980).

Madsen, David B., and Richard Fike. "Archaeological Investigations in Utah at Fish Springs, Clay Basin, Northern San Rafael Swell, Southern Henry Mountains." Bureau of Land Management, Utah Cultural Resource Series, No. 12 (1982).

Madsen, David B., and James O'Connell, eds. *Man and Environment in the Great Basin.* Society of American Archaeologists Papers No. 2. (1982).

Mammoth Ward Records to 1898, and Historical Records 1890 to 1896. Church of Jesus Christ of Latter-day Saints Family History Library, Salt Lake City, Utah.

Marwitt, John P. "Fremont Cultures." In *Handbook of North American Indians: Great Basin,* ed. by Warren L. D'Azevedo. Washington, D.C.: Smithsonian Institution, 1986.

McCune, Alice Paxman. *History of Juab County, 1847–1947.* Springville, Utah: Art City Publishing Co., 1947.

Miller, Glen."The Geology and Mineral Deposits of Juab County." 1998. Written especially for this study, and in possession of the author.

Mooney, Bernice Maher. *Salt of the Earth: The History of the Catholic Church in Utah, 1776–1987.* Salt Lake City: Intermountain Catholic Press, 1992.

Morgan, Dale L. *Jedediah Smith and the Opening of the West.* Lincoln: University of Nebraska Press, 1969.

Murphy, Miriam B. "'If only I shall have the right stuff': Utah Women in World War I." *Utah Historical Quarterly* 58 (1998): 334–50.

National Register of Historic Places Files. Historic Preservation Office, Utah State Historical Society.

Nephi City Council Minutes. Nephi, Utah.

Newell, M. Clark. *Mona and Its Pioneers.* Mona, Utah: Mt. Nebo Camp Daughters of Utah Pioneers, c. 1991.

Notarianni, Philip F. *Faith, Hope, & Prosperity: The Tintic Mining District.* Eureka, Utah: Tintic Historical Society, 1982.

Openshaw, Fred H.C. "The Benefits of Small School Systems as Perceived by the Staff, Students, and Residents of the Ten Smallest School Districts in Utah." Ed.D. Dissertation, Brigham Young University, 1976.

Papanikolas, Helen Z., ed. *The Peoples of Utah.* Salt Lake City: Utah State Historical Society, 1981.

"Papers of the Knight Investment Company." Manuscript 278, Special Collections, Harold B. Lee Library, Brigham Young University, Provo, Utah.

Poll, Richard D., Thomas G. Alexander, Eugene E. Campbell, and David E. Miller, eds. *Utah's History.* Provo, Utah: Brigham Young University Press, 1978.

Powell, Bert. Interview with Pearl Wilson, 8 January 1999.

"A Report of the Works Division 15 April 1934–31 October 1935." Utah Emergency Relief Administration.

Richardson, Philip D., James R. Wilson, and Paula N. Wilson. "Mineral Collecting in Utah." *Rocks and Minerals* 68 (November-December 1993).

Roberts, Richard Campbell. "History of the Utah National Guard." Ph.D. Dissertation, University of Utah, 1973.

Schroedl, Alan R. "Paleo-Indian Occupation in the Eastern Great Basin and Northern Colorado Plateau." *Utah Archaeology* 4 (1991): 1–16.

Scoville, Sherry. "Samuel McIntyre: Founder and Builder in Utah History." 1980. Unpublished manuscript in possession of Pearl Wilson.

Sharrock, Floyd W., and John P. Marwitt. "Excavations at Nephi, Utah, 1965–1966." University of Utah Anthropological Papers, No. 88 (1967).

Sperry, George A., C.W. Johnson, Sadie H. Greenhalgh, Grace J. McCune, Martha C. Eager, and Iris Garrett. *Nephi's Centennial Jubilee.* Nephi: Times News, 1951.

Statistical Abstract of Utah 1996. Salt Lake City: Bureau of Economic and Business Research, 1997.

Stephensen, Maurine P. *A History of Levan.* Levan, Utah: Chicken Creek Daughters of Utah Pioneers, 1990.

Stucki, Roland. *Commercial Banking in Utah, 1847–1966.* Salt Lake City: Bureau of Economic and Business Research, 1967.

"Thermoid Western at Nephi, Utah." *Utah Economic and Business Review* 13 (April 1953): 4–5.

Twain, Mark. *Roughing It.* New York: Holt, Rinehart and Winston, Inc., 1953.

Utah Atlas and Gazetteer. Freeport, Maine: DeLorme Mapping, 1993.

Utah Directory and Gazetteer for 1879–80. Salt Lake City: H.L.A. Culmer & Co., 1879.

"Utah Historical Markers and Monuments Site Form." Utah State Historical Society.

Utah State Gazetteer and Business Directory, 1900. Salt Lake City: R.L. Polk & Co., 1901.

Utah State Gazetteer and Business Directory, 1912–1913. Salt Lake City: R.L. Polk & Co., ca. 1913.

Warner, Ted J., ed., and Fray Angelico Chavez, trans. *The Dominguez-Escalante Journal. Their Expedition through Colorado, Utah, Arizona, and New Mexico in 1776.* Provo, Utah: Brigham Young University Press, 1976.

Warrum, Noble, ed. *Utah Since Statehood.* Salt Lake City: J.S. Clark Publishing Co., 1919.

Wolf's Mercantile Guide, Gazetteer, and Business Directory. Omaha, Nebraska: Omaha Republican Book and Job Printing House, 1878.

Worthington, Keith N., Sadie H. Greenhalgh, and Fred Chapman. *They Left a Record. A Comprehensive History of Nephi, Utah, 1851–1978.* Provo, Utah: United States of America Community Press, 1979.

Index